GUATEMALA

El Petén
p111

The
Highlands
p160

Central &
Eastern Guatemala
p43

The Pacific Slope
p80

D1475183

Ray Bartlett, Lucas Vidgen

CONTENTS

Plan Your Trip

PHOTOTRIP/GETTY IMAGES ©

The Guide

P A THOMPSON/GETTY IMAGES ©

Top: Resplendent quetzal (p195);
Bottom: Antigua (p166)

YGGDRASILL/SHUTTERSTOCK ©, BOTTOM: MARITZA LUNA/SHUTTERSTOCK ©

Volcán Fuego (p176)

Guatemalan food (p30)

Toolkit

Storybook

RAY BARTLETT/LONELYPLANET ©

Naranjo (p131)

GUATEMALA
THE JOURNEY BEGINS HERE

Having traveled through Mexico for decades and seen that country's side of Yucatán, I'd always assumed Guatemala was essentially the same. How wrong I was, and how lucky, too, to discover it thanks to my love of Maya ruins. Guatemala deserves to be explored in depth and in detail. Each time I visit I find something new that amazes me, whether it's a ruin deep in the jungle or the astonishing degree of skill needed to make something on a backstrap loom. I love crossing a mountain ridge to meet people so different that not even the language is shared. Whether you come as a casual tourist just passing through or someone hoping to stay for weeks, months or years, Guatemala and its people will become a part of you, the experience will enrich you and the memories you take with you will be precious.

Ray Bartlett

@kaisoradotcom

My favourite experience is exploring the lost city of Naranjo (p131), in the eastern Petén jungle. The magnificent structures and challenges of getting there feel like living in an adventure movie.

WHO GOES WHERE

Our second writer and expert chooses
the place which, for him, defines Guatemala

The waterfall at Finca El Paraíso (pictured, p65) is a favorite for me. It's just absurdly underdeveloped. The car park is a mud pit, there are no changing rooms, the steps down to it are slippery bare earth carved into the hillside with broken handrails, and you have to hobble across razor-sharp rocks to get into the water. But once you're in, you forget all of that because you're in a truly spectacular, unique corner of the earth.

Lucas Vidgen

@LucasVidgen

Lucas is a writer and bicycle mechanic.

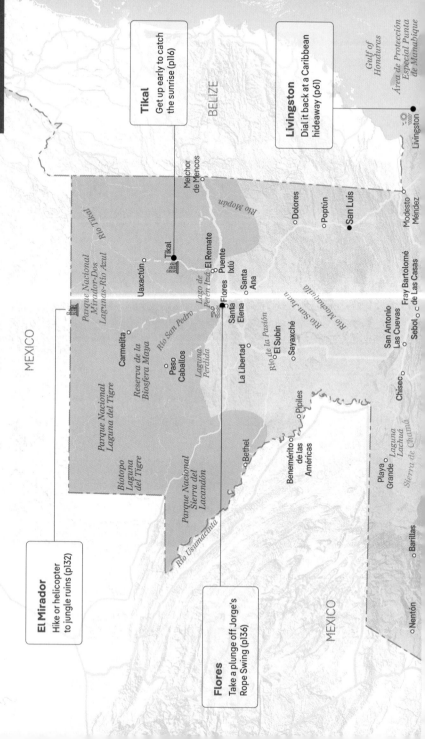

Tikal
Get up early to catch the sunrise (p116)

Livingston
Dial it back at a Caribbean hideaway (p61)

El Mirador
Hike or helicopter to jungle ruins (p132)

Flores
Take a plunge off Jorge's Rope Swing (p136)

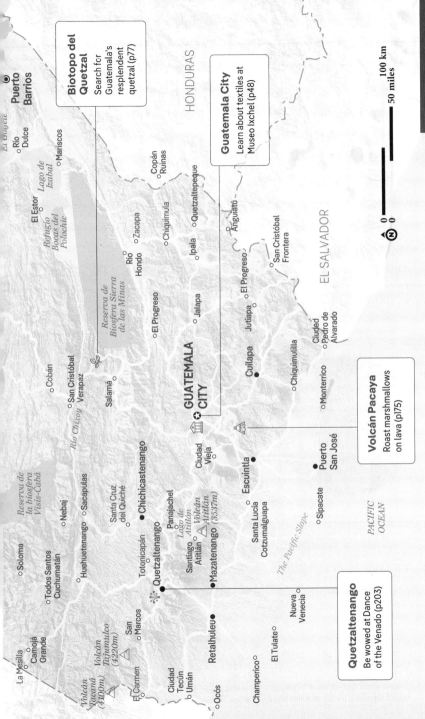

Biotopo del Quetzal
Search for Guatemala's resplendent quetzal (p77)

Guatemala City
Learn about textiles at Museo Ixchel (p48)

Volcán Pacaya
Roast marshmallows on lava (p175)

Quetzaltenango
Be wowed at Dance of the Venado (p203)

HONDURAS

EL SALVADOR

PACIFIC OCEAN

100 km
50 miles

La Bodega
Puerto Barrios
Río Dulce
Mariscos
Lago de Izabal
El Estor
Refugio Bocas del Polochic
Copán Ruinas
Zacapa
Chiquimula
Quetzaltepeque
Ipala
Anguiatú
San Cristóbal Frontera
Río Hondo
El Progreso
Jalapa
El Progreso
Jutiapa
Cuilapa
Ciudad Pedro de Alvarado
Chiquimulilla
Monterrico
Reserva de Biosfera Sierra de las Minas
Cobán
San Cristóbal Verapaz
Salamá
Río Chixoy
GUATEMALA CITY
Ciudad Vieja
Escuintla
Puerto San José
Sipacate
Santa Lucía Cotzumalguapa
Reserva de la biosfera Visis-Cabá
Soloma
Todos Santos Cuchumatán
Nebaj
Sacapulas
Santa Cruz del Quiché
Chichicastenango
Panajachel
Lago de Atitlán
Volcán Atitlán (3537m)
Santiago Atitlán
Mazatenango
Totonicapán
Quetzaltenango
Huehuetenango
La Mesilla
Camojá Grande
Volcán Tacaná (4100m)
Volcán Tajumulco (4220m)
San Marcos
El Carmen
Ciudad Tecún Umán
Ocós
Champerico
El Tulate
Nueva Venecia
Retalhuleu

7

ETCHED IN STONE

Amongst other things, Guatemala's original inhabitants were prodigious stonemasons, and left some fabulous reminders of their civilizations that have weathered the elements and can still be appreciated today. Towering temples and intricate carvings are dotted around the country – some are a short walk out of town and others require grueling treks through the jungle to visit. This is living history – many sites are still active today, used by worshippers to keep the old customs alive.

Getting In

Most archaeological sites charge a modest entrance fee that is often much higher for tourists than for locals. Even so, entry to Tikal costs about US$15.

Ruins Everywhere

There are archaeological sites all over the country, 18 of which are easily accessible to visitors. The greatest concentrations are in the Petén and highlands regions.

Be Prepared

Sites are often remote, with few services. Bring good walking shoes, insect repellent, plenty of water and a hat to keep the midday sun at bay.

BEST ARCHAEOLOGICAL EXPERIENCES

Get up early to catch the sunrise over ❶ **Tikal** (p116), accompanied by a soundtrack of howler monkeys.

Nip across the border into neighboring Honduras to check out the breathtaking site at ❷ **Copán** (p67).

Trek through the jungle (or cheat with a helicopter ride) to the hottest archaeological ruin in the country, ❸ **El Mirador** (p132).

Investigate the mix of Maya and Olmec cultures in the little-visited Pacific Slope site of ❹ **Takalik Abaj** (p90).

Check out the largest stelae in the Maya world, nestled amongst the banana plantations at ❺ **Quiriguá** (p66).

FROM LEFT: SIMON DANNHAUER/SHUTTERSTOCK ©, KOBBY DAGAN/SHUTTERSTOCK ©, TATI NOVA PHOTO MEXICO/SHUTTERSTOCK ©

Lago de Atitlán (p183)

WATERFRONT

Some of Guatemala's most beautiful places are found around its various lakes. Volcano-ringed Lago de Atitlán is the obvious superstar, but there's something magical about Lago de Petén Itzá (p137), the small towns on its shore and, of course, the island town of Flores. Further south, the massive Lago de Izabal is home to a staggering array of wildlife.

Into the Depths

With a maximum depth of 340m, Lago de Atitlán is thought to be the deepest lake in Central America.

Staying Afloat

Lake transport is often boat-only and lifejackets are sometimes available. If you want one, ask. If they don't have one, wait for the next boat.

BEST LAKESIDE EXPERIENCES

Go birding, swimming and canoeing in the rainforest-shrouded waters of the lovely, remote and rarely visited ❶ **Laguna Lachuá** (p77).

Take the stunning boat ride from the lake town of ❷ **Río Dulce** (p62), down the river to the Caribbean port town of Livingston.

Explore Guatemala's pirate past at ❸ **El Castillo de San Felipe** on the banks of the Lago de Izabal (p69).

Find yourself grounded and calm in a yoga retreat overlooking ❹ **Lago de Atitlán** (p183).

Laze in hammocks and dive off ❺ **Jorge's Rope Swing in Flores** (p144).

A WOVEN TRADITION

One of the things you'll be struck by when you first get to Guatemala is the wild array of colors that are used in everyday life thanks to the country's strong tradition of weaving. Traditionally woven garments are used particularly by indigenous women in daily life, and the elaborately woven and embroidered designs you see walking around the streets make their way into markets, decorations and shops.

Style Guide

Weaving designs are very specific to towns and regions – experts can tell where a woman is from just by the style of clothes she is wearing.

Menswear

Although traditional dress is mostly used by indigenous women, the equivalent for men is still used in some towns like Santiago Atitlán and Todos Santos Cuchumatán.

Learning the Ropes

You can learn to weave on a traditional backstrap loom at schools in San Pedro La Laguna, Quetzaltenango and Antigua.

BEST TEXTILE EXPERIENCES

Immerse yourself in the **❶ Museo Ixchel** (p50) in Guatemala City dedicated to the culture and history of weaving and traditional dress.

Strike a bargain in Guatemala City's Mercado Central or **❷ Mercado de Artesanías** (p54) – both excellent places to browse and buy.

Peruse the stunning textiles in **❸ Chichicastenango's** market (p208).

Learn about dyes and fabrics at **❹ Atitlán Women Weavers** (p191), a women's weaving collective in San Pedro Atitlán.

Visit **❺ Nebaj** (p209) and the Ixil Triangle, where women proudly wear traditional *traje*.

11

THE FESTIVE SPIRIT

Guatemalans love to party and, no matter where you are in the country, there's pretty much guaranteed to be a festival popping off within half a day's travel from where you are. To begin with, each town has a patron saint and each saint has a day on the calendar, so most towns hold a festival at that time of year to honor their patron. Other festivals celebrate specific ethnic groups, historic events and sacred days.

Old Time Fun

Town festivals are becoming more generic, but some maintain old traditions like catching greased pigs or the *palo volador*, the Maya version of the maypole.

Burning the Devil

The Quema del Diablo (burning of the devil) is celebrated in early December, with fireworks, processions and residents burning trash in the street.

A Picnic with a Difference

On All Saints' Day (November 1) families take food to the cemetery to have picnics with departed loved ones and tend their graves.

BEST FESTIVAL EXPERIENCES

Hop a boat to Livingston to celebrate ❶ **Garifuna Day** (November 26, p27), with Garifuna music, food and dancing.

Follow the skulls as they get paraded around town in the ❷ **Procesión de la Santa Calavera** (p27) in San José on All Saints Day (November 1).

Watch as men fly around the *palo volador* – a pre-Hispanic version of the maypole – in ❸ **Cubulco's** (p79) annual festival.

Be wowed with the festivities at ❹ **Dance of the Venado** (p205) in Quetzaltenango.

Enjoy a carnival-type atmosphere at ❺ **Baile de la Chatona y el Caballito** (p114), in Flores.

13

FROM LEFT: MILOSZ MASLANKA/SHUTTERSTOCK ©, ALEKSANDAR TODOROVIC/SHUTTERSTOCK ©, SARINE ARSLANIAN/SHUTTERSTOCK ©

Hammocks, Lago de Atitlán (p183)

KICK BACK

Sure, there's plenty to do in Guatemala, but sometimes the best thing to do is to do nothing. Guatemalans love to take it easy and if you've run down your batteries traipsing around archaeological sites, scaling volcanoes and exploring markets, there are some fantastic places to settle back for a recharge before diving back into the fray.

Get Swinging

Loving the hammock? If your back can handle it, some budget hotels along the coast will rent you a hammock to sleep in.

Settling In

Found somewhere you'd like to stay for a while? If you're in for some serious downtime, ask your hotel for their weekly (or monthly!) rates.

BEST DO-NOTHING EXPERIENCES

Hit the hills and blend in with the growing backpacker scene in the lush surrounds of ❶ **Lanquín** (p75).

Pull up a hammock and consider taking some surfing lessons (tomorrow, maybe?) in the laidback surfer haven of ❷ **El Paredón** (p108).

Dial it back Caribbean-style in the small town of ❸ **Livingston** (p61), where white sands, blue water, cold beer and sea breezes are all on hand.

Laze around the lakeside sipping coffee or getting plastered in ❹ **Flores** (p136).

People-watch in ❺ **Antigua's** central plaza. (p166).

GRINGO-FREE GUATEMALA

The tourist trail is well-worn in Guatemala, but there are hundreds of opportunities to get off it and experience a whole other side of the country. Being the only foreigner in town may sound intimidating, but the basics are easy to organise and Guatemalans are so welcoming that they'll be happy (and probably slightly curious) to see you.

❺

❸   **❷**

❹

❶

Getting There

Guatemalan buses go nearly everywhere. Just tell the driver's helper where you're heading – they'll make sure you get off at the right spot.

Staying There

Nearly every small town has at least one hotel – the humbler ones are called *hospedaje*. Look for them near where the bus stops.

Making Connections

English is rare outside of the main tourist areas, and a couple of weeks of Spanish classes will give you the basics to make some friends.

BEST OFF-THE-BEATEN-TRACK EXPERIENCES

Hit the beach but skip the crowds in the tiny Pacific coast beach town of **❶ Tilapita** (p91).

Go back to nature in the lush surrounds of the **❷ Punta de Manabique** (p63) reserve on the Caribbean coast.

Base yourself in **❸ Raxruhá** (p66), an excellent staging post to explore nearby caves, lagoons and Maya sites.

Helicopter or hike to rarely visited **❹ El Mirador** (p132).

Go deep into the jungle to visit the ruins of **❺ Naranjo** (p131).

15

FIERY PEAKS

Throughout western Guatemala, almost wherever you look, the horizon is defined by volcanoes. There are 33 of them all up, the majority extinct or dormant, and only three classified as currently active. Volcanoes have shaped the history of the country, causing catastrophes and forcing the capital city to relocate multiple times, but they're also sacred to the Maya and a favorite hiking destination for locals and visitors alike.

The Fiery One

Guatemala's most active volcano, Volcán Fuego, looms over Antigua – it regularly spits ash and gas, and has erupted seven times in the last decade.

Going Up?

It's recommended to climb most volcanoes in Guatemala with a guide. You'll find specialized tour operators in Antigua, Quetzaltenango and around Lago de Atitlán.

A Way to Pay the Bills

Geothermal energy is an obvious possibility for Guatemala – it's estimated that two thirds of the country's energy requirements could be met this way.

BEST VOLCANIC EXPERIENCES

Explore the **❶ Tecuamburro** (p59) volcanic complex, a set of three volcanoes, on the outskirts of the small town of Cuilapa.

From Quetzaltenango, scale the nearby **❷ Volcán Cerro Quemado** (p207), an active volcano revered by the Maya as a pilgrimage spot.

Challenge yourself on **❸ Volcán Atitlán** (p183), Lake Volcán Atitlán's highest volcano and a known hangout for the resplendent quetzal.

Hike the **❹ Rostro Maya** (p188) to view the sunrise over Lago de Atitlán.

Roast marshmallows in the still-warm lava flow of **❺ Volcán Pacaya** (p157).

ANIMAL CROSSINGS

Guatemala's wide range of landscapes and climatic zones are home to a staggering array of animals – 600 species of birds, 250 types of mammals and over 200 reptiles and amphibians, not counting butterflies and other insects. Some are endangered, some have grown wary of humans, and others are so common you'll be brushing them out the way.

For the Birds

Guatemala is a world-renowned bird-watching destination. Over 300 bird species (including nine hummingbirds and four trogons) have been recorded at Tikal alone.

Fanged Friends

Guatemala doesn't have many poisonous snakes, but the tropical rattlesnake and the fer-de-lance are both highly venomous and worth avoiding at all costs.

To Spot a Manatee...

The marine reserves around Río Dulce are where you'll have your best chance of spotting the notoriously shy manatee – take a canoe and paddle softly.

④
⑤

②

③①

BEST WILDLIFE EXPERIENCES

Rescue turtle eggs or release the hatchlings back into the sea in the coastal town of ❶ **Monterrico** (p102).

Try your luck at spotting Guatemala's elusive national bird, the resplendent quetzal, at the ❷ Biotopo del Quetzal (p77).

Rescue turtle eggs or release the hatchlings back into the sea in the coastal town of ❶ **Monterrico** (p102).

Take the drive-thru approach to wildlife spotting at ❸ Autosafari Chapín (p109).

See jaguars and learn about the illegal wildlife trade at ❹ **ARCAS**. (p142)

Watch howler monkeys dance above you on ❺ **Chiminos Island** (p156).

REGIONS & CITIES

Find the places that tick all your boxes.

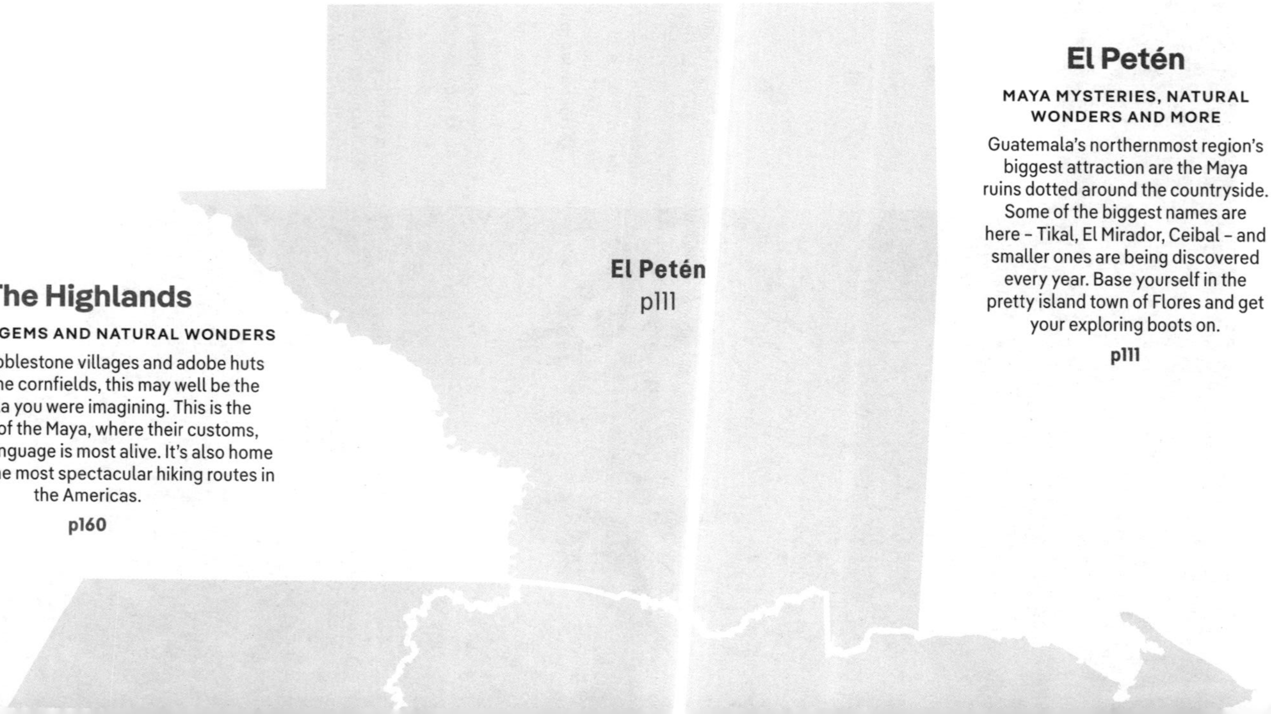

The Highlands

CULTURAL GEMS AND NATURAL WONDERS

With its cobblestone villages and adobe huts amongst the cornfields, this may well be the Guatemala you were imagining. This is the heartland of the Maya, where their customs, dress and language is most alive. It's also home to some of the most spectacular hiking routes in the Americas.

p160

El Petén

MAYA MYSTERIES, NATURAL WONDERS AND MORE

Guatemala's northernmost region's biggest attraction are the Maya ruins dotted around the countryside. Some of the biggest names are here – Tikal, El Mirador, Ceibal – and smaller ones are being discovered every year. Base yourself in the pretty island town of Flores and get your exploring boots on.

p111

El Petén
p111

Central & Eastern Guatemala

BIG CITIES AND LUSH SURROUNDS

Love it or hate it, Guatemala City is ground zero for museums, galleries, live music, theater and other big-city delights. In the cloud forests in the middle of the country, crops turn to coffee and cardamom, orchids abound, and you might just see a quetzal bird in the wild.

p43

Central & Eastern Guatemala
p43

The Pacific Slope
p80

The Highlands
p160

The Pacific Slope

GUATEMALA'S PLAYGROUND

Suffering sensory overload from the sights, sounds and smells of the rest of the country? Kick back and put in some serious hammock time in Guatemala's sun-drenched playground where the beer is cold, the seafood is fresh and the pace of life is dialed waaaaaaay back.

p80

ITINERARIES

The Big Three

Allow: 8 days
Distance: 1200km

This classic itinerary takes in Guatemala's superstars that appear on pretty much any visitor's 'must-see' list. There's some nice variation here – Antigua's good for architecture, foodies and nightlife, Lago de Atitlán is Guatemalan nature and traditional culture at its finest, and Tikal offers glimpses into the splendor of the peaks of Maya civilization.

Tikal (p116)

❶ ANTIGUA ⏱ 2 DAYS

You'll probably land in Guatemala City, but leave that for later – the tranquil, tourist-friendly town of **Antigua** (pictured, p166) is a much better place to find your feet. Get ready to take some photographs – there are stunning vistas at every turn. Wander the streets, explore the ruins, climb a volcano. Once you're done, hop one of the regular shuttles heading for Lago de Atitlán.

🚌 *2 hours by minibus*

❷ LAGO DE ATITLÁN ⏱ 2 DAYS

Panajachel has the most bustle, San Marcos is a hippy enclave, San Pedro is the laidback party town, or there are more traditional options in San Juan or Santiago. Wherever you stay, don't miss a boat ride across **Lago de Atitlán** (p183) – it's a truly memorable experience.

🚐 **Detour:** *If you're here on a Thursday or Saturday, hop over to Chichicastenango market.* ⏱ *1½ hours*
🚌 *4 hours by bus*

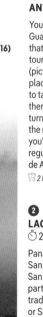

③ GUATEMALA CITY ⏱ 1 DAY

Many avoid it, but given that you have to pass through anyway, consider stopping off in **Guatemala City** (p48) to check out the world-class museums in Zona 13 and crumbling grandeur of the Centro Historico. You might also be interested to see how the other 1% live – Zonas 10 and 15 are the affluent side of Guatemala that you don't really see elsewhere.

✈ 1 hour by plane; 🚌 9 hours by bus

④ FLORES & TIKAL ⏱ 2 DAYS

Your best bets for getting here are overnight first-class bus or plane. You'll arrive near the charming island town of **Flores** (p136), which makes a good launching point for Tikal. Get out to the site early to avoid the crowds and the heat, and spend the day scrambling up ancient pyramids, as monkeys swing through the trees and *tepezcuintles* scurry along the ground.

ITINERARIES

Into the Mountains

Allow: at least 9 days
Distance: 785km

Guatemala's most traditional regions are in the western highlands and the high plateau that forms the center of the country. Ancient customs live and breathe here. There's not much English spoken and in some remote communities even Spanish is a distant second language. For many, this is the real Guatemala.

Todos Santos Cuchumatán **2**

Huehuetenango — 5hr

Cuilco

Volcán Tajumulco (4220m) — San Sebastián

Momostenango

San Cristóbal Totonicapán

San Marcos

Totonicapán

El Tumbador

START **1**

Quetzaltenango **1**

❶ QUETZALTENANGO
⏱ 2 DAYS

The largest city in the highlands and second-largest in the country, **Quetzaltenango** (p203) is a bit of a cultural hub. It's home to many artists and literary figures, with a population swollen by students from the seven universities in town. People come here to learn Spanish, hike and climb nearby volcanoes or simply take in life in an everyday Guatemalan town.
🚌 *5 hours by bus*

❷ TODOS SANTOS CUCHUMATÁN
⏱ 2 DAYS

At the foot of a valley high in the mountains, the little town of **Todos Santos Cuchumatán** (p216) is frequently enveloped by fog by 4pm; otherwise, the views of the surrounding countryside are breathtaking, and it's a favorite hiking destination. The Mam culture is strongly preserved here, and this is one of the few places where you'll see men in traditional dress.
🚌 *5 hours by bus*

❸ NEBAJ ⏱ 3 DAYS

Pushing further into the mountains brings you to **Nebaj** (p209), where local guides offer a plethora of hikes visiting local communities along the way. In many ways, this is a forgotten part of Guatemala – it suffered brutally during the civil war and conditions are slow to improve. To see what life is really like for many rural Guatemalans, this is a good place to start.
🚌 *7 hours by bus*

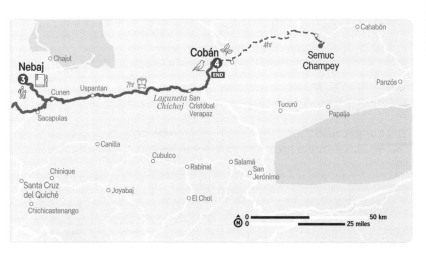

Volcán Tajumulco (p202)

HUMBERTO DIAZ/SHUTTERSTOCK ©

❹ COBÁN ⏱ 2 DAYS

With a couple of bus connections, you'll reach the modern, bustling town of **Cobán** (p70), nestled in the cloud forests at the center of the country. Just out of town you can tour coffee and cardamom plantations, or search for orchids or birdlife, including the resplendent quetzal.

🔄 *Detour:* Visit the limestone pools of Semuc Champey (pictured), a truly divine swimming spot. ⏱ 4 hours

WHEN TO GO

Answer: whenever you want. The Land of the Eternal Spring has comfy weather year-round and there's always something happening.

You don't have to worry too much about peak season in Guatemala – the country sees more of a steady trickle of foreign tourists than any wild influxes. Probably the spring break in the United States sees the biggest wave of tourists, but don't worry – this is no Cancún.

The only time things get complicated is during the rainy season, which runs roughly May to September and tends to culminate with a hurricane or two. Up in the mountains it gets chilly. Down on the coast and in the jungle it gets steamy. If you're planning on moving around, bring layers that you can add and subtract accordingly.

The Local Crush

The only time you're ever likely to struggle with accommodation is around Christmas and Easter – Guatemalans love to travel during those periods and hotels book out with locals and tourists from neighboring countries. Prices tend to spike at these times, then remain stable for the rest of the year.

LUCY BROWN/SHUTTERSTOCK ©
FAR RIGHT: NOBITO/SHUTTERSTOCK ©

Easter celebrations, Antigua (p166)

⊕ I LIVE HERE

EASTER IN ANTIGUA

Brenda Vasquéz is an IT contractor based in Guatemala City. She has lived and worked all over Central America and in the United States.

We go to Antigua every Easter. Sometimes the crowds get crazy. If you don't like being around lots of people, avoid the main days. But it's such a special atmosphere – everybody is happy, there's never trouble. We love the processions, the carpets, everything – it's like nothing else. Everybody should see it at least once.

LA CANÍCULA

A glorious little respite from the daily downpours, La Canícula or *veranillo* (little summer) is a 10- to 15-day break in the rainy season when the rain just stops and the whole country gets a chance to dry out a bit.

Weather Through the Year

	JANUARY	FEBRUARY	MARCH	APRIL	MAY	JUNE
Ave. daytime max:	24°C	25°C	26°C	27°C	27°C	25°C
Days of rainfall:	2	2	2	5	13	23

MICROCLIMATES EVERYWHERE

Guatemala has dozens of microclimates as well as larger climate zones. Going from Quetzaltenango (altitude 2330m) to Retalhuleu (239m) takes about an hour; the trip passes through an estimated 30 microclimates and sees the temperature rise around 20°C.

Sacred Days

As you'd expect, Guatemala goes all out on the Christian calendar's two big events. **Semana Santa** (Easter) sees statues paraded through the streets, carried by hooded devotees. This goes off all over the country, but **Antigua** (p166) sees the most elaborate parades, with **Guatemala City** (p48) a close second. 🌤 **April**

Christmas is slightly more subdued, except for the national obsession of letting off fireworks at midnight on Christmas Eve. ☀ **December**

Smaller towns have their own traditions – in the south, **Esquipulas** (p56) pays homage to the Black Christ idol on January 15 and thousands of pilgrims flock into town. ☀ **January**

All Saints Day (November 1) is commemorated across the country as cemeteries take on a festive air, with families visiting deceased relatives. Enormous multicolored kites are flown in the small towns of Santiago Sacatapéquez and Sumpango. ☀ **November**

 I LIVE HERE

HIKING SEASON

Mario Carvallo is a tour guide specializing in volcano hikes. He has been leading hiking expeditions in Guatemala for over 20 years.

I'll go to the mountains any time, but the best time for me is just after the rainy season. There's something different in the light – the visibility is better than any other time of the year and this is when the wildflowers come out. You can't see the ground for all the different colored flowers there are.

Regional Flavor

Guatemala's cultural diversity is really on display in the smaller festivals that take place around the country throughout the year. November 26 is **Garifuna Day**, most fervently celebrated in the small coastal town of **Livingston** (p61) – expect lots of live music, traditional food, dancing and general partying into the night. ☀ **November**

The Fiesta de Cabulco is one of the few places in the country

to maintain the tradition of the *palo volador* (flying pole) where men swing by their feet from ropes attached to the top of a 30m pole – you can see it on the last day of their five-day festival at the end of July. Other ancient rituals are kept alive when the highly traditional town of **Rabinal** (p78) has its festival around the middle of January. ☀ **January**

Christmas, San Andres Xecul

DREAMING OF A WHITE CHRISTMAS?

With sub-zero temperatures and altitudes above 2000m, you'd expect at least a little snow in these parts, but nope – when it's hot, it rains, and when it's cold, it stops. No snow for you.

	JULY	AUGUST	SEPTEMBER	OCTOBER	NOVEMBER	DECEMBER
Ave. daytime max:	**25°C**	**25°C**	**25°C**	**24°C**	**24°C**	**24°C**
Days of rainfall:	19	19	21	15	7	3

Hiking, Volcán Acatenango (p176)

GET PREPARED FOR GUATEMALA

Useful things to load in your bag, your ears and your brain

Clothes

Layers: The big questions are where and when. If you'll be in the mountains, bring extra – it gets chilly at night. The lowlands are steamy, so you'll want loose-fitting clothes with long sleeves and pants to keep the mosquitos away. An umbrella is much more useful than a rain jacket in the hot rainy season.

Boots and shoes: It's unlikely that you'll be needing formal shoes, but some cleanish newish street shoes will give you a break from those heavy hiking boots and be good enough for a night out at a nice restaurant. Flip-flops are a must for shared showers and coastal regions.

Manners

Eating: It's customary to say 'buen provecho' (bon apetit) to other diners as you enter or leave a restaurant.

Bargaining: This is acceptable pretty much anywhere that doesn't have price tags on the products.

Church: Dress respectfully if you're going inside – for men this means long pants; for women, covered shoulders and a reasonably high neckline.

If you forget something: Don't panic – clothes of varying quality are sold all over the country.

READ

Men of Maize (Miguel Ángel Asturias; 1949) The most famous novel by Guatemala's most famous novelist.

A Mayan Life (Gaspar Pedro Gonzáles; 1995) A beautiful and at times heart-wrenching study of rural Guatemalan life.

Time Among the Maya (Ronald Wright; 1989) A classic travelogue with history, politics, anthropology and archaeology.

The Art of Political Murder (Francisco Goldman; 2008) Looks at the dictatorship's role in Catholic Bishop Gerardi's assassination.

Words

'Hola' Hello, often followed by a 'qué tal?' or 'qué onda?' (what's up?).

'Chapín' is what Guatemalans call themselves.

'Vos' is a very informal way to say 'you' – only use it with friends, or better yet, wait to see if the other person uses it on you first.

'Camioneta/parilla' the famous 'chicken bus'; the repurposed US school buses that go everywhere and are the cheapest (and least comfortable) form of transportation.

'Porfa' Guatemalans love abbreviations – this one is short for 'por favor' (please). If you want to get more relaxed, try 'porfis'.

'La refa' is short for la 'refacción' (a snack).

'Orale' is borrowed from Mexico but used extensively here. This multi-use word is most useful when you want to agree to a proposal: 'Let's go to the beach'... 'Orale'

'Cafecito' Guatemalans love putting diminutives on words, like putting a 'y' on the end of an English word. So a coffee (café) becomes a 'cafecito'. The queen (reina) is a 'reinita'. You can refer to Lucas as Luquito. Note that actual size has nothing to do with it – a plane can be an 'avioncito'.

'De nada' is the standard way of saying 'you're welcome'.

'Buenos días'/'buenas tardes'/'buenas noches' means good day (anytime before noon)/good afternoon (any time before the sun goes down)/good evening (after dark).

'Que te vaya bien' literally translates as 'that you go well'; a cool way of saying goodbye.

WATCH

Aquí me Quedo (Rodolfo Espinoza; 2010) Comedy using a kidnapping to tease out political satire.

When the Mountains Tremble (Pamela Yates & Newton Thomas Sigel; 1983) Story of the conflict between the Maya and the military.

Capsulas (Verónica Riedel; 2011) From one of the country's few female directors, looking at greed, corruption and the drug trade.

Ixcanúl (Jayro Bustamante; 2015, pictured) A beautifully shot tale of a young Kaqchiquel girl's coming of age.

La Llorona (Jayro Bustamante; 2019) An ex-dictator is haunted by the spirits of his victims.

LISTEN

Galería Caribe (Ricardo Arjona; 2000) The first Billboard number one for Guatemala's most famous pop singer still sounds pretty good today.

Ilusión (Gabby Moreno; 2016) Grammy-nominated album from LA-based folk-pop superstar, mostly sung in Spanish.

Mil Palabras Con Sus Dientes (Bohemia Suburbana; 1999) The breakthrough album of arguably the best of the '90s Guatemalan rock bands.

Jun Winaq' Rajawal Q'ij (Balam Ajpu; 2020) Debut release from Maya hip-hop outfit, rapping in Tz'utujil, K'iche', Kaqchiquel and Spanish.

Guatemalan breakfast of beans, eggs, tortillas and plantains

THE FOOD SCENE

If you've got a few quetzals in your pocket you'll never go
hungry in Guatemala – delicious, nutritious food is everywhere.

From fast and tasty street food to luxurious fine dining, Guatemala's food scene is rich, varied and often surprising. What you eat depends greatly on where you are – down on the coast, seafood is king, while up in the mountains, hearty stews and broths keep the cold at bay. The cattle country to the east is unsurprisingly a beef-eater's paradise. More cosmopolitan areas like Antigua and parts of Guatemala City offer up international dining and experimental cuisine, often with unique Guatemalan twists added.

All of this is powered by Guatemala's extensive farmlands – visit any local market and be prepared to be blown away by the sheer variety of fresh produce on display. Foods that feel luxurious back home like avocados, mangoes, rambutan and dragon fruit are everyday items here, sitting alongside the apples and bananas.

Food is one of the great, simple unifiers of Guatemalan culture and mealtimes are often joyous occasions, offering everyone a chance to take a break, relax and enjoy the company.

The Guatemalan Staples

Here we have to begin with corn, and more specifically, the tortilla. No traditional Guatemalan meal is complete without it. Tortillas are made from cornmeal, traditionally slapped into a patty shape and grilled on a flat plate called a comal. Tortilla-making machines are beginning to take over this laborious process, but purists swear by

Best Guatemalan Dishes	PEPIÁN	TAPADO	JOCÓN	CHUCHITOS
	Chicken or turkey in a spicy sesame seed and tomato sauce.	The traditional Garifuna seafood and plantain stew.	Green stew of herbs, vegetables and chicken or turkey.	Beans or meat wrapped in corn dough, steamed in corn husks.

the handmade variety. The tortilla's rival in ubiquity would be frijoles (beans). Eaten any time, the humble frijoles tend to come pureed into a paste (volteados) and served as a purplish-black lump on your plate. Runners-up in the popularity stakes are eggs and plantains. The former come any way you want them – scrambled (revueltos) being the most popular, with fried (fritos) as a close second. Plantains are generally fried, too, although some dishes call for them to be boiled.

With a little side dish of cream and maybe a sliver of fresh white cheese, the above describes the classic Guatemalan meal. All this is washed down with coffee, which tends to be of the weak, filtered variety, served black (negro), unless you specify that you want milk (con leche).

Vegetarians & Vegans

It's not hard being vegetarian in Guatemala, but it's not particularly easy. A lot of dishes are prepared with animal stock, making it hard to be 100% vegetarian. Unless something is specifically advertised as being vegetarian, it's worthwhile being very specific about your diet. *Sin carne* (without meat) means 'without beef' to many Guatemalans and may get you a plate with chicken, ham or fish instead.

It's much easier to find meat-free options in larger cities and places used to catering to foreign tourists. Chinese restaurants are the huge exception here – they always have vegetarian options on the menu and quite often have tofu. Elsewhere, you may find yourself buying your own ingredients and cooking a lot. Backpacker hostels often have kitchen facilities and if you're staying in a homestay, your host family will no doubt let you use their kitchen.

Chuchitos

CHOCOLATE

Next time you're enjoying a steaming cup of hot chocolate, bear in mind that you're engaging in a ritual going back thousands of years.

The earliest evidence of cacao consumption is from the Olmec culture, around 1750 BCE. Chocolate soon gained luxury status amongst the Aztecs and Maya who used it in rituals and even as currency (which of course lead to cacao counterfeiting – emptying out the seed pod and filling it with mud).

The rest of the world had never seen cacao before the Spanish conquest – along with potatoes, tomatoes, corn, beans, squash, chili, avocados and vanilla, it's one of the foods we take for granted, but it was completely unknown outside of Mesoamerica a few hundred years ago.

Hot cacao

KAK'IK	BOXBOL	FIAMBRE	CHILES RELLENOS
Traditional turkey stew from the Alta Verapaz region.	Balls of corn dough and meat, wrapped in squash leaves and boiled.	A technicolor multi-ingredient salad, usually eaten on Día de los Muertos.	Breaded and fried bell peppers, stuffed with meat and vegetables.

Specialties

Savor our selection of culinary classics and gastro challenges.

Snacks & Street Food

Tacos The classic roadside snack, available everywhere in portions of three.

Pupusas Fried cornmeal patties stuffed with beans or cheese.

Tamalitos de chipilín Corn flour mixed with chipilín leaves, steamed in corn husks.

Sweet Treats

Buñuelos Like little donut balls, deep fried, rolled in sugar and swimming in anise syrup.

Rellenitos A beguiling mixture of plantain, bean paste, cinnamon and vanilla, often served with cream.

Arroz con leche For fans of rice pudding, this one is made by boiling rice, sugar, vanilla and cinnamon in milk.

Dare to Try

Revolcado An extremely tasty stew often made with a pig's head, liver and heart along with tomato, onion, garlic, cumin and bell peppers.

Elote Loco Scarier than it

Ceviche

sounds, 'crazy corn' is basically steamed or grilled corn, covered with everything the vendor can get their hands on – ketchup, cheese, mayonnaise, mustard, Worcestershire sauce, chili and lemon. You can choose your ingredients, but purists go for *con todo* (with everything).

Ceviche Seafood (usually shrimp and fish) that is 'cooked' simply by letting it marinade in lemon juice. If that doesn't sound that daring, consider that you can buy it from car-trunk vendors, hundreds of miles from the ocean!

MEALS OF A LIFETIME

Las Tres Garifunas (p61) The *tapado* is great (everything on the menu is good) and the atmosphere is spot-on Garifuna hospitality; in Livingston.

Swell (p108) Shrimp tacos in El Paredón like you've always hoped for, with fresh ingredients and a tangy sauce.

Xkape Koba'n (p72) Check out the traditional Kak'ik in their lovely Cobán garden dining area.

Maracuya (p138) Delicious *pepián* in Flores, in either chicken or vegan varieties.

Romeo y Julieta (p168) Housemade pastas in a quaint Antigua restaurant that feels like you're in the Italian countryside.

THE YEAR IN FOOD

EASTER

Traditionally eaten on Good Wednesday, there are many varieties of *pan de Semana Santa* (Easter bread), but the one to look out for is *pan de yemas*, made with egg yolk.

DÍA DE LOS MUERTOS

The biggest party in town is at the cemetery, where elaborate plates of cold cuts, pickles and everything else imaginable form part of the feast to honor the dead.

CHRISTMAS

Tamales are eaten year-round, but no Christmas is complete without these delicious banana-leaf-wrapped parcels whose ingredients include corn mash, meat and spices.

NEW YEAR'S EVE

When the clock strikes midnight, make sure you have 12 grapes on hand (not 11, not 13). Custom says that eating them at that time will bring you luck for the New Year.

Pepián

SIMON DANNHAUER/SHUTTERSTOCK ©

Lago de Atitlán (p183)

THE OUTDOORS

Few countries can match Guatemala in the range and sheer awesomeness of its outdoors, from jungles and erupting volcanoes to cloud forests and crocodile-filled lagoons.

Guatemala's spectacular elevation changes make for fantastic variety in what you can do, see and experience while you're here. You can look down from a high volcanic peak at sunrise and then be swimming, kayaking or even diving in the azure waters below a few hours later. Hike in a misty cloud forest in the morning, then hop on a bus and be ready to swim or surf on the Pacific coast an hour later.

Jungle Trekking

For those who are up for a true jungle experience, prepare to get those hiking boots muddy and hit the jungle trails of El Petén, visiting ruins lost and long-forgotten that still sit waiting to be excavated. On the way, spot beautiful birds, *curious* pizotes (coatis) or maybe, just maybe, a jaguar.

It's not for the faint of heart. On the way you can expect to have temperatures over 30°C, sweat buckets and swat mosquitoes who think DEET is merely a tasty seasoning.

Trips like this will make you feel like Indiana Jones, and while you can count on plenty of unexpected things happening, one thing we can say is: this is no walk in the park.

Summiting Volcanoes

Whatever your religious views, even the most jaded agnostic can't help but look out

More to Explore

RUINS
Uncover rarely seen Maya mysteries at remote **Uaxactún** (p121).

CAVING
Meet a vampire (vampire bat, that is!) as you go underground in **Cuevas de Candelaria** (p75).

KAYAKING
Take in a lake or lakeshore and even see crocodiles in **Lago de Petén Itzá** (p137).

FAMILY ADVENTURES

Visit the incredible ruin of **Tikal** (p116) and learn about the vanished Maya who built the city.

Helicopter to El Mirador (p132) and climb Guatemala's largest pyramid, getting a view of unbroken jungle as far as the eye can see.

Learn how to protect wildlife at the animal rehab center **ARCAS** (p142), and see jaguars, parrots and macaws.

Explore the abandoned 17th-century **Castillo de San Felipe de Lara** (p69), with canons and lots of narrow passageways.

Be wowed by the beauty of orchids on a tour of the **Orquigonia** (p73). Some are only a few millimeters high!

Spot a brilliantly colored resplendent quetzal in the cloud forest reserves outside **Cobán** (p67).

---

from atop a Guatemalan volcanic peak and think there's something grander, bigger, more cosmic out there.

If you camp overnight you'll look up and think the stars are close enough to pluck from the night sky.

With the infernal glow of a nearby erupting volcano, you may even wonder if you've been hiking down, into a fiery hell, instead of up.

But when the sun's rays pierce the darkness and you see the majestic tapestry of the country stretching out below as far as you can see, nothing earthly seems to matter any-

more. It's an ineffable, beautiful and, yes, we'll say it, spiritual experience that rewards those who don't mind steep trails, loose gravel and a slip or slide along the way.

Boating

Some of the best outdoor fun you'll have in Guatemala isn't on land, but on the water: whether you're riding a *lancha* across a flat lagoon surface to visit the other side, zipping through a twisty river or diving off a gunwale into a pristine swimming hole, there's no end to the possibilities when it comes to boats and water.

Look for manatees on a quiet cruise between Livingston and Río Dulce.

Grab the camera and get some great birding in as you head up narrow tributaries to visit the Dos Pilas or Aguateca ruins around quiet Sayaxché.

Lean over (or dive off!) the boat that's taken you to beautiful azure Crater Azul. Hunt for rare waterlilies and other riparian flowers in the reedy shores of Lago de Izabal.

Or if all that's too humdrum for your tastes, hit Lago de Petén Itzá after dark, partying and drinking with friends on a night cruise as the music blares.

BEST SPOTS

For the best outdoor spots and routes, see the map on page 36.

CARRERAARDON/SHUTTERSTOCK ©

Crater Azul (p153)

HIKING
Find monkeys, birds, and more in a hike in the beautiful **Biotopo Cerro Cahuí** (p151).

BIRDWATCHING
Seek out trogons and other rare birds as you explore **Tikal** (p116).

HORSEBACK RIDING
Ride along the shores at **Monterrico** (p102).

ZIPLINING
See the canopy like a bird would at **Reserva Natural Atitlán** (p178).

ACTION AREAS

Where to find Guatemala's best outdoor activities.

Walking/Hiking
1 Acul (p209)
2 Biotopo del Quetzal (p77)
3 El Mirador (p132)
4 Nakum (p132)
5 Naranjo (p131)

Ruins
1 Copán (p67)
2 El Ceibal (p154)
3 Iglesia y Convento de la Recolección (p168)
4 Takalik Abaj (p90)
5 Uaxactún (p121)

National Parks
1 Biotopo Monterrico-Hawaii (p104)
2 Los Tarrales Nature Reserve (p195)
3 Punta de Manabique (p63)
4 Parque Nacional Laguna Lachuá (p77)
5 Tikal (116)

MEXICO

BELIZE

Gulf of Honduras

Livingston

MEXICO

Parque Nacional Mirador-Dos Lagunas-Río Azul

Río Tikal

Parque Nacional Laguna del Tigre

Reserva de la Biosfera Maya

Carmelita

Biotopo Laguna del Tigre

Paso Caballos

Laguna Perdida

Río San Pedro

Parque Nacional Sierra del Lacandón

Bethel

Río Usumacinta

Benemérito de las Américas

Pipiles

La Libertad

Sayaxché

Río de la Pasión

El Subin

Río San Juan

Río Machaquilá

San Antonio Las Cuevas

Chisec

Playa Grande

Laguna Lachuá

Nentón

Barillas

Uaxactún

Tikal

El Remate

Puente Ixlú

Santa Ana

Lago de Petén Itzá

Flores

Santa Elena

Lago de Yaxhá

Melchor de Mencos

Dolores

Poptún

San Luis

Fray Bartolomé de Las Casas

Sebol

Modesto Méndez

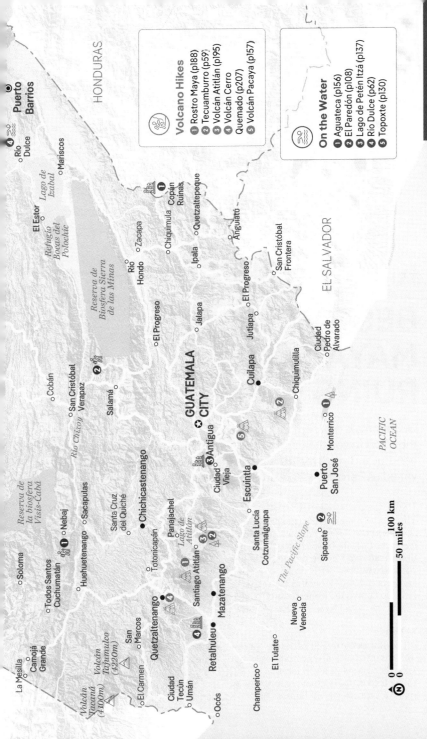

Volcano Hikes

❶ Rostro Maya (p188)
❷ Tecuamburro (p59)
❸ Volcán Atitlán (p195)
❹ Volcán Cerro Quemado (p207)
❺ Volcán Pacaya (p157)

On the Water

❶ Aguateca (p156)
❷ El Paredón (p108)
❸ Lago de Petén Itzá (p137)
❹ Río Dulce (p62)
❺ Topoxte (p130)

HONDURAS

EL SALVADOR

Puerto Barrios

Río Dulce

Copán Ruinas

Chiquimula

Quetzaltepeque

Anguiatú

San Cristóbal Frontera

Ipala

Jalapa

El Progreso

Jutiapa

Ciudad Pedro de Alvarado

Chiquimulilla

Cuilapa

GUATEMALA CITY

Antigua

Ciudad Vieja

Escuintla

Puerto San José

Monterrico

Santa Lucía Cotzumalguapa

Sipacate

El Tulate

Champerico

Nueva Venecia

Ocós

Ciudad Tecún Umán

El Carmen

San Marcos

Retalhuleu

Mazatenango

Quetzaltenango

Totonicapán

Santiago Atitlán

Lago de Atitlán

Panajachel

Chichicastenango

Santa Cruz del Quiché

Sacapulas

Huehuetenango

Todos Santos Cuchumatán

Soloma

Nebaj

Camoja Grande

La Mesilla

Volcán Tacaná (4100m)

Volcán Tajumulco (4220m)

Reserva de la biosfera Visis-Cabá

San Cristóbal Verapaz

Cobán

Salamá

Río Chixoy

Reserva de Biosfera Sierra de las Minas

El Progreso

Río Hondo

Zacapa

El Estor

Lago de Izabal

Refugio Bocas del Polochic

Mariscos

PACIFIC OCEAN

The Pacific Slope

0   50 miles
0   100 km

37

MEXICO

El Mirador • • Río Azul

Piedras Negras • • Uaxactún • San Bartolo
El Zota •
Tikal • • Yaxhá
La Blanca

MEXICO

Dos Pilas • • El Ceibal
Aguateca •
• Cancuén

Gulf of Honduras

El Golfete

BELIZE

• Zaculeu

Quiriguá •

• Gumarcaaj
Ixlmché • • GUATEMALA CITY
Takalik Abaj Kaminaljuyu ✪

• Copán

HONDURAS

• Santa Lucía Cotzumalguapa

PACIFIC OCEAN

EL SALVADOR

Ⓝ 0 ──── 100 km
0 ──── 50 miles

TRIP PLANNER

BEST MAYA RUINS

Guatemala is peppered with spectacular ruins and it's well worth the effort to see the best of them. Spend time visiting more than a handful and you'll realize that the Maya cities were as different and varied as Paris, New York and Tokyo are today.

TIKAL

Tikal (p116) is the classic Guatemalan Maya ruin site; a vast reserve filled with hundreds of structures, many of which have been beautifully restored. You can ascend pyramids, visit observatories, see ballcourts. Spotting monkeys and birds is another key reason to visit. Don't miss the iconic spots of Templo IV and the Gran Plaza.

YAXHÁ

Off to the eastern side of Petén, **Yaxhá** (p129) is often included as a side visit from Tikal. Because of its lovely location next to Yaxhá lagoon, tours often try to time this spot for late afternoon. Sunsets here are

spectacular, and a viewing platform atop Templo 216 allows for magnificent photography.

COPÁN

Often confused with the Guatemalan city of Cobán, to reach **Copán** (p67) you'll cross the border into Honduras. The ruin is known for incredible ornate carvings and astonishingly well-preserved structures that were discovered within larger ones. Don't miss the Templo Rosalila, the hieroglyphic staircase, or some of the more ornate stelae, such as H or N. It's also home to a spectacular population of rare scarlet macaws.

TIPS FOR VISITING RUINS

Be prepared Ruins are often hot, sometimes buggy, and you'll likely be doing a hefty bit of walking and (oof!) climbing stairs. Take water, sunscreen, bug spray and protective clothing.

Zigzag Most injuries happen while ascending or descending structures, where rough rocks or slippery moss can lead to falls. Minimize risk by zigzagging, making your line of direction more horizontal than vertical.

No drone zones No Guatemalan ruins currently allow drones.

Pick up trash Don't leave water bottles or wrappers at the ruins. Better yet, if you see trash, dispose of it even if it's not yours.

QUIRIGUÁ

A good spot to add to a trip to Copán, **Quiriguá** (p66) is notable for its incredibly tall stelae, which dwarf – sometimes by twice – most other cities' monuments. Many are very well-preserved and the site is also a good spot for birding among the avocado and fruit trees.

CANCUÉN

You'll have to take a riverboat to reach this ruin located deep in the jungle. **Cancuén** (p77) was the terminal city for river trade down the Río Pasión, and as such, controlled much of the region's trade. The largest palace of the Maya world is at this site, as well as a unique cistern in which many ancient bodies were found.

EL MIRADOR

Accessible by helicopter as a day trip from Flores or by a multi-day hike through the jungle, **El Mirador** (p132) makes Tikal seem like child's play. It has by some calculations the world's largest pyramid, La Danta. There's a commanding view of the jungle from its peak, as well as impressive friezes.

STEPHENS & CATHERWOOD

History is rife with examples of how contact with the West had unfathomably dark consequences for the people of Mesoamerica, including the Maya.

Conquest led to near complete destruction of a civilization that even today we're only beginning to recreate and understand, much of it inexcusably lost as the Spanish tried to erase and eradicate a culture.

They succeeded in many ways, and for centuries once-great cities lay hidden in impenetrable jungle.

The rediscovery of Maya civilization began in the mid-1800s, when a New York writer named John Lloyd Stephens and a British artist named Frederick Catherwood teamed up on a journey that would shine the spotlight on this great civilization.

The book *Incidents of Travel in Central America, Chiapas, and Yucatán* was a bestseller, and details their journeys through the region as they visited Maya site after Maya site, enduring wars, thefts, weather and sickness in the interests of bringing these wonderful places to the attention of the Western world.

Often explorers of that time had an agenda of racial and religious superiority, viewing other cultures as inferior.

These two men, however, understood the majesty of the Maya civilization, and though it was published nearly 200 years ago, the book still resonates today.

MEHDI KASUMOV/SHUTTERSTOCK ©

Yaxhá (p129)

GUATEMALA

THE GUIDE

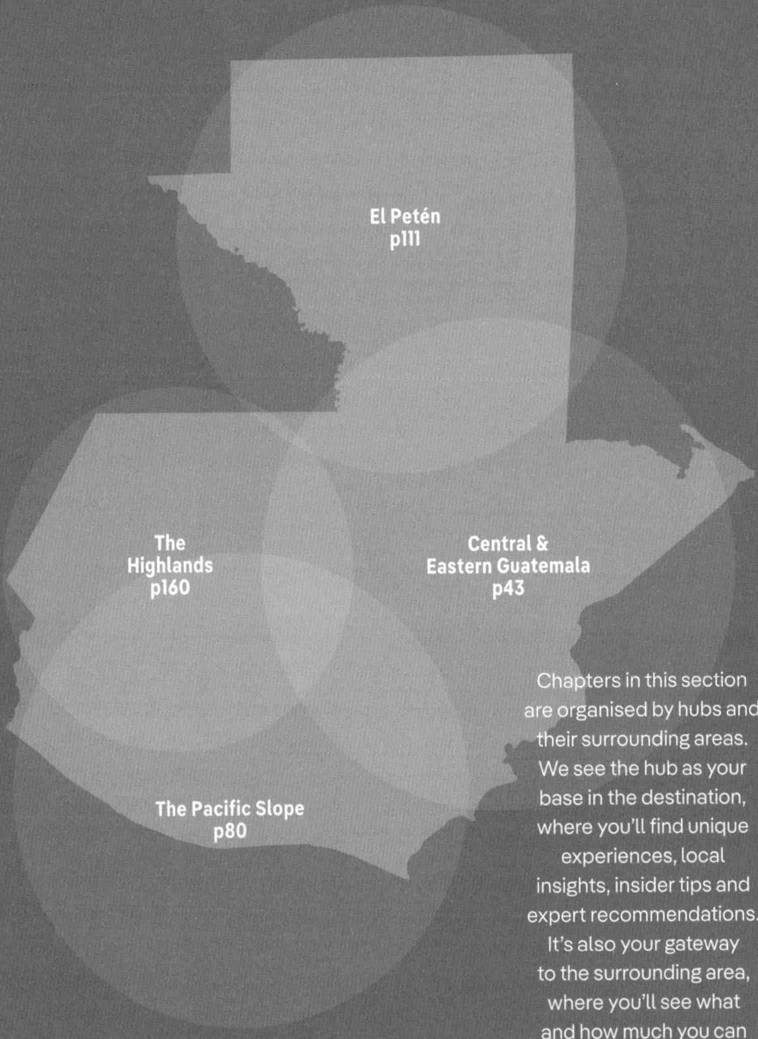
El Petén
p111
The Highlands
p160
Central & Eastern Guatemala
p43
The Pacific Slope
p80

Chapters in this section are organised by hubs and their surrounding areas. We see the hub as your base in the destination, where you'll find unique experiences, local insights, insider tips and expert recommendations. It's also your gateway to the surrounding area, where you'll see what and how much you can do from there.

Antigua (p166)

OLEH_SLOBODENIUK/GETTY IMAGES ©

Semuc Champey (p75)

CENTRAL & EASTERN GUATEMALA

BIG CITIES AND LUSH SURROUNDS

The most diverse region in Guatemala, taking in the capital city, cloud forests, small indigenous villages and the Caribbean charms of the east coast.

There are very few common threads running through this region. Guatemala City at its southern edge is all big city bustle with the usual capital city drawcards: good nightlife, great places to eat and the best museums in the country. Venture northwards and you pass through the arid terrain of eastern Guatemala before moving into the lush landscapes and cloud forests around Cobán. This is coffee and spice country, but visitors come for the amazing karst formations – a spelunker's delight – and to see the dazzling array of bird- and wildlife that make the forests their home.

Further east, things take a decidedly tropical turn. This is banana country –

in fact, the crops that came from here were the inspiration for Guatemala being labeled as the first Banana Republic. Nowadays African palm tree plantations are taking over with equal amounts of controversy.

Río Dulce (the 'sweet river') remains a boater's haven – you'll find boaters here especially during the hurricane season, taking refuge and stocking up before setting sail again. Further towards the coast is the enchanting Garifuna enclave of Livingston, a settlement unlike any other in the country. You can only get here by boat, but that boat ride down the Río Dulce through steep leafy canyons is one more not-to-be-missed experience.

LUKAS UHER/SHUTTERSTOCK ©

THE MAIN AREAS

GUATEMALA CITY
The bustling capital city with a buzz that you won't find in the rest of the country.
p48

CARIBBEAN COAST
White sands, turquoise waters - this is banana and palm tree country.
p60

COBÁN
Lush vistas in the hill country nestled amongst the cloud forests.
p70

Find Your Way

There are some serious distances here, but the bus network is good and the roads are passable year-round. Down on the coast, boats are the practical option where roads are few or nonexistent.

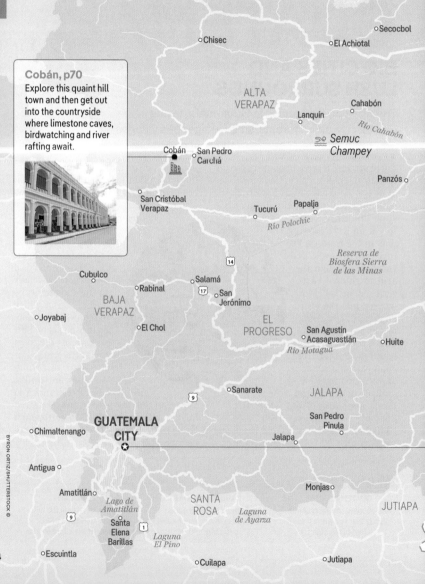

Cobán, p70
Explore this quaint hill town and then get out into the countryside where limestone caves, birdwatching and river rafting await.

Secocbol

El Achiotal

Chisec

ALTA VERAPAZ

Cahabón

Lanquín

Río Cahabón

Semuc Champey

Cobán   San Pedro Carchá

Panzós

San Cristóbal Verapaz

Tucurú   Papalja

Río Polochic

Reserva de Biosfera Sierra de las Minas

Cubulco

Rabinal

Salamá

San Jerónimo

BAJA VERAPAZ

Joyabaj

El Chol

EL PROGRESO

San Agustín Acasaguastlán   Huite

Río Motagua

Sanarate

JALAPA

GUATEMALA CITY

San Pedro Pinula

Chimaltenango

Jalapa

Antigua

Amatitlán

Monjas

Lago de Amatitlán

SANTA ROSA

Laguna de Ayarza

JUTIAPA

Santa Elena Barillas

Laguna El Pino

Escuintla

Cuilapa

Jutiapa

BYRON ORTIZ/SHUTTERSTOCK ©

44

San Luís

BELIZE

[13]

Chacalté

Bahía de
Amatique

Caribbean Coast, p60
Hammocks, palm trees, seafood,
reggae bars. This is still Guatemala,
but only just. You've seen the
movie, now live the lifestyle.

San Juan

Biotopo
Chocón
Machacas

Livingston

Gulf of
Honduras

Laguna
Santa
Isabel

Área de Protección
Especial Punta
de Manabique

El Golfete

Cayo
Piedra

Puerto Santo
Tomás De
Castilla

Puerto
Barrios

Laguna
Tinta

La Ensenada

Río San Marcos

El Estor

IZABAL

Cacáo

Lago de
Izabal

Refugio
Bocas del
Polochic

Morales

Los
Amates

[9]

CAR
You do not want to drive in
Guatemala City, but having your
own wheels for the rest of the
region makes sense for the not
too faint-at-heart.

Gualan

ZACAPA

HONDURAS

BUS
Bus services in Guatemala are
regular and of good quality.
There are few 'chicken buses'
here – minibuses are popular
for medium distances while
first-class Pullmans take the long
hauls.

Zacapa

La Union

[10]

Chiquimula

CHIQUIMULA

**Guatemala City,
p48**
Love it or hate it, you're
going to pass through
at some point. Why
not stop off and soak
up some culture while
you're there?

Quezaltepeque

Esquipulas

BOAT
If you're anywhere coast-side, the
option to go by boat will almost
always be there – bear it in mind
for a bit of variety, but also be
aware that sometimes there is no
other option.

N   0 ────── 100 km
    0 ────── 50 miles

45

Plan Your Time

Bouncing around or staying put is equally easy here – the key is deciding which parts of this diverse region you want to experience.

Livingston (p61)

If You Only Do One Thing

● Make a beeline for **Río Dulce** (p62) and hop on a boat bound for **Livingston** (p61). Public lanchas (small motorboats) run regularly, but if you have a group together, ask about hiring a private one. You'll get more time to float through the lily gardens, check out the birds at Isla de Pájaros and stop for a dip at the hot springs.

● Landing in Livingston, stop off for a drink or some delicious traditional Garifuna cuisine at the community-minded restaurant **Buga Mama** (p61), and catch a cool breeze from the balcony overlooking the river.

Seasonal Highlights

Any time is good to visit. A dampener is the rainy season – you can expect downpours most mornings from May to October.

JANUARY

Traditional festivals in towns around Salama kick off – Rabinal's 6-day **Festival de San Pablo** is well worth a mention.

MARCH/APRIL

Antigua gets all the **Semana Santa** fame, but Guatemala City's Centro Historico has elaborate floats and processions, too.

MAY

The start of the **rainy season** brings a few showers, but things won't get serious for another month or so.

A Week-Long Stay

● Hit up a museum or two in **Guatemala City** (p48) before jumping on a bus for the verdant hill country surrounding Cobán. Soak up the atmosphere for a day or two, but your real destination is **Semuc Champey** (p75), a series of limestone pools that form the best natural swimming hole in the country.

● Once you're done there, keep heading east, following the Río Cahabón and visiting the traditional villages and logging towns along the way until you reach **Lago de Izabal** (p65). From there, it's a short hop to Río Dulce and the boat trip to Livingston.

If You Have More Time

● Spend some more time in Guatemala City – the museums are great, but Zona 1 and the Centro Historicos where the real heart of the city is. The **Parque Central** (p48) is always a hive of activity, featuring buskers, preachers and the occasional live concert. A wander down the pedestrian strip of **6a Avenida** (p48) is a great way to soak in the big city bustle.

● For some contrast, hop on a bus for **Salamá** (p78), a cute enough town in its own right, but especially noteworthy for the atmospheric little villages in its surrounds. There's some good hiking in the area, too.

JULY/AUGUST
Cobán hosts **Rabin Ajau**, the country's most impressive folklore festival, which brings together communities from all over the country.

SEPTEMBER
The height of the Caribbean **hurricane season** sees the town of Río Dulce packed with yachties seeking some shelter.

NOVEMBER
Garifuna National Day is celebrated on 26th November and the town of Livingston cranks it up appropriately.

DECEMBER
As the **grape harvests** come in, you'll see roadside vendors all throughout eastern Guatemala offering boxes to motorists.

GUATEMALA CITY

Guatemala City

Love it or hate it, there's an undeniable buzz to Guatemala City that you won't find in the rest of the country. This is the commercial and political hub of the nation, a sprawling mass of low-slung buildings that grows every year as migrants pour in from the countryside in search of opportunity. Laid out across a series of plateaus and ravines, 'Guate', as it is almost universally known, became the capital back in 1773 after nearby Antigua was razed by an earthquake.

There are pockets of brilliance amongst Guate's sea of mediocrity. Parque Central, the central plaza, is ringed by impressive architectural feats, and the plaza itself buzzes with life all through the week. The surrounding Zona 1 is busy reinventing itself as a culture and nightlife district, and many abandoned buildings are being reinhabited by urban professionals as the inner city comes back to life.

TOP TIP

Guate is laid out more or less on a grid: *avenidas* (avenues) run north–south, while *calles* (streets) run east–west. Sports cars and skyscrapers are the norm in the affluent Zonas 9, 10 and 15 – a stark contrast to much of the country.

BEST PLACES TO DRINK IN GUATEMALA CITY

Las Cien Puertas
The graffiti-covered walls, cheap beer and rock music make this a perennial favorite with university students.

Rayuela
Live folk music, good food and eclectic decor combine to make this a great spot to start your night.

El Gran Hotel
Featuring Zona 1's best dance floor, with live salsa and merengue bands most weekends.

Zona 1

THE HISTORIC HEART OF THE CITY

The bustling heart of Guatemala's biggest city, **Zona 1** is the area you're likely to get warned about, but stick to the main streets in daylight hours and it's well worth a visit. The classic start would be with a stroll up the pedestrianized 6a Avenida – you're likely to catch a busker or two and there's plenty of street food and market stalls to catch your eye.

Palacio Nacional de la Cultura

Stop off at **Bar y Restaurante El Portal**, a famous drinking hole just off the central plaza, where it's said that Che Guevara did some early recruiting before heading off to Cuba, and from there it's on to the plaza itself. Officially named Parque Central (like all the other main plazas in the country) you won't find much park here, but you will find a hubbub of street entertainers, preachers, day-trippers, food vendors and selfie-snapping sweethearts.

While you're in the neighborhood, get a guided tour of the Palacio Nacional de la Cultura as much for its neoclassical architecture as the art exhibitions it hosts. A short stroll away is the Mercado Central, with its top floors devoted to handicrafts and other souvenir ideas from around the country, while the bottom floors serve up everything from cheap lunches to cut flowers, cooking utensils and bulk pet food.

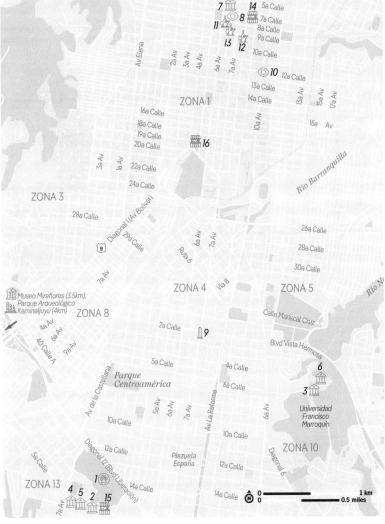

ZONA 1

ZONA 3

ZONA 4

ZONA 5

ZONA 8

ZONA 13

ZONA 10

Parque Centroamérica

Plazuela España

Universidad Francisco Marroquín

Museo Miraflores (3.5km);
Parque Arqueológico
Kaminaljuyú (4km)

Río Barranquilla

0   1 km
0   0.5 miles

SIGHTS
1 La Aurora Zoo
2 Museo de los Niños
3 Museo Ixchel
4 Museo Nacional de Arqueología y Etnología
5 Museo Nacional de Arte Moderno
6 Museo Popol Vuh
7 Palacio Nacional de la Cultura
8 Parque Central
9 Torre del Reformador
10 Zona 1

NIGHTLIFE
11 Bar y Restaurante El Portal
12 El Gran Hotel
13 Las Cien Puertas

SHOPPING
14 Mercado Central
15 Mercado de Artesanías
16 Plaza El Amate

Guatemala City

Museo Nacional de Arqueología y Etnología

I LIVE HERE: WHAT TO DO IN GUATEMALA CITY

Rubén Martínez, taxi driver, shares what he does on a day off in the capital

Sundays are the best time to be in Guatemala City. There's not so much traffic around and most people are a bit more relaxed than usual. 6a Avenida in Zona 1 is good for people-watching. Walk up to the plaza (Parque Central) where there's usually something going on. Sometimes I go to play football with friends. There's not a lot of open space in the center, so we go out to the university campus, or to Parque Minerva in Zona 2, and have a picnic.

The Museums

ART, HISTORY AND CULTURE

Guatemala City has the best collection of museums in the country and they're mostly clustered together – you could hit them all in one (somewhat exhausting) day, but you would have to be a real enthusiast.

Zona 13 down by the airport is home to the Museo Nacional de Arqueología y Etnología, which hosts the country's largest collection of Maya artefacts, beautifully displayed in modern surrounds. Information is sparse, but the pieces – particularly the stone sculptures and jewelry collections – are amazing to look at, without explanation. Next door is the Museo Nacional de Arte Moderno, which hosts revolving exhibits of modern art from around the world and has a sizeable collection of works by Guatemalan artists from the last century or so.

Nearby in Zona 10 are another two notable museums. The Museo Popol Vuh is dedicated to pre-Hispanic culture, with a heavy focus on Maya culture. The standout exhibit is a faithful copy of the Dresden Codex, one of the precious 'painted books' of the Maya. The Museo Ixchel, named after the Maya moon goddess, focuses more on contemporary Maya life, exhibiting weavings, photographs and traditional crafts of the

WHERE TO EAT IN GUATEMALA CITY

Aida
Take a break from Zona 1's bustle and chow down on delicious local and international dishes. **$**

Tamarindos
Guatemalan/Asian fusion? Who cares what they call it, it's all delicious. **$$$**

Restaurante Altuna
Featuring Guatemalan and Spanish dishes, in a formal but not quite stuffy atmosphere. **$$$**

highlands towns. On the other side of town, the Museo Mira-flores has an excellent collection of pieces from nearby Kaminaljuyú and a fascinating garden showcasing plants that were cultivated by the Maya for food and medicine.

Kaminaljuyú

WHERE IT ALL BEGAN

Long before the Spanish arrived, the site of Parque Arqueológico Kaminaljuyú was one of the most important in the region and was thought to have dominated over much of the highlands. We'll never know its full extent as houses have been built over much of it, but what remains is interesting enough and its park-like setting can make for a nice break from the hustle outside.

Restoration and excavation work proceeds painstakingly – much of the site has not been excavated yet and grassy mounds dot the landscape, waiting for someone with time and money to see what's underneath. What was open to the elements was damaged by neglect and the climate before anybody took a real interest in it, but now roofs have been constructed over the main work areas. The impressive carvings found here have mostly been moved to the museums in town, but you can still get an idea of the scope of the place from what is being uncovered – at its peak, it's estimated that there were thousands of inhabitants and dozens of temples here.

Currently, the most serious excavations are happening around the ball court, which is thought to have been built by invaders from Teotihuacán in Mexico around 400 CE. Nearby are several *talud-tablero* structures, constructed in a distinctive stepped building style generally recognised to be from Teotihuacán.

Guatemala City for Kids

SOMETHING FOR THE LITTLE ONES

Guatemala is heavy on cultural attractions that may not captivate the kids if you've brought them along, so it's a good idea to jump on kid-friendly experiences when you get the chance. Guatemala City does OK for kids – there are plenty of familiar chain restaurants around and some interesting little day-tour options.

If they're even remotely interested in science, a trip to the Museo de los Niños (Children's Museum) is pretty much a must. It takes inspiration from similar science museums from around the world, but has a few Guatemala-specific exhibits – the earthquake simulator is generally a big hit and the massive jigsaw puzzle of the departments of Guatemala will keep

THE PARIS END OF GUATEMALA CITY

Guatemala City can be a fairly straitlaced affair, but every now and then it catches you by surprise. One such example is the replica of the Eiffel Tower located at the corner of 7a Avenida and 2a Calle in Zona 9. Originally called the Torre Conmemorativa de 19 de Julio, it is now known as the Torre del Reformador and stands at 75m high. It was manufactured in the United States and constructed here in 1935 to commemorate the birth of General Justo Rufino Barrios, the liberal reformer president who is contributed by many to have brought Guatemala into the modern era and whose likeness appears on the 5 quetzal bank note.

 WHERE TO EAT IN GUATEMALA CITY

Kacao
Set under a palm-thatched roof, this is the best place for *comida típica* (typical regional food) in Zona 10. **$$**

La Cocina de Señora Pu
Excellent, down-home cooking with a couple of modern twists is on offer at this family-run favourite. **$$**

Roque Rosito
Part of Zona 1's burgeoning cafe scene, with great coffee and some interesting sandwiches and snacks. **$**

them occupied for a while. Just across the road is La Aurora Zoo, a surprisingly well-kept place where most of the animals have spacious natural enclosures. There's your usual range of African animals, the occasional surprise like the kangaroos, plus a large area devoted to animals from the Americas.

While you're on this side of town, if the kids still have some energy to burn, you could try X-Park, an 'extreme adventure' park featuring rock-climbing walls, ziplines, giant trampolines, a mechanical bull and other such activities.

Life After Dark

DRINK, DANCE AND BE MERRY

The well-heeled inner-southern suburbs (Zonas 9, 10 and 15) of Guatemala City are a world away from much of the country. You'll hear plenty of English spoken here – Miami is a favorite holiday destination – and see plenty of brands, sports cars, fancy shopping malls and other status symbols.

Perhaps not surprisingly, this area has long been labeled the Zona Viva: literally, the 'alive zone'; perhaps more accurately the nightlife zone. Weekends are obviously when it all heats up, and if you're on foot, you could start around the corner of 14a Calle and 2a Avenida – just go for a wander, listen for the beats and you'll find the party. The Zona Viva is mostly a place for bars – there are a few dance clubs, but the majority of those have moved out to the **Carretera a El Salvador**, right on the outskirts of town.

Once shunned by much of the country after dark, Zona 1 is making a strong comeback in the nightlife stakes. The area south of Parque Central has the best concentration of options – Las Cien Puertas has been going forever and now forms the center of a cluster of venues playing everything from EDM to thrash metal. Nearby, El Gran Hotel has regular live music and a good dance floor.

Pasos y Pedales

WALKING AND PEDALLING

If you're looking for something completely wholesome to do on a Sunday morning, get out with the rest of active Guatemala City and go for a walk. Started back in 2001, this is a municipal initiative to make the city more friendly to its inhabitants. Between 10am and 2pm, some of the city's wider streets are closed to traffic and immediately overtaken by pedestrians, bike riders, dog walkers, skaters, street artists, food vendors and all sorts of other entertainment, including dance and tai chi classes, games and jumping castles.

WHY I LOVE GUATEMALA CITY

Lucas Vidgen, writer

Part of what I love about Guatemala City is how underappreciated it is. It's had a bad reputation for years and people tend to land at the airport and make a beeline for elsewhere. But in many ways, Guate is where it's at – downtown Zona 1 is thriving now, with an optimism unseen for many years. There are always new places popping up that are worth exploring and a few classics that have been around for decades, and deservedly so. It has all the usual big city problems – crowds, crime, pollution – but if you give it a chance, you're bound to find a few gems of your own.

 WHERE TO STAY IN GUATEMALA CITY ———————————————

Hostal Nostalgic
Zona 1's best hostel is simple, with a good range of rooms and a fantastic, central location. $

Hotel Ajau
Handy for the downtown bus terminals, the Ajau is tastefully decorated and spotlessly clean. $

Hotel Colonial
Sprawling and sedate, the Colonial offers spacious rooms, a full-service dining area and on-site parking. $$

La Aurora Zoo

BEST LIVE MUSIC VENUES IN GUATEMALA CITY

Trovajazz
For folk, jazz and the occasional standup comedy night, Trovajazz has been a cultural center for decades and continues to attract high-quality acts throughout the week.

Proyecto Poporopo
In Zona 1, this cool little gallery/bar/music venue has regular performances.

Rayuela
Serves good cocktails, live music (folk, jazz and blues) and the occasional poetry reading.

La Casona
Live music, art exhibitions and dance classes.

It's a great opportunity to see everyday city-dwellers take some time off and enjoy themselves. There are plenty of friendly municipal police around and nobody's causing trouble.

Five parts of town currently host Pasos y Pedales (steps and pedals) on Sundays – in Zonas 2, 9, 7 and 11. The one that started it all is probably the most interesting in terms of the variety of activities on offer and is the most accessible for tourists, too – it goes along Avenida la Reforma in Zona 9 down to Avenida de las Américas in Zona 13, about a 5km stretch, running roughly from the US embassy down to the monument commemorating Pope John Paul II.

The Civic Center Murals

ARCHITECTURE AND ART COLLIDE

Much of Guatemala City's modern architecture is strictly utilitarian, the major exception being the buildings in Zona 4's Civic Center. Conceived in the 1950s, the idea was to gather the most important civic buildings such as the town hall, central bank and High Court in one central location. Leading architects and visual artists of the time collaborated on the design of the buildings and their facades. Some murals

 WHERE TO STAY IN GUATEMALA CITY

Villa Toscana
Handy for the airport, this B&B has spacious, modern rooms, and a lovely garden. **$$**

La Inmaculada
Walking distance to the Zona Viva, with deluxe touches like rainforest showers and Egyptian cotton bedding. **$$$**

Hotel Barceló
A business class hotel with enough touches of style to make the casual visitor feel at ease. **$$$**

Sunset, Guatemala City

GUATEMALA CITY'S BEST SOUVENIR SHOPPING

Guatemala City's craft markets have products from all over the country.

Mercado Central
Just off the main plaza, Zona 1's Mercado Central has an enormous variety of stalls on its upper floors, with plenty of weavings, jewelry and knickknacks.

Mercado de Artesanías
The Mercado de Artesanías beside the zoo is fun and relaxed, but can get a bit pricey.

Plaza El Amate
On the borders of Zonas 1 and 4, Plaza El Amate has cheap clothing, knock-off watches and a couple of good souvenir stalls.

are housed in the building lobbies, but many are visible from the outside, including relief sculptures and mosaics by famous Guatemalan artists such as Dagoberto Vásquez, Carlos Mérida, Roberto González Goyri and Efraín Recinos, with themes ranging from aspects of contemporary Guatemalan life to scenes of the Spanish conquest and episodes from the *Popul Vuh* (Maya creation story).

GETTING AROUND

If you stick within the same zone, Guatemala City is compact enough to walk. Public transport is plentiful, but the large red buses aren't recommended for first-time visitors. For trips across town, the green Transmetro buses are the only really recommendable public transport option for the casual visitor, as they are much safer and more orderly. In the end, most tourists opt for taxis, which are cheap, usually metered and readily available. Don't use taxis unless they are clearly marked as such.

Beyond Guatemala City

Estanzuela

Guatemala City

Esquipulas

Amatitlán

Cuilapa

Antigua and the coast are the obvious choices, but there are some other worthy day trips out of the capital.

Just on the outskirts of Guatemala City is Lago de Amatitlán. The lake fades in comparison to pretty much every other lake in the country, but its carnival atmosphere can keep you amused for a few hours, particularly if you've got the kids along.

Pushing further towards the El Salvador border, the altitude drops as you hit the coastal flatlands and reach the small, largely nondescript town of Cuilapa. You could hang out and soak up the laidback cowboy ambience, but most visitors are here to climb the nearby volcanoes. To the west are the arid lowlands of El Oriente, where the pilgrimage center of Esquipulas and small vacation town of Río Hondo make for good detours.

TOP TIP

Buses for Amatitlán and Cuilapa leave from Guatemala City's CentraSur terminal. The highways in this region are good if you're up for renting a car.

Esquipulas (p56)

WILLIAM BARQUERO/GETTY IMAGES ©

Amatitlán

THE OTHER LAKE

If you're stuck in Guatemala City and need to escape for a few hours, the lake town of **Amatitlán** makes for a great little getaway.

The lake itself is way too polluted for swimming (and eating the locally caught fish would be a brave act), but the surroundings are pleasantly green and there's a carefree attitude of the day-trippers who end up here.

Heavy industry used to surround the lake (hence the pollution problem), but local conservation efforts have done a lot to help clean it up, and some of nearby Guatemala City's jet set have started buying up land for holiday houses on its shores.

The town of Amatitlán offers very little of interest to the average tourist, but there's a carnival-like atmosphere down on the waterfront where all the action is.

You can hire paddleboats or go out on a motorboat cruise, and the little eateries scattered along the waterfront offer good cheap food.

A fairly ordinary amusement park, run by the IRTRA franchise, offers a couple of big swimming pools, manicured grounds and some play areas for kids.

The one don't-miss attraction here is the *teleférico* (cable car) which runs from the lakeside all the way up the mountainside. The views are superb and the equipment appears to be reasonably well-maintained. You can reach the lake from Guatemala City's CentraSur bus terminal – the ride takes about 30 minutes.

Esquipulas

HOME OF THE BLACK CHRIST

An important pilgrimage center, **Esquipulas** packs out in mid-January for its Cristo de Esquipulas festival, but it sees a steady stream of visitors year-round – it's rated as one of the country's top tourist draws.

An estimated one million pilgrims from all over Central America, Mexico and the United States visit this little town annually, all to be in the presence of a small, darkened wood statue of Jesus on the cross.

Sculpted in the late 1500s, El Cristo Negro (Black Christ) as it came to be known, gained a reputation for healing supplicants who visited and worshipped him.

One theory as to his popularity is that this is another example of syncretism; a blending of pre-Hispanic and Catholic beliefs that the Maya employed as a way of being able to

CLEANING UP AMATITLÁN

The story of Lago de Amatitlán is one of many waterways in Guatemala. Once a sleepy little rural pocket, urban pressures from nearby Guatemala City saw the population here explode just as industry moved in to take advantage of cheap land, a plentiful water supply and lax restrictions on industrial waste management.

It wasn't long before the lake's waters were a toxic nightmare – unfit for swimming, much less fishing or drinking.

Grassroots organisations have been trying to clean up the lake for years, often working at cross-purposes with government initiatives, many of which have been marred by corruption scandals. As environmental consciousness grows in Guatemala, the water quality is improving, but it has a long way to go.

 WHERE TO EAT IN AMATITLÁN

Mengalita's
A fantastic balcony overlooking the water and good typical dishes like beef foot stew. **$$**

Pupuseria Gloria
For a quick snack on the run; located down by the waterfront. **$**

La Rocarena
Up the hill and away from the crowds, with lush grounds and great views. **$$**

BRUNO ADRIAN/SHUTTERSTOCK ©. BOTTOM: BYRONORTIZA/GETTY IMAGES ©

Lago de Amatitlán

NON-RELIGIOUS THINGS TO DO IN ESQUIPULAS

Cueva de las Minas
If the religious slant of Esquipulas is getting a bit heavy for you, make a quick dash out of town to visit Cueva de las Minas. Bring a flashlight to explore the 50m-deep cave and a swimsuit for a dip in the Río El Milagro.

Parque Chatún
Offers waterslides, horseback rides, ziplines and other amusement park attractions. Free shuttle buses circulate Esquipulas' downtown area.

continue with their traditional beliefs without suffering religious persecution from the invading Spaniards.

Whatever the reason, Esquipulas got a big boost in popularity when Pope John Paul II visited in 1996. It also has a place in many Central Americans hearts as the peace accords that ended the decades-long civil wars in the region began talks here and bear the town's name.

The town itself is a pleasant enough place to wander around, with plenty of tourist infrastructure. It's very relaxed outside of January. You can get here on a first-class bus from Guatemala City in about four hours.

Estanzuela & Río Hondo

DINOSAURS AND WATERPARKS

Looking out at the arid expanses of land that make up El Oriente, as this part of the country is known, it's not too hard to imagine dinosaurs wandering through it. And wander they did, although there is some debate about the size of the creatures. What is known is that large mammals such as giant sloths and sabre-toothed tigers made this corner of the world their home.

Paddleboats on Lago de Amatitlán

 WHERE TO STAY IN ESQUIPULAS

Hotel Legendario
The finest hotel in town, with spacious rooms set around an enormous swimming pool. **$$$**

Hotel Vistana al Señor
Good-value rooms in the middle of downtown. The upstairs balcony has great views. **$$**

Hotel Portal de la Fe
Touches of style and a handy, central location make this a good choice. **$$**

WHERE'S THE RUM?

One of Guatemala's proud exports is Zacapa rum – it's won a bunch of international prizes and is a favored gift for visiting dignitaries. While you're out this way, you might think of dropping in to the small town of Zacapa to see how it's made, but you would go away disappointed – the rum was named after Zacapa to celebrate its 100th anniversary, but it's truly a national product: it uses sugarcane from around Retalhuleu, is aged in the highlands around Quetzaltenango, and it's bottled in Mixco, just outside of Guatemala City. A small band of woven palm fiber known as *petate* is the only thing that comes from this region, from the even smaller town of Jocotán.

Museo de Paleontología, Arqueología y Geología

Over 5000 fragments, fossils and skeletons are on display in the Museo de Paleontología, Arqueología y Geología in the small town of **Estanzuela** – if you're even vaguely interested in paleontology and prehistoric life, it's well worth making the detour for this free museum whose collection features remains of mastodons, armadillos, a tiny prehistoric horse and mammoth teeth.

If you've got the kids along (or you're simply melting in the Oriente heat), consider following the crowds to one of the local water parks.

Parque Acuático Longarone is a humble affair, with a few slides and swimming pools scattered around, while Valle Dorado goes all out with giant slides, lazy rivers, mini golf, ziplines and a whole lot more.

 WHERE TO STAY IN RÍO HONDO

Hotel El Atlantico
The best-looking hotel in the area is all dark wood, spacious rooms and manicured grounds. **$$**

Hotel Longarone
The rooms here are spacious and clean, and the restaurant is the best in town. **$$**

Hotel Nuevo Pasabien
Almost a resort feel, with multiple swimming pools, restaurants and nightly activities. **$$**

Resort-style accommodation is available if the place really catches your fancy.

Estanzuela and **Río Hondo** are easily reachable from Guatemala City by first-class bus. The trip takes about three hours.

Cuilapa & Its Volcanoes

TICK ANOTHER COUPLE OFF THE LIST

Deep in Guatemala's south, the little town of **Cuilapa** serves as an excellent jumping-off point for ascending a couple of the region's less-visited volcanoes. Although it's the capital of the Santa Rosa department, Cuilapa has much more of a small-town feel to it, and most of the population makes its living from the citrus and coffee plantations that surround the town. Getting to Cuilapa is easy enough – it's about a two-hour bus ride from Guatemala City.

From there, visiting the volcanoes can get a little trickier. Climbing the towering Volcán Cruz Quemada (1700m) is easy enough, but involves hiking 12km from the town of Santa María Ixhuatán at its foothills. You can hire a guide in Santa María or make your own way up, asking for plenty of directions.

Tecuamburro is actually a complex of three volcanoes – Cerro la Soledad (1850m), Cerro de Miraflores (1950m) and Cerro Peña Blanca (1850m). Peña Blanca is the most popular climb, with small vents releasing steam and sulfur at regular intervals.

The climb isn't hard, but again starts at the town at the base (Tecuamburro) from where it's about 14km to the top. Low scrub and trees mean that you don't get much of a view until you're nearly at the top.

Regular minibuses leave Cuilapa for both Santa Maria and Tecuamburro.

I LIVE HERE: WHERE TO GO OUT IN CUILAPA

Ángel Ruíz, a student, shares where to find some nighttime action in his hometown of Cuilapa.

We don't get many tourists around here. In fact, we're kind of surprised when we do see them. I go to university in the capital, I come back most weekends and always for holidays. We sometimes go to the Vintage Bar and if I have friends who come to visit, I always take them to CasaMia, just near the park. It's like a bar and a restaurant. Sometimes they have parties or live music, but it's pretty relaxed.

Tecuamburro

GETTING AROUND

First-class buses run to the east from Guatemala City's CentraNorte bus terminal. All buses heading south leave from the CentraSur terminal. All the towns listed in this section are small enough to be walkable, but *tuk-tuks* zip around, offering a cheap way to get across town and also an easy way to find addresses.

CARIBBEAN COAST

Caribbean Coast

Guatemala City

Guatemala doesn't have much Caribbean coastline, but what it does have is the real deal. This is banana and palm tree country. It's been a contested area for centuries – Guatemala still lays claim to all of neighboring Belize and the pirate situation was so bad at one point that the Spanish built a fort at San Felipe to ward off unwelcome visitors who came sailing up the Río Dulce.

The Garífuna began populating land around Livingston in the early 1800s and while their population is small, their cultural influence is writ large in the town.

Expats love the Caribbean side, and you'll find many scattered around Lago de Izabal, up and down the Río Dulce, and in Río Dulce town itself.

Puerto Barrios is the only town of any real size in the area; a pleasingly ramshackle port town with its seedy sides, storied history and good transport connections to Belize and Honduras.

TOP TIP

Outside of Puerto Barrios and Río Dulce town, much of this region is remote and sometimes only reachable by boat. Prices can be higher and luxuries fewer, where everything needs to be shipped in. Stock up before heading out.

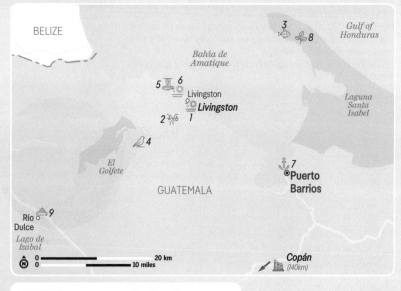

BELIZE

Gulf of Honduras

3

8

Bahía de Amatique

5   6
Livingston
Livingston

2   1

4

El Golfete

Laguna Santa Isabel

GUATEMALA

7
Puerto Barrios

Río Dulce

Lago de Izabal

0   20 km
0   10 miles

Copán
(140km)

TOP SIGHTS
1 Livingston

SIGHTS
2 Cueva de la Vaca
3 Estero Lagarto
4 Isla de Pájaros

5 Los Siete Altares
6 Playa Blanca
7 Puerto Barrios
8 Punta de Manabique

TRANSPORT
9 Río Dulce

FRANCKY38/SHUTTERSTOCK ©

Livingston

Livingston

HOME OF THE GARIFUNA

As if Guatemala didn't have enough cultural diversity, the little Caribbean town of **Livingston** adds another piece to the puzzle.

The Garifuna first arrived here in the early 1800s, having migrated from neighboring Belize in the latest of a series of migrations going back hundreds of years. While the census puts Livingston's population at around 9% Garifuna, the town proudly maintains its heritage and customs.

The town itself is made up of wooden houses, small hotels and very low-key tourism. There's plenty of delicious local food on offer here – the Garifuna have always dwelt close to the sea, so seafood is an obvious element, but cassava and a delicious side dish known as rice and beans (better than it sounds, we promise) is never far away.

The town itself is small enough to explore on foot, and a couple of bars feature regular live music and impromptu jam sessions. The town beaches are OK for a quick dip, but to get that true white-sand, turquoise-water experience, consider a

THE GARIFUNA FOOD GUIDE

One of the most enduring aspects of Garifuna culture is the food, which is quite different from what you will taste elsewhere in Guatemala. Traditional Garifuna food is generally prepared at home or for ceremonial occasions – you don't see it a lot on restaurant menus, but when you do, you should grab the chance to try it. Keep an eye out for:

Conch soup Conch meat and vegetables simmered in a coconut broth.

Darasa Coconut-flavored tamales, wrapped in a banana leaf and boiled until solid.

Tapado Seafood, green and ripe plantains, herbs and spices in a coconut-based broth.

Gifiti A herb-infused rum drink, used for medicine but also drunk socially.

WHERE TO EAT IN LIVINGSTON

Buga Mama
Delicious Garifuna food and great coffee, served on a balcony overlooking the river. $

Happy Fish
A long-standing favorite in the middle of town, with good breakfasts and plentiful tourist info. $

Las Tres Garifunas
Part cultural center, part restaurant serving good home-style meals in a friendly atmosphere. $

RÍO DULCE: A SANCTUARY FROM THE STORMS

During hurricane season, the marinas and hotels around Río Dulce fill up with yacht sailors who come here from all over the Caribbean. They come here because Río Dulce provides the necessary condition of deep water (that allows a yacht's keel to pass), which stretches far inland – hurricanes lose force as they make landfall, so the further inland you go, the safer you are. Once the hurricane season passes, the town empties out again, but if you're looking to crew on a yacht or hop a ride to your next Caribbean destination, Río Dulce around the end of October is the place to be.

Río Dulce

boat tour out to the aptly named Playa Blanca, with a stop-off at the jungle-shrouded Los Siete Altares waterfall along the way. Longer boat tours and snorkeling trips out to the nearby cays are also available.

Touring the Río Dulce

GUATEMALA'S BEST BOAT RIDE

Given that Livingston is only approachable by water, the boat ride from **Río Dulce** town is a question of necessity for many locals, but it's an absolute stunner for visitors to the region.

You can get on board a public boat, but if you have a few people together, consider hiring a private one – they're not that much more expensive and you'll be able to stop and enjoy at a more leisurely pace.

From Río Dulce, the first sight you'll pass is the **Isla de Pájaros**, where hundreds of seabirds regularly nest. There are detours through lily-covered estuaries, a stop at a hot spring where steamy water from the mountain mixes with the cool river water, and a few other stops along the way to visit small fishing communities that line the river banks.

WHERE TO STAY IN RÍO DULCE

Bruno's Marina
Waterfront yachtie favorite with clean rooms, a good restaurant/bar and a sweet little swimming pool. **$$**

Tortugal
As close as Río Dulce gets to boutique, with stylish, modern rooms and lush grounds down to the waterfront. **$$$**

Hacienda Tijax
A short boat ride from Bruno's with a range of elegant rooms set in the mangroves. **$$**

The trip culminates as you enter the **Cueva de la Vaca**, a steep-walled gorge whose sides are covered in thick tangled jungle.

Be on the lookout for freshwater dolphins who have been known to appear around here. If you return to Río Dulce by boat, your driver may offer to take you a bit further to cruise around the outside of El Castillo de San Felipe, built in 1652 by the Spanish to repel pirates who would come sailing up the river.

Puerto Barrios & Punta de Manabique

ECHOES OF A BYGONE ERA

Once an opulent port town and now showing some serious signs of wear, **Puerto Barrios** was at one point the busiest port town on the Caribbean. Boatloads of bananas were sailed out of here and the port is still very active, as the massive container yard in town testifies. Much of the town exists in that classic Caribbean slumber – the streets empty out around midday and nobody moves anywhere fast. Most tourists are here to catch a boat – either to Livingston or across the bay to Punta Gorda in Belize. Tour operators sometimes offer snorkeling or sailing trips out to the Belize Cayes.

Puerto Barrios also makes an excellent staging post for a trip to the **Punta de Manabique**, a large Caribbean wetland stretching all the way from Amatique Bay to the Honduran border. The remote reserve is known for its untouched beaches, mangroves, birdwatching and wildlife, including crocodiles and manatees.

There's not much comfort out here, which is part of the charm, of course. This is community tourism at its most basic: staying in a rustic ecolodge in the small village of **Estero Lagarto**, eating simple, fresh meals, snorkeling, canoeing, fishing and hiring locals to take you out to explore the beaches and mangroves and visit small fishing communities living very much like they have done for hundreds of years.

MOVING ON FROM PUERTO BARRIOS

Puerto Barrios isn't much of a destination in its own right, but it provides a couple of important border crossings. There's a seaward connection with the town of Punta Gorda in southern Belize – there tends to be one departure daily, early in the morning. Regular direct buses also go to the Honduran border town of El Corinto, with connections from there to La Ceiba, San Pedro Sula and beyond. Every now and then somebody offers yacht connections direct to Roatán in Honduras, often stopping at the reefs along the way for fishing and snorkeling. If you're interested, ask around the port area to see if anybody is doing this.

MORE ABOUT THE GARIFUNA

You can read more about the fascinating history and unique culture of **the Garifuna** as well as more on their delicious food and infectious music on page 245.

GETTING AROUND

Tuk-tuks are the main form of transportation within towns in this region. Minibuses cover short hops between towns, and large first-class buses cover the highways.

Caribbean Coast

El Estor •

• San Felipe

• Mariscos

Quiriguá •

• Copán

Beyond the Caribbean Coast

Often overlooked by travelers passing through, eastern Guatemala is home to hidden gems and a couple of world-class attractions.

Heading east from the coast, the land flattens out and the landscape is dominated by banana and African palm plantations. Bananas have been here forever, of course – the term 'banana republic' was coined to describe countries under the sway of fruit corporations, as Guatemala was in the early 20th century. African palm is a newer colonizing crop – large swathes of farmland are being dedicated to the fast profits it generates, bringing with it a worrying drop in biodiversity.

Travel here can be extremely uncomfortable – the rains are monsoonal, and the heat is furnace-like. The Maya ruins at Quiriguá make a good stop, as do the small towns dotted around Lago de Izabal.

TOP TIP

The midday sun is serious business here – if you're going to be walking, plan for early morning or late afternoon.

Maya ruins, Quiriguá (p66)

INSPIRED BY MAPS/SPS/SHUTTERSTOCK ©

Finca El Paraíso

El Estor & Lago de Izabal

LAKE BREEZES AND NATURAL WONDERS

East of Río Dulce is Lago de Izabal proper – Guatemala's largest lake. **El Estor** is the biggest settlement on the lake and is a short minibus ride from Río Dulce. The town gets its name from when the English established it as a trading post – El Store eventually morphed into El Estor.

It makes for a comfortable base from which to explore the natural wonders of the area. The excellent nature-conservancy NGO Fundación Defensores de la Naturaleza offers ecotourism to nearby nature reserves where you stand a very good chance of seeing howler monkeys, an array of birdlife and the occasional manatee.

Closer to town is El Boquerón, a beautiful canyon that you can explore via canoe with a local guide, stopping off to swim in its chilly, pristine waters. If the water's too cold, just down the road is Finca El Paraíso.

The main attraction here are the thermally heated waters that seep from the mountainside, mixing with cool creek water before tumbling over a steamy waterfall. It's both a fascinating and breathtakingly beautiful spot and you could

THOSE MANATEES ARE NOT MERMAIDS

You have to be very quiet and a little bit lucky, but paddling around the inlets and mangroves of Lago de Izabal and Río Dulce, you might just see a manatee. Also known as sea cows, these huge (up to 900kg) mammals are quite shy, and some species are currently endangered. It's thought that the mermaid myth came from (possibly homesick) sailors mistaking manatees spotted in the distance for half-woman, half-fish creatures. Christopher Columbus himself wrote that mermaids are 'not half as beautiful as they are painted' when he made the same mistake after having seen a group of manatees near what is now the Dominican Republic.

WHERE TO EAT IN EL ESTOR

Restaurante Típico Chaabil
The waterfront location is better than the food, but it offers the widest menu in town. $$

Gardenia's Café
Simple, economic meals in the center of town. Best coffee for miles around. $

Restaurante Elsita
More no-frills downtown dining. Good fish, tacos and ceviche dishes and plenty of ice-cold beer. $

GETTING TO THE RUINS AT QUIRIGUÁ

If you're just passing through and not planning on staying the night in Quiriguá, ask the bus driver to drop you at the 'cruce para las ruinas', which is outside of Quiriguá town itself, on the main highway. From there you should be able to get a *tuk-tuk* or pickup down to the ruins – it's about 3km, which is walkable if the heat isn't too bad. If you're staying in town, the obvious choice is a *tuk-tuk* out to the site, but again it's a pleasant enough 4km walk if you start early enough – you can take the more direct route by following the railroad instead of staying on the road.

ODESSA25/SHUTTERSTOCK ©

Carved stone, Quiriguá

spend many hours here, alternating between the hot and cold waters and ducking into small caves in the creek bank for a natural steam bath. If you really like the place, simple lake-front huts are available about 10 minutes' walk away.

Quiriguá

INTRICATE CARVINGS AND BANANA PLANTS

One of Guatemala's three UNESCO World Heritage Sights, **Quiriguá** was once one of the most important cities in the Maya world, with strong connections to Copán in modern-day Honduras, a mere 50km away across the border.

It's an excellent site, made all the more enticing for how unvisited it is – get your timing right and you may have the place to yourself, plus a few archaeologists.

A couple of temples and the requisite ball court have been unearthed, but the real attraction here are the stelae – monolithic, intricately carved slabs of stone scattered around the site that were used to record important moments in history, such as the ascension of new kings to the throne or the events of large battles.

 WHERE TO STAY IN QUIRIGUÁ

Posada Quiriguá
A bit out of the way, but worth the hike for clean, stylish rooms and friendly service. **$$**

Hotel Royal
Basic but functional rooms with a good little restaurant set on the front porch. **$**

Hotel El Quetzal
Simple rooms at a reasonable price, located on the road to the ruins. **$**

Despite being such an important site, Quiriguá was unknown to Europeans until around 1840, and excavations in earnest didn't start for another 50 years. The whole site can be visited in a few hours – it's not that big, but the level of detail in much of the carving may have you pausing longer than expected.

A small museum at the entrance is worth a quick visit, particularly for the model depicting how the site would have looked in its heyday.

The town of Quiriguá is about two hours by bus from Puerto Barrios. *Tuk-tuks* make the short run from the town to the ruins.

Mariscos

THE FORGOTTEN LAKE TOWN

The only town of any note on Lago de Izabal's southern shore, **Mariscos** was once a bustling spot from which ferries left to cross the lake to El Estor. Once the road from Río Dulce to El Estor was built, the town has begun to languish, but it's still a lovely little spot – tranquil and just far enough off the highway that it never really sees any sorts of crowds. The water here is clean and perfect for swimming year-round.

The atmosphere is captivatingly Caribbean – giant palm trees sway everywhere and nobody is in much of a rush to do anything.

Although the town is connected by road to the main highway, it feels very much like a lake town – most businesses around here communicate by two-way radio, and transport to Río Dulce and El Estor is easily arranged via water taxi.

There are a couple of little waterfront eateries in town, but if you've come this far, you'll want to stay a while, and the best place by far to do so is at the expat-run Denny's Beach.

There is indeed a beach here, lovingly tended by its owner; the rooms and bungalows have been developed as a labor of love over decades. Kayaks, horseback riding, fishing tours and general lazing about in hammocks are some of the attractions.

Copán

A TRIP ACROSS THE BORDER

Just across the border in neighboring Honduras, **Copán** is one of the most impressive and easily accessible Maya sites. You could make it in a (long) day trip from anywhere in Eastern Guatemala, but the lovely town of Copán Ruinas is just down the road and provides every sort of comfort that a tourist could be seeking.

RUBBER PLANTATIONS

In the early days of Guatemala's commercial agricultural development, the constant heat and heavy rains of Guatemala's coastal regions made them especially suitable for rubber farming. Production began here as early as 1736 and Guatemala was soon exporting rubber all over the world. With the advent of vulcanization and the subsequent industrialization of rubber, the market really took off. There are still some working rubber farms in the coastal regions – look for evenly planted forests of tall spindly trees, often with a bucket attached to catch the sap – but as the market becomes less lucrative, many are being replanted with African palm trees, a fast-growing tree whose oil provides a more profitable harvest.

 WHERE TO EAT IN MARISCOS

Restaurante Marinita
Simple Guatemalan fare served up lakeside. The excellent swimming dock is a bonus. **$**

Restaurante Karilinda
A variety of seafood dishes and snacks, and a lovely, breezy balcony overlooking the water. **$**

El Costeño
To the west of town, specializing in ceviche but offering all the Guatemalan standards as well. **$**

BEST THINGS TO DO AROUND COPÁN RUINAS

Macaw Mountain Bird Park

Even if you're not particularly into birds, a trip to the Macaw Mountain Bird Park is worth the trip – it's an animal rescue center that hosts a dazzling collection of rescued birds (mostly macaws) in large natural enclosures.

Luna Jaguar Spa Resort

Further out of town, the Luna Jaguar Spa Resort is an open-air Maya-themed spa featuring thirteen stations where you can soak in thermal waters and take natural steam baths.

El Castillo de San Felipe de Lara

Rubber plantation (p67)

The site itself is sprawling, but it's easy enough to visit the main buildings within a day. Restoration work is ongoing here – you're likely to see working archaeologists reconstructing stairways and documenting finds.

There are no looming pyramids here, but the scale of some of the principal buildings is spectacular, the site has an impressively restored ball court and many of the carvings on the staircases and stelae are intact and have been well-preserved.

Copán is famous in the Maya world for the quantity and quality of sculptures that have been found here. Some of the best examples are on display in the on-site Museo de las Esculturas – definitely worth your time for a detour and a bonus escape from the midday sun.

A small store at the entrance sells informative books if you want to self-guide. Another option would be to contract a guide at the site's entrance – look for the ones with the of-

 WHERE TO STAY IN COPÁN

Café ViaVia
Belgian-run, with a good variety of rooms and an excellent bar/restaurant attached. **$**

Hotel Madrugada
Large rooms featuring colonial-style decorations and an excellent balcony overlooking the valley. **$$**

Terramaya
Boutique luxury with excellent views at a reasonable price. Rooms upstairs have fantastic balconies. **$$$**

ficial name badge, as they work for a cooperative of guides that ensures fair pay and knowledgeable, professional service.

Buses run from Puerto Barrios to Chiquimula frequently. From there you can get a minibus that goes to the border crossing near Copán Ruinas. Minibuses and pickups wait on the Honduran side of the border to complete the trip.

San Felipe

DEFENDING AGAINST THE PIRATES

A small town on the banks of Lago de Izabal, **San Felipe** makes it onto the map for the fort which goes by the grand name of El Castillo de San Felipe de Lara. Built in 1652, it's wonderfully situated on a small promontory jutting out into the lake's northern shore.

The grounds themselves make a pleasant place for a wander – there are plenty of shady grassy spots for picnics and the swimming is fine from the lake banks here.

The fort was originally built to fend off marauding pirates who would sail up the Río Dulce to attack cargo ships and small lakeside villages like El Estor. It was used as a prison for a while, then fell into disrepair before being restored in the 1950s.

As far as these things go, it's a pretty good restoration effort – the site definitely captures the atmosphere of those buccaneering days with plenty of old cannons positioned around its outskirts and bits of memorabilia scattered around its sparsely decorated rooms.

Small restaurants by the entrance to the site offer good simple meals, and San Felipe itself offers a surprisingly decent selection of accommodation in case you're tempted to stay.

San Felipe can be reached by boat or bus from Río Dulce. It's about a 4km walk if the sun isn't too blazing.

PIRATES OF THE CARIBBEAN

El Castillo de San Felipe stands as a reminder of a time when real-life pirates of the Caribbean roamed the seas, plundering ships carrying cargo (itself most likely plundered) back to Europe. The fort was constructed to defend against attackers who sailed up the Río Dulce, and it was attacked by Irish, English and Colombian pirates more than 30 times. As a sign of its importance, it was reconstructed each time and never abandoned until trade shifted further up the coast.

As the Guatemalan and Belizean navies developed, piracy became a more dangerous and less profitable exercise and many pirates converted to semi-legitimate businessmen, trading in precious woods extracted from Guatemala's forests.

GETTING AROUND

Tuk-tuks are available in all the towns mentioned here. First-class buses run along the main highway serving long and medium-distance destinations. Minibuses do short runs between neighboring towns.

COBÁN

Cobán

Guatemala City

Nestled amongst the cloud forests in the region known as Alta Verapaz, Cobán has been a population center for centuries. The rich farmland, abundant water and mild climate supported large settlements before the Spanish arrived and the conquistadors met some of their fiercest resistance in this region. Adherence to traditional pre-colonial customs is particularly strong in this area.

Cobán itself is a delightful little town – prosperous and growing, but not yet exhibiting any big city problems. There's a very mild German influence here – the town saw a large influx of Europeans in the 19th century and the newcomers found fortune planting the coffee and cardamom that still fuel much of the local economy.

There's so much to do in the surrounding countryside that the temptation is to get here and move on, but give Cobán a chance – it might just grow on you.

TOP TIP

Owing to its small size, pretty much everything in Cobán is within walking distance. This is hill country, though, with the central plaza perched right at the high point of the town – be prepared for plenty of ups and downs.

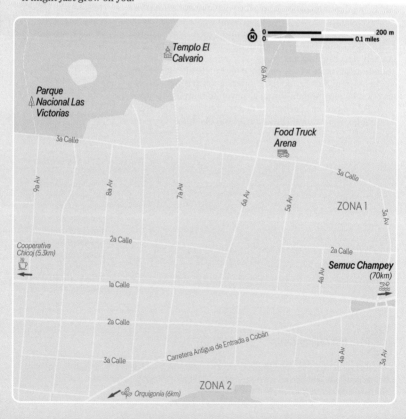

SALMONNEGRO-STOCK/SHUTTERSTOCK ©

Cobán

Downtown Cobán

A CHARMING LITTLE HILL TOWN

Once little more than a stopping-off point for more exciting adventures in its surrounds, Cobán is starting to make it onto tourists' radar as a destination in its own right. The downtown area around the Parque Central is safe and pretty, if not quite as visually stunning as Antigua. There's not a whole lot to do here – just wandering the streets in the mild climate can easily while away a few hours.

The Parque itself is a good place to start, with some pretty gardens and a baffling Soviet-era gazebo obscuring your view of the cathedral.

The occasional handicrafts market springs up on the south side of the plaza in the eaves of the Gobernación building. There's a covered market just to the east of the plaza and another sprawling open-air one block to the north.

For a view out over town, make your way to the Templo El Calvario, right next to the Parque Nacional Las Victorias. If you can make it up the long flight of steps, you'll be rewarded with views out over the countryside – try to go early before the fog settles in.

NATIONAL SYMBOLS

Cobán is home to two of Guatemala's national symbols. You'll recognise the national bird – the resplendent quetzal is front and center on the country's flag. From Southern Mexico to Panama, the quetzal makes its home in cloud forests such as those surrounding Cobán. Also in these forests is the *monja blanca* (white nun orchid), Guatemala's national flower. Happiest in areas above 1600m with moderate temperatures, little humidity and low-hanging clouds, the *monja blanca* is also found in Mexico and Central America. The quetzal is hard to spot in the wild, but you can easily see a *monja blanca* at Orquigonea. A quetzal is shown on the Q1 coin, and a *monja blanca* on the 50 centavo coin.

 WHERE TO STAY IN COBÁN

Hotel Central
Great location, spacious rooms, a sweet little patio and good views out the back windows. $

Hotel La Posada
Spacious and well-decorated rooms just off the plaza with a very good attached restaurant. $$

Hostal Casa Tenango
Cobán's one true hostel does a pretty good job with a range of rooms at fair prices. $

I LIVE HERE: WHY I STAY IN COBÁN

Esteban Choc, Cobán-based Barista, explains why he's here to stay.

I was born in the capital, but my family moved here when I was small – I don't really remember living anywhere else. I've been to plenty of other places, but I can't imagine living in another place. The air here feels fresh; even when you're in the middle of the city it doesn't feel dirty or polluted like it does In Guate. Cobán is really growing. Lots of people are moving here because it's a safe place to live, to raise your family. People make fun of the weather in Cobán. The mornings are always misty and we have this rain we call *chipi chipi* (drizzle), but I love it. God willing, I'm here to stay.

Coffee, Cobán

If you're looking for a bit of outdoor dining, food trucks are the latest craze to hit Cobán – check out the **Food Truck Arena**, a dedicated space where they congregate.

Natural Wonders

GET INTO THE CLOUD FORESTS

Alta Verapaz is so packed full of natural attractions that it may not come as a surprise to know that you don't even need to leave Cobán to start appreciating them. Just on the outskirts of the downtown area is the gloriously named Parque Nacional Las Victorias.

There's 82 hectares of densely forested land reserved here, crisscrossed by walking trails that pass by lookout spots and cute little ponds. There's even a (very basic) campground if you're feeling that way inclined.

 WHERE TO EAT IN COBÁN

Kardamomuss
Some of the most inventive dishes in town, often featuring cardamom in chic, modern surrounds. **$$**

La Abadia
A cozy atmosphere, beautifully presented dishes and a good wine list make this a date night favorite. **$$**

Xkape Koba'n
Good traditional dishes with some vegetarian and vegan options, served in a lovely garden setting. **$**

Further out of town but still very doable by public transport is Orquigonia, an absolute must-see for orchid lovers or even the orchid-curious.

The cool, moist climate around Cobán is perfect for orchids and the town even has an annual festival celebrating them.

At this privately run sanctuary, tours run for around an hour, taking you on a journey through the forest. The guide will point out interesting species along the way and fill you with more orchid-related facts than you probably knew existed, starting with the Maya's relationship with them and continuing up to the challenges of species preservation that exist today.

If you really like it out here, they have cosy little cabins sleeping up to six people where you can stay the night – call to find out if you're interested.

Cooperativa Chicoj

COMMUNITY-BASED COFFEE TOURISM

The other thing that Cobán is famous for is, of course, coffee, and if you've ever been curious about how the good stuff gets into your cup, Cooperativa Chicoj, a community tourism initiative 15 minutes from downtown Cobán, is the place to find out.

Knowledgeable guides literally walk you through the entire process from planting the seed to filling your cup, with interesting tidbits about how Guatemala's climatic diversity contributes to the wide range of coffee available from the different regions and the various roasting techniques used to produce the perfect bean.

One interesting aspect of the tour is the optional zipline component – there are seven of them in total that weave across the property.

As highlighted by the rise in fair-trade coffee over recent years, the coffee industry is hugely problematic and it feels good to be supporting a cooperative that supports the local community. If you're interested, your guide will tell you about the burgeoning industry that is community tourism in Guatemala and the troubled history that growers collectives like this one have faced.

Once the tour is done, there's the obligatory tasting and the chance to buy some freshly roasted coffee, bakery goods and souvenirs.

GUATEMALAN COFFEE

There are eight main coffee-growing regions:

Acatenango, Antigua & Fraijanes
Coffee grown in these volcanic mineral-rich regions is known for its marked acidity and fragrant aroma.

Atitlán
Grown in rich organic soils, Atitlán coffee is full-bodied and aromatic, with notes of citrus.

Cobán
Limestone and clay soils and year-round drizzle give Cobán coffee fruity flavours and a mild aroma.

Huehuetenango
Non-volcanic soil gives Huehuetenango coffee an intense acidity and a full body.

El Oriente
Mild, chocolaty coffee with low acidity.

San Marcos
This warm, rainy region produces coffee with floral notes and a mild acidity.

GETTING AROUND

Cobán is small enough to walk around, but taxis hang out in the Parque Central. A municipal ordinance has prohibited *tuk-tuks* from operating within the city limits. Minibuses serve the small villages around the outskirts of town.

Lagunas de
Sepalau

Raxruhá

Grutas de
Lanquín

Cobán

Semuc
Champey

Biotopo del
Quetzal

Rabinal

Salamá

Beyond Cobán

Enjoy Cobán, but don't get stuck there
– there are plenty of worthwhile attractions
in the surrounding countryside.

Some of the country's most impressive natural wonders are within striking distance of Cobán. The mild climate, vast swathes of protected forest and impressive limestone formations almost beg to be explored. You'll see posters of Semuc Champey all over the country; the Laguna Lachuá is a remote lake surrounded by untouched forest; the cave systems around Raxruhá offer exciting possibilities for serious spelunkers to casual strollers alike. Birdlife is especially abundant – there are no guarantees, but there's a chance you might see the national bird, the resplendent quetzal. Community tourism is particularly strong in this region and gives visitors a great way of learning about these remote locations while supporting the people who make them their home.

TOP TIP

Buses go everywhere, but hiring a car in Cobán is a decent option – some roads are only passable with 4WD.

Semuc Champey

GALYNA ANDRUSHKO/SHUTTERSTOCK ©

Grutas de Lanquín

Lanquín & Semuc Champey

BAT CAVES AND SWIMMING HOLES

Chances are you'll know what **Semuc Champey** looks like before you even get close. The jungle-shrouded limestone pools here are one of Guatemala's iconic tourist attractions, thought by some to be the most beautiful spot in the country. If their location were any less remote, the place would be packed out every day, but as it is, the sparse crowds and large area mean that you often feel like you have the place to yourself, even if that's not quite the case.

You can camp out here on the grounds. A couple of basic accommodation options have sprung up near the entrance, but most people choose to make the pretty village of **Lanquín** their base and catch one of the regular pickups out to the site.

Lanquín itself is almost worth the visit in its own right. It's an extremely picturesque spot, nestled between the mountains on the banks of the Río Cahabón.

The main village sits on a hilltop, surrounding a central plaza that is overtaken most days by a lively market. Just on the edge of town are the Grutas de Lanquín, a bat-filled cave system that extends several kilometers into the earth.

LIMESTONE FORMATIONS

The amazing rock formations and turquoise waters in the rivers around Lanquín and in all of the Verapaces region come from the fact that the ground is rich in limestone. Being softer and slightly soluble in rainwater means that this rock gets moulded over time by the elements. The majority of the world's caves can be found in limestone deposits, such as eastern Mexico's famous cenotes which, along with caves, are sacred to the Maya as portals to the underworld. The stepped terraces of Semuc Champey are composed of a specific type of limestone known as travertine, which forms when mineral-rich water emerges from beneath the ground at force, leaving granular deposits that build up over time.

 WHERE TO STAY IN LANQUÍN

Zephyr Lodge
Firmly planted on the backpacker trail, this full-service hostel has a great location and decent rooms. $

Hostal Oasis
A fine range of bungalows spread around a grassy property right down on the riverbank. $$

El Sueño De Tansú
Simple but stylish rooms, an on-site bar and an excellent balcony looking out over the valley. $$

THE FRANJA TRANSVERSAL DEL NORTE

If you're enjoying the relative peace around Raxrujá, make the most of it – one of Guatemala's most ambitious infrastructure projects is coming through here. Called the Franja Transversal del Norte, this highway stretches 265km from the border of southwestern Mexico to the Belizean border just north of Río Dulce. The project has been planned since the 1970s but has been mired in a series of scandals and revelations. The route passes through sensitive environmental and cultural areas, but detractors claim that proper impact studies were never made. Local communities are also very wary that it passes by areas that are rich in petroleum and minerals and they fear that once it opens, mining companies won't be far behind.

MARIA JOSE LOU/SHUTTERSTOCK ©

Resplendent quetzal, Biotopo del Quetzal

Lanquín is served by regular minibuses from Cobán; it's roughly a three-hour trip. From there it takes around another half-hour to Semuc Champey by pickup. All Lanquín hotels offer tours, but don't buy one on the street – this town is rife with scammers.

Around Raxruhá

CAVES, RUINS AND LAGOONS

Sitting at the crossroads between El Petén to the north, the Verapaces to the south, the highlands to the west and the Ca-

 WHERE TO STAY IN RAXRUJÁ

Hotel Cancuen
Just on the edge of town. Rooms range from basic and fan-cooled to modern with air-con. $

Candelaria Lodge
Just out of town, this French-run hotel is stylish and comfortable and offers a predictably good restaurant. $$

Las Bugambilias
Simple, clean rooms set around a pretty garden. The attached restaurant serves good traditional food. $

ribbean coast to the east, **Raxruhá** feels like it should be a lot more important than it is. All of the attractions are out of town.

The limestone rock formations offer several excellent cave systems to explore – Cuevas de Candelaria are impressive at 22km long, with enormous chambers and a subterranean river where tubing is sometimes offered.

North of Raxruhá, the remote Maya site of Cancuén is reachable only by boat or foot from the even smaller village of La Unión. It's a complicated journey that's well worth it.

Cancuén was an important trading center in its heyday, and ongoing excavations suggest that it may have been larger than Tikal.

The buildings that have been unearthed are impressive, both for their size and the intricate carvings that are still in good condition. Further to the west is the Parque Nacional Laguna Lachuá, an idyllic spot where a large national park surrounds a near-circular pristine turquoise lake. The park is popular with birdwatchers and several kilometers of trails wind through the forest.

A rustic bunkhouse on the lake's shore provides accommodation for those wanting to stay.

Raxruhá is about two hours by bus from Cobán.

Biotopo del Quetzal

A CHANCE TO SPOT A QUETZAL

Officially known as the Biotopo Mario Dary Rivera, the 1,044-hectare Biotopo del Quetzal nature reserve is administered by Guatemala's public university, the Universidad de San Carlos.

Only a fraction of the park is open to visitors, but it's well worth the trip if only to get up close to the lush ecosystem known in these parts as cloud forest.

The reserve gets its more popular name because quetzal birds have been spotted here. They often feed on fruits of the aguacatillo tree and are most active between February and September.

Even taking that into account, a sighting is not at all guaranteed – despite being the national bird, quetzals have been teetering on extinction in this region for some time, as their wonderful plumage is prized amongst collectors.

Even if they don't spot a quetzal, few people go away from this reserve disappointed. Two gorgeous walking trails lead away from the visitors center, winding their way past mosses, ferns, orchids, waterfalls and swimming holes.

The trails total about 6km altogether and are fairly easy

THE QUETZAL & THE MAYA

The quetzal features heavily in Mesoamerican mythology and was considered a sacred bird to the Maya. The punishment for killing a quetzal was death. Quetzal-related imagery frequently appears in pre-Columbian cultures, probably most famously in the quetzal feathers that formed the centerpiece of the headdress that the Aztec ruler Moctezuma II used at the time of Spanish conquest. The Maya god of the air, Kukulcán, is represented as a feathered serpent, obviously related to a similar god in Aztec-Toltec culture named Quetzalcoatl. Kukulcán is worshipped at such sites as Chichén Itzá when the sun in the spring equinox casts shadows on the staircase of the Temple of Kukulcán, revealing his likeness to worshippers.

 WHERE TO STAY NEAR THE BIOTOPO DEL QUETZAL

Ranchitos del Quetzal
Right by the entrance to the reserve with clean, simple rooms and friendly service. $

Ram Tzul
A birdwatchers paradise, set on 1,000 hectares of nature reserve. Rooms are comfortable and stylish. $$

Posada Montaña Del Quetzal
Popular with tour groups, the restaurant is great and the rooms are OK. $$$

walking, with a couple of steep sections and slippery steps. The visitors center sells maps with checklists of the 75 other species of bird you are likely to see.

The Biotopo is about 50km south of Cobán; around 90 minutes by bus.

Lagunas de Sepalau

SECLUDED LAGOONS

Outside of the small town of Chisec, the Lagunas de Sepalau take their name from the local Q'eqchi' word meaning 'place of the sea'. One look at their dazzling, crystal waters and you'll understand why.

They get their startling blue colors by being fed from mineral-rich underground springs. The lagoons are connected by rustic paths that weave through near-virgin rainforest. The whole area is pristine, and swimming is permitted (and recommended) in all except the first of the lagoons, which serves as a water supply for local communities.

There's a small rowboat on hand that you can hire to paddle around the place, and sightings of a variety of wildlife have been reported – keep your eye out for tapirs, iguanas, howler monkeys and jaguars, as well as parrots, toucans and many other bird species.

The area is administered by a local community tourism initiative based in the village of Sepalau Catalzul – stop off there to pay your modest entrance fee before proceeding.

You can camp here if you have your own tent. If you don't, the community sometimes have one to rent, but don't count on it. Eating options are limited in the area – you're better off eating in Chisec or bringing a picnic.

Chisec is about two hours from Cobán by bus. From there you can get a regular pickup to Sepalau Catalzul.

Salamá & Rabinal

TRADITION AND NATURAL BEAUTY

An unspoilt little hill town with an ornate church and a sleepy air, **Salamá** is many travelers' introduction to the Verapaces region – the low plateau that forms much of the center of the country. There's not much to do here, which is part of the charm, but the Sunday market gets lively and there are some great hiking and birdwatching opportunities in the surrounding countryside. Nestled amongst the Minas mountain range on the banks of the Salamá River, the town is mostly surrounded by cattle farms.

The Ach'ie Maya were here originally, but after the Span-

BEST COMMUNITY TOURISM PROJECTS AROUND CHISEC

Lagunas de Sepalau
These wonderful, wild lagoons are easily accessible from Chisec.

Laguna Lachuá
Nature lovers can stay in Rocjá Pomtilá, enjoy the village life and use it as a base for exploring the nearby Laguna Lachuá.

B'ombi'l Pek
Hike through the corn fields and abseil into the caves at B'ombi'l Pek – a truly unforgettable experience.

Cuevas de Candelaria
This extensive cave system has multiple entry points allowing for anything from a pleasant walk to full-on spelunking or river tubing.

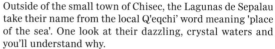

WHERE TO STAY IN CHISEC

Hotel Estancia De La Virgen	**Casa Vieja**	**Hotel El Potrillo**
Spacious, plain rooms set around a large patio featuring an enormous swimming pool. **$$**	A friendly family-run hotel on the outskirts of town. Rooms are simple, quiet and clean. **$**	Budget digs in the center of town. Rooms vary greatly – ask to see a few. **$**

Lagunas de Sepalau

BEST PLACES TO STAY IN SALAMÁ & RABINAL

Hotel Verapaz
Surprisingly chic for Salamá, with lush grounds, a great pool and some well-appointed rooms. $$

Hotel del Centro
Reasonably clean budget rooms right by the plaza in Salamá. The ones at the front can get a lot of street noise. $

Hotel Maria De Los Ángeles
Hotels are basic in Rabinal – the clean, medium-sized rooms here are the pick of the bunch. $

ish conquest, Dominican monks took control of the area with the plan of cultivating grapes for winemaking. Remnants of the elaborate Roman-inspired system of aqueducts that they constructed can be seen today.

To the west of Salamá, the small towns of San Miguel Chicaj and **Rabinal** are mildly interesting at any time of year, but things really heat up during their festivals – this is where the region's pride in its indigenous heritage really comes to the fore. Rabinal in particular put up some of the fiercest opposition to the Spanish invasion.

Even further west is the tiny town of Cubulco – if you're around here in July, definitely check out their festival, which is one of the last in the country to feature the *palo volador* (Maya flying pole).

Buses to Salama and Rabinal leave regularly from Cobán. The trip to Salamá takes about two hours.

Palo volador,
Cubulco

GETTING AROUND

Minibuses connect the outlying towns with Cobán. All towns listed here have *tuk-tuks* for local transportation, but are small enough to walk around. Tours and pickups go from Lanquín to Semuc Champey. If you're driving, you'll need a 4WD for this stretch of road.

THE PACIFIC SLOPE

GUATEMALA'S PLAYGROUND

Sleepy beach towns, once-opulent cities, surfers' hideouts and relics of non-Maya pre-Columbian civilizations. Welcome to La Costa.

The Olmecs were here first, having come south from what is now Mexico as early as 1,500 BCE. They didn't leave much trace except for the distinctive stone statues found around Santa Lucía Cotzumalguapa. As the highland civilizations were crumbling, some Maya tribes moved down to the coast, but the Spanish were soon to arrive and they met little resistance in this region.

The heavy rains, blazing sun and fertile volcanic soil proved perfectly suited to crops such as cotton and sugarcane, and towns like Retalhuleu took on a grandeur that you can see slowly fading as you pass through. The cotton has long gone, but there's still plenty of cane around – it forms the backbone of the local economy. There's

very little commercial fishing going on, but there is a number of small fishing villages, some of which are reinventing themselves as tourist destinations.

El Paredón has the best waves in Guatemala and attracts a steady stream of surfers from around the world – towards, the end of hurricane season the swells can be impressive.

Further south is Monterrico, the closest beach town to Guatemala City and accordingly busy during local holiday periods. The beaches may not be what you expect – they're all black volcanic sand, the waves are wild and the rip tides can be deadly. Just keep your head about you – it's almost impossible not to have fun in this part of the world.

BYRON OBED SAGASTUME BRAN/GETTY IMAGES ©

THE MAIN AREAS

RETALHULEU
Once the pearl of Guatemala's Pacific coast, 'Reu' is now an agricultural hub.
p86

SANTA LUCÍA COTZUMALGUAPA
It's worth the effort to see the Olmec-style sculptures.
p94

MONTERRICO
There's plenty to like about Guatemala's most popular beach town.
p102

Resplendent quetzal

Find Your Way

The coast is a narrow strip of land bisected by the coastal highway, so most of its attractions are naturally beach-side, but there are a few inland options worth exploring.

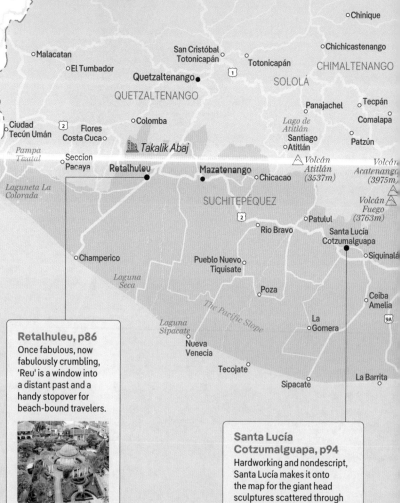

Sacapulas

Chinique

Chichicastenango

CHIMALTENANGO

Malacatan

San Cristóbal
Totonicapán

Totonicapán

El Tumbador

Quetzaltenango

SOLOLÁ

QUETZALTENANGO

Panajachel

Tecpán

Colomba

Lago de
Atitlán

Comalapa

Ciudad
Tecún Umán

Flores
Costa Cuca

Santiago
Atitlán

Patzún

Takalik Abaj

Pampa
Tizatal

Seccion
Pacaya

Retalhuleu

Mazatenango

Chicacao

Volcán
Atitlán
(3537m)

Volcán
Acatenango
(3975m)

Laguneta La
Colorada

SUCHITEPÉQUEZ

Volcán
Fuego
(3763m)

Rio Bravo

Patulul

Santa Lucía
Cotzumalguapa

Champerico

Pueblo Nuevo
Tiquisate

Siquinalá

Laguna
Seca

Poza

Ceiba
Amelia

9A

The Pacific Slope

La
Gomera

Laguna
Sipacate

Nueva
Venecia

Tecojate

Sipacate

La Barrita

Retalhuleu, p86
Once fabulous, now fabulously crumbling, 'Reu' is a window into a distant past and a handy stopover for beach-bound travelers.

Santa Lucía Cotzumalguapa, p94
Hardworking and nondescript, Santa Lucía makes it onto the map for the giant head sculptures scattered through the surrounding countryside.

0   100 km
0   50 miles

CAR

Sugarcane trucks barrelling along the highway and roads of varying quality off it don't make for relaxed driving around here. Take the bus or hire a driver.

BUS

First-class buses run up and down the highway at regular intervals. Some only stop in larger towns. 2nd class ("chicken") buses service the smaller towns and most coastal communities.

TUK-TUK

More often used for short hops around town, these little three-wheelers will take you to the next town over as well – it's a fun, breezy ride if you can keep your wits about you.

Monterrico, p102
Guatemala City's closest party town packs out in the holidays and winds way back mid-week. It's a great place to rest up and recharge the batteries.

Plan Your Time

Nobody's in a rush here and for most of the year the heat is so vicious that you won't want to be moving around too much anyway.

Santa Lucía, Cotzumalguapa (p94)

If You Only Do One Thing

● Just make a beeline for **Monterrico** (p102). Popular as it is, this is still more fishing village than Cancún super-resort. Relax on the beach and explore the little bars and restaurants along the coastline. If you're looking for some movement, take a tour through the mangroves – early morning is best for the birdlife.

● If you feel like going further afield, visit the turtle sanctuary down at **Biotopo Monterrico-Hawaii** (p104) – if you're there in hatching season, you can help release the newborns into the sea, a sight guaranteed to melt even the hardest traveler's heart.

Seasonal Hghlights

The temperature here swings between 'hot' and 'really hot'. If you need air-conditioning, make sure you check if your hotel has it.

JANUARY

The first week or two of the year it seems everybody heads to the coast. Join in or avoid accordingly.

FEBRUARY

Carnaval kicks off around the country, but is at its liveliest in Retalhuleu.

MARCH

Surf season starts, with some nice little swells for beginners. The big waves come with the rains later in the year.

4 Days to Travel Around

● Spend a couple of days at Monterrico, then hop on a bus for the little town of **Santa Lucía Cotzumalguapa** (p94) – there's not much for tourists here, but it's a comfortable enough place to spend a couple of nights.

● The reason you're here is to see the nearby archaeological sites of El Baúl and Bilbao, which feature large, Olmec-style heads, elaborate carvings and interconnected stone causeways that have been uncovered in the surrounding countryside over the last 150 years.

If You Have a Week

● Once you're done visiting Monterrico and Santa Lucía, keep heading north for the regional capital at **Retalhuleu** (p86). A reasonably sized town at an important crossroads, 'Reu' as it's mostly known has good places to eat and sleep and a downtown that is lively enough to make an aimless wander worthwhile.

● If you've got the kids along, they'll probably be quite happy at the nearby fun parks of **Xetulul** and **Xocomil** (p90). If you're up for more Maya ruins, **Takalik Abaj** (p90) makes for a good day trip.

JUNE

Turtle-nesting season starts, running through to December. Volunteers are always needed to save eggs from predators.

SEPTEMBER

Turtles start hatching and are released back into the ocean between now and January.

NOVEMBER

Whale-watching season begins, with humpback and sperm whales in migration until March.

DECEMBER

The surf starts to calm down a bit, making it a good time for beginners to get some lessons in.

RETALHULEU

Once the pearl of Guatemala's Pacific coast, Retalhuleu, or 'Reu' (*ray-oo*) to pretty much everybody, saw its heyday during the cotton boom. When the bottom fell out of that market, local farmers turned to cattle, sugarcane and bananas. The city itself has a moderately prosperous, pleasingly crumbling atmosphere. The central plaza and surrounding buildings seem grandiose now, but offer a glimpse into a bygone era, as does the ostentatious, palm-lined boulevard that leads into town from the highway.

There's not much to do in Reu itself, apart from wander its winding streets and admire such curiosities as its pot-plant-covered police station and sprawling open-air shopping mall.

There's plenty to do in the surrounding area, though, and the city offers the most comfort and widest variety of amenities in the nearby area.

Retalhuleu   ✪ Guatemala
City

TOP TIP

Long-distance buses stop in the center of town at a stop called La Galera before continuing to the main terminal on the outskirts. The city is small enough to be walkable, but *tuk-tuks* zip around everywhere, offering cheap hops around town.

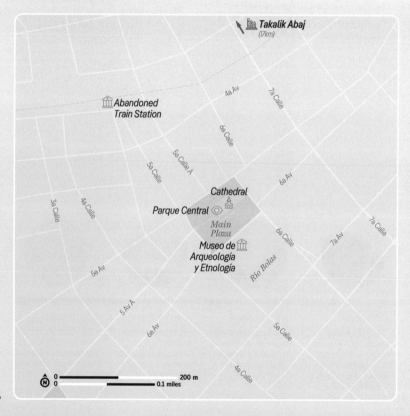

ANGEL AJANEL/SHUTTERSTOCK ©

Retalhuleu Cathedral

Retalhuleu's Night Market

ALFRESCO DINING, COASTAL STYLE

A stroll around Retalhuleu's lovely **Parque Central** is a worth-while activity at any time of day – the carefully manicured gardens and brightly painted benches, which are all over-looked by Reu's stately and dominating cathedral, stand in stark contrast to the somewhat rundown nature of the rest of the downtown area. During the day, a quick pass through the Museo de Arqueología y Etnología is worth your time for a small archaeological collection on the ground floor.

Like much of Reu, though, the plaza is a pretty empty place while the midday sun is blazing down. Once the sun goes down, the locals emerge from their homes and the town really comes to life. Food vendors set up stalls along the plaza's southwest side, putting little benches and tables out on the street, with the area taking on a festive air.

There are no real gourmet options along here; it's mostly ta-cos, *tostadas* (crunchy tortillas accompanied by various top-pings), *garnachas* (fried corn dough topped with meat and beans), hot dogs and various permutations on the 'fruit in a bag' theme. But the atmosphere is relaxed and friendly – feel free to wander around asking questions. The vendors are

BEST PLACES TO EAT IN RETALHULEU

Café Kiut'z
The coolest cafe in town, with a great garden serving up burgers, pasta snacks and good coffee from early to late. **$**

Hotel Astor
Patio dining in this hotel's restaurant is as fine as it gets in downtown Reu. International and local dishes in relaxed, formal surrounds. **$$**

Temos
People on the coast love their steak, and this place delivers some very fine cuts. A good wine list and a few seafood dishes round out the menu. **$$**

 WHERE TO STAY IN RETALHULEU

Hotel Posada de Don José
Just a block from the plaza, with large spacious rooms set around a lovely pool area. **$$**

Hotel La Estancia
Budget hotels can be hit and miss in Reu, but this one's clean, quiet and renovated. **$**

Hotel San Gabriel
A few blocks from the plaza, with bright airy rooms around a central parking lot. A solid choice. **$**

RAILWAYS IN GUATEMALA

As a once-burgeoning industrial nation, Guatemala used to be crisscrossed with train tracks. The longest stretches connected Tecún Umán at the Mexican border and Puerto Barrios on the Caribbean coast with Guatemala City. The line between Quetzaltenango and Retalhuleu only lasted three years before being wiped out by a hurricane, never to be rebuilt.

There have been various attempts at reviving the rail network, but many of the tracks have been pilfered and sold for scrap or repurposed, and a lot of the land has been taken over by squatters. Getting the trains back on the tracks will be a massive, expensive task, and Guatemala's extensive network of trucks for cargo and buses for passengers make it a low priority.

ANGEL AJANEL/SHUTTERSTOCK ©

The old train station

chatty and welcoming and overall the market offers the visitor a wonderful window into how life is down on the coast.

The Old Train Station

AN ICON FROM THE PAST

There is probably no one more emblematic image of Retalhuleu's past than the abandoned train station that sits in the center of town, just off the Parque Central. If photography is your thing or you're just looking for an atmospheric reminder of the way things used to be here, it's worth wandering over to check it out. Opened in 1884, the station was once the pride of the city, which still, without irony, calls itself the 'Capital of the World'. Steam trains covered the 66km journey between Reu and the port town of Champerico, carrying cargo – cotton, coffee and sugar exports – and passengers as part of the problematic and ultimately doomed Guatemalan train network.

There's not much to see here now. In its heyday, this would have been a hive of activity, with three-story buildings holding offices, warehouses and workshops, and people and goods moving to and from the port, destined for or arriving from Europe. You can't enter the graffiti-strewn buildings, but the area is completely open and you're welcome to wander and photograph to your heart's content. The facade on 4 Calle A is probably the most impressive: a stately construction with columns and arched windows, and the station clock still intact on the corner of the building is stuck in time.

GETTING AROUND

The city center is small enough to walk around, but the plentiful *tuk-tuks* can be a welcome sight in Reu's stifling heat. Buses coming into town arrive first at a stop called La Galera, which is better for downtown hotels than the main terminal on the outskirts of town.

Beyond Retalhuleu

Aldea Loma
Linda
    Reserva
    El Patrocinio
Takalik Abaj   Xocomil &
Tilapita   Xetulul
   Retalhuleu
    Finca Santa
    Elena
Champerico

The lush, rolling hill country around Retalhuleu offers a little bit of something for everyone.

Takalik Abaj, one of Guatemala's oldest known archaeological sites, makes for an easy day trip from Retalhuleu. There are no soaring pyramids here – this site was inhabited by a mixture of Olmec and Maya cultures and is known more for ornate carvings than feats of architecture.

To the north of town are a collection of amusement parks that pack out during school holidays. They're surprisingly well-kept, and a must-visit if you have kids along or just enjoy goofy fun and waterslides.

And then of course there's the beach. There are a few worthwhile beach towns within striking distance of Reu – Champerico gets the crowds, while Tilapita is much more sedate.

TOP TIP

Shared taxis with fixed routes and their destinations written on the windshield are safe and can be hailed anywhere.

Takalik Abaj (p90)

LEV LEVIN/SHUTTERSTOCK ©

Guatemala shows signs of being the longest inhabited country in Central America – some evidence suggests that there were people here around as early as 18,000 BCE. Much of the activity was migration, though, with people moving south and eventually ending up in South America. Early settlers include the Olmecs who are believed to have inhabited the area around Takalik Abaj from 1500 BCE. It is thought that the Olmec-style heads in La Democracia were actually carved by Pipil settlers, who arrived in Guatemala around 900 BCE, but much of this is guesswork as these cultures borrowed traded objects and icons heavily. What is known from the carvings at Takalik Abaj is that the Maya were firmly ensconced there from 300 BCE onwards.

Takalik Abaj
A MIX OF CULTURES

The most impressive archaeological site on the Pacific Slope, Takalik Abaj (or Abaj Tajalik, depending on who you ask) spreads across nearly 10 sq km, cascading over nine terraces. The site's name translates to 'standing stones' and there are indeed stelae here, but probably the most interesting exhibits are the large carved stone heads showing a strong influence from Mexico's Olmec culture and establishing a link that some of the inhabitants here came from the north at some point.

Around 280 structures have been unearthed. The highest of these is Structure 5, which measures around 16m. Fine carvings, mostly in the Maya style, are evidenced all around the site, and there are also various examples of the pot-bellied figures known as *barrigones*, which were found near La Democracia and are on display in the central plaza there.

Much of Takalik Abaj was destroyed when the city was sacked around 300 CE, and a large portion of the original site has not been excavated, as it lies underneath nearby coffee plantations. Thankfully, some plantation owners are interested in Maya culture and support excavation of the site, and have ceded various parts of their properties to excavation and exploration efforts.

The site itself can be seen within a couple of hours. There isn't much else in the way of services out here. Drink and snack vendors sometimes congregate at the entrance, but don't count on it. The park is about a 30-minute drive from Reu. Coming by public transport, get a shared taxi to El Asintal and a pickup from there to the site.

The IRTRA Parks
FUN IN THE SUN

Yes, ancient cultures are fascinating and volcanoes are great to look at and climb, but even the most hardened traveler needs a little mindless fun now and then, and this is where the IRTRA parks outside of Retalhuleu shine.

There are two main parks here. Parque Acuático Xocomil is the water park, and it contains all the attractions you know and love – the lazy river, the dunking stalls, the wave pool, dedicated children's areas and a mind-boggling assortment of waterslides, from terrifying vertical drops to more mellow winding, twisting numbers that you ride in a raft with four people aboard. Lockers are available and there's OK fast food on sale at various restaurants at reasonable prices.

Situated right next door, Parque de Diversiones Xetulul is

WHERE TO STAY NEAR THE IRTRA PARKS

Hostales de IRTRA	**Zafra Hotel**	**Hotel Gran Karmel**
Some of the coast's best accommodations; run with the same meticulous care as the fun parks. **$$$**	Large, cool but ageing rooms with wide shady porches and a great restaurant/pool area. **$$**	Fancy setup, with landscaped grounds, huge rooms and all the amenities you'd expect. **$$$**

Parque Acuático Xocomil

THE IRTRA STORY

The organization that runs the fun parks outside of Reu, IRTRA (the Instituto de Recreación de los Trabajadores de la Empresa Privada – the Institute of Recreation for Workers of Private Companies) is probably the best-functioning example of public-private collaboration in Guatemala's history. The idea is simple – an Act of Congress mandates that every employer pays one day's salary per worker per year to a fund that develops parks such as these around the country. All workers get a card that entitles them to heavily discounted entry and accommodations. Apart from providing affordable vacations to working families, the parks are so well run that they have won international awards and attract visitors from all over Central America and Mexico.

your classic amusement park featuring roller coasters, the swinging pirate ship and other heart-stopping amusements. Hourly shows (magic, dance exhibitions etc) take place in a couple of different theaters on site.

If you don't feel like walking, a small train runs around the perimeter of the site, stopping at various 'stations' along the way.

First-time visitors to the parks are often surprised by the level of cleanliness, professionalism and maintenance on display. This isn't some village *feria* – the parks pride themselves on their quality. As a result, you'll see visitors from Mexico and all over Central America who come to this region just to visit the parks on vacation.

 WHERE TO EAT IN CHAMPERICO

Restaurante La Mariscada
A laid-back place, with tables under palm trees. The swimming pool is a bonus. **$**

Restaurante 7 Mares
Attached to the hotel of the same name, with tables set out right on the beachfront. **$$**

Rancho Hermanitos Morales
One of many beachfront joints serving up fresh seafood and cold drinks at rock-bottom prices. **$**

I LIVE HERE: BEACHES & BEYOND

Edgar Martínez, agricultural consultant, breaks down the best options in and around Reu. There are lots of things for tourists to do around here. When friends visit I like to be the guide, to take them to places that they don't expect. Lots of the most beautiful places are on private land, but one place that's open to the public is Takalik Abaj Lodge – that has some really beautiful grounds where you can walk and a waterfall where you can swim. Everybody wants to go to the beach when they come. If we want to party, we go to Champerico. If we're with our families, we go to Tulate – it's good there for kids.

Champerico

The parks are about a 30-minute drive from Reu. Shared taxis make the run or you could hop on any bus heading towards Quetzaltenango and jump off at the entrance.

Champerico & Tilapita

A DAY AT THE BEACH

If this is your first time on the Pacific coast, there are some things you need to know about beach life here. The most important one is that the riptides can be deadly and lifesavers (if there are any) tend to be more of the 'stand on the shore and blow whistles at people' persuasion rather than the 'jump in, paddle out and save people' type that you might be accustomed to.

Slightly less life-threatening is the sand. It's black because it's made of volcanic rock. All the Pacific coast beaches have

WHERE TO STAY IN CHAMPERICO & TILAPITA

Hotel 7 Mares
Large, sparse rooms around an inviting pool area, right on the Champerico beachfront. **$**

Hotel Pacifico Mar
Very basic rooms, great food and a pool, a couple of hundred meters from the water's edge in Tilapita. **$**

Sol Palmeras
Under construction at the time of writing, but promises to be Tilapita's fanciest option. **$$**

sand this color – it has nothing to do with cleanliness. If you're looking for white sand, that would be on the other side of the country, on the Caribbean coast.

There are two very good beaches within striking distance of Retalhuleu, and they couldn't be more different. The old port town of **Champerico** is the most accessible, about an hour from Reu by bus. During normal weekdays it's a pretty relaxed place, but on weekends and during school holidays it packs out to an almost comical degree. There are a bunch of seafood restaurants set up right on the beachfront and a few places to stay, but most people come for the day and the town really empties out at night.

On the opposite end of the spectrum is **Tilapita**, a couple of hours from Reu, where just one hotel/restaurant awaits you (and one other is preparing to open). It's the definition of laid-back and rarely sees any sort of crowd, even in high season.

Agrotourism

DOWN ON THE FARM

With the instability of agricultural markets and the rise of tourism in Guatemala, a new industry has emerged – that of agrotourism. At its most basic, the idea is simple enough: local farmers open up a few rooms in their farmhouse and start accepting guests. It gets a fair bit more elaborate than that, though, as some places have put in purpose-built accommodations and now earn a healthy slice of their income from hosting guests year-round.

There are a few very good options within an hour of Reu. On the rustic end of the scale is **Aldea Loma Linda**. This community tourism project is based in the village of the same name, in a delightful location at the foothills of the Volcán Santa María. Apart from participating in everyday farming activities, visitors can explore the many walking trails in the area and have a good chance of seeing the rare quetzal bird in its habitat.

A couple of steps up in comfort is the **Finca Santa Elena**, a working farm that produces coffee and a range of dehydrated fruit products (bananas being the best seller). Educational tours of the beautifully maintained property are conducted by the farm's friendly English-speaking owner.

If you're looking for rural but fancy, Reserva El Patrocinio is about the most formal option in the area. Set amongst 140 hectares of coffee, macadamia and rambutan plantations, this place offers hotel-style accommodations, gourmet meals, a range of seven different tours of the reserve and the obligatory zipline tour.

TEPACHE

If you spend any time out on the highway on the Pacific coast, it's quite likely that you will be offered *tepache* by a roadside vendor. Curiously absent from restaurant menus, this fermented (but largely non-alcoholic) drink is sold almost exclusively to passing motorists. Originally from Sonora in Mexico, the drink is made from pineapple rinds and is usually served cold, in a little plastic bag with straw, and is sometimes further flavored with brown sugar and cinnamon. The fermentation process produces various bacteria which are supposedly beneficial for gut health, but mostly it's just a tasty, refreshing (slightly strange) drink. Give it a go – you just might like it!

GETTING AROUND

Chicken buses make the runs between Reu and the beach towns. For Tilapita you might need to get a connection in Coatepeque.

Places closer to Reu are served by shared taxis that have their destinations painted on the windshield.

SANTA LUCÍA COTZUMALGUAPA

Like many other working towns along the coastal flatlands, the economy in Santa Lucía Cotzumalguapa revolves around sugarcane, and the town is like an island in a sea of it. It's a pretty crop while growing, but during burn-off season (November to May) the air is thick with smoke and soot. Once the harvest starts, the roads and highways fill up with double and triple trailers, stacked almost comically high with freshly cut cane on its way to the refineries.

Chances are you're not here for any of that – Santa Lucía's great claim to fame are the great stone heads that are discovered in the surrounding farmlands on a regular basis. They're not easy to get to – in fact, the entire area is curiously underexploited as a tourist destination – but are well worth the effort to experience some of Guatemala's few visible remnants of its connections to pre-Maya cultures.

Santa Lucía
Cotzumalguapa

Guatemala
City

TOP TIP

The hotels in the downtown area are really not recommendable – the best place to look for accommodations is out at the entrance to town, about a kilometer west of the central plaza.

View of Volcán de Agua from Santa Lucía Cotzumalguapa

Santa Lucía's Museums

GIANT STONES FROM ALL OVER

Santa Lucía has two very good museums, both of which showcase findings that have been dug up on nearby sugarcane farms.

Museo El Baúl is the most unique. The museum itself occupies a couple of sheds on the working cane farm located on the outskirts of Santa Lucía.

What's interesting here is that the figures that you see are unlike those anywhere else on display in Guatemala. These are large, anthropomorphic representations of birds, jaguars and humans, carved from huge slabs of volcanic stone and standing 6ft tall in some cases.

Before you go anywhere, make some inquiries – this museum closed down during the COVID lockdowns and has been slow to reopen.

 WHERE TO STAY IN SANTA LUCÍA COTZUMALGUAPA ⸻

Hotel Santiaguito
Cool, shady grounds, an excellent pool area and friendly staff make up for the slightly worn rooms. **$$**

Hotel Internacional
Clean and decent budget rooms off the highway. Nothing fancy but good for a night. **$**

Hotel El Camino
Large, somewhat modern rooms that don't quite live up to the promises of the fancy lobby. **$$**

At the time of writing, to visit you needed to apply for permission a week in advance from the nearby El Pantaleón refinery, and even they didn't know the procedure for doing so. Hopefully by the time you read this, regular visits will be allowed again.

The town's other museum, Museo Cultura Cotzumalguapa, is much less problematic. Sitting on the grounds of Finca La Ilusión to the east of town, it houses a collection of much more familiar Maya-style findings, including altars, stelae obsidian blades, tools and jewelry.

The claim is that all the pieces are originals with the exception of one large fiberglass reconstruction of a piece that was too large to move from its original location.

You could walk to either of these two museums, but it would be a hot, slow and uninteresting trudge. Consider hiring a taxi if you don't have a vehicle.

Santa Lucía's Maya Sites

LIVING HISTORY

While the museums in town hold the most impressive archaeological findings, Santa Lucía also has a couple of nearby active Maya worship sites. Visitors are allowed to approach, but should act respectfully.

These are spiritual ceremonies and modest dress, a minimum of noise and requesting permission before taking photos are the minimum standards here.

VISITING THE SITES

Santa Lucía's attractions are spread out, public transport is patchy and there is nobody offering tours as such. Each of the places mentioned here is within (long) walking distance from town, but visiting each on foot would be a grueling couple of days of joyless trudging through the coastal heat. If you don't have your own vehicle, the best option is to hire a taxi driver to take you around – there are plenty lounging around the Parque Central and they know all of the sites mentioned here. Don't be afraid to bargain – their first offer is almost guaranteed to be outrageous.

Sugarcane field

FRANCISCO SANDOVAL GUATE/SHUTTERSTOCK ©

DANIELSALDANAPHOTO/SHUTTERSTOCK ©

Museo El Baúl (p95)

BEST PLACES TO EAT IN SANTA LUCÍA COTZUMALGUAPA

Robert's
Probably the fanciest place in town, this steakhouse does good steak and seafood dishes in relaxed, formal surrounds. $$

Hotel Santiaguito
It seems like half the town rolls through at some point for the Santiago's big breakfast buffet. Later in the day, cheap set meals and a tasty burger selection round out the picture. $

La Mera Utz
Down-home cooking out on the highway, offering a good range of snacks and *churrascos* (grilled meat). $

The sites are identified by the sugarcane *finca* that surrounds them. The **Bilbao Stones** site is just north of town. There are a few examples of fine carvings here, including glyphs from the Maya calendar and a ball player surrounded by birds and animals.

The other site, at **Finca El Baúl** (not to be confused with the museum on the same *finca*), is further to the north, just to the west of the small village of Colonia Maya.

This site is frequently used for ceremonial purposes and you will most likely see remnants such as flowers, grains and candle wax.

There are many altars here, but the most interesting piece lies half-buried in the dirt – a large, grimacing head with an ornate headdress and beaked nose. Interestingly, none of these stones have been dated or even studied in any great depth.

Both sites are in remote locations, out in the sugarcane fields with not much else around.

Although there have been no bad reports, it's better to err on the side of caution if visiting – don't go alone, don't carry more valuables than are necessary and consider taking a local guide (a taxi driver will do) for extra reassurance.

GETTING AROUND

*Tuk-tuk*s and taxis are all over the place. Some local buses go close to the Maya sites and museums, but not really close enough to be useful. The hotels listed here are all out on the highway, about a kilometer from the Parque Central.

Beyond Santa Lucía Cotzumalguapa

Santa Lucía
Cotzumalguapa

Tulate   La Democracia

Sipacate

You're still technically on the coast here, so take advantage of the beaches and check out some more giant heads while you're at it.

There's no escaping the heat in Santa Lucía, so the obvious move is to head for the beach. From here you can backtrack a bit to get to Tulate, one of the more mellow beach spots along this coast with a few decent spots to eat and sleep, and some slightly gentler wave action than you generally see around here.

Heading directly for the coast, though, would land you in Sipacate, which is not a bad spot and offers an interesting back-door route to the much more popular surfing town of El Paredón. On your way through, leave time to stop off at La Democracia where further giant heads are on display in the central plaza and community-run museum.

TOP TIP

Bus schedules and routes are notoriously changeable here – if you're going somewhere remote, it's worth triple-checking your options before heading out.

Stone head (p101), La Democracia

BARBARA ASH/SHUTTERSTOCK ©

BYRON SAGASTUME/SHUTTERSTOCK ©

Sipacate (p99)

La Democracia

GIANT HEADS IN A TINY TOWN

The southernmost link in the chain of Pipil-Olmec sites with Takalik Abaj and Santa Lucía Cotzumalguapa, **La Democracia** is one of the stranger archaeological experiences you're likely to have. The large, Olmecoid heads and pot-bellied *barrigones* here were found on the nearby Finca Monte Alto and transported for display in the town's central plaza. That's where they sit today, under purpose-built shelters that provide some protection from the elements. It's an arresting sight, made all the more so for locals lounging against them, catching some shade from the midday sun as if having a dozen enormous stone heads in the middle of your plaza was the most normal thing in the world.

While you're here, you might as well check out the Museo Regional de Arqueología, which faces the plaza and houses a small but important collection of artefacts that were also unearthed at Monte Alto and nearby sites. The most impressive piece in the collection is a nearly intact jade mask, which was allegedly removed illegally from the country, and taken all the way to Austria to appear in a museum exhibit before being returned to Guatemala. At last accounts, it was being

WHY I LOVE LA DEMOCRACIA

Lucas Vidgen, writer

There's just something quintessentially Guatemalan about the giant heads in La Democracia. Anywhere else these would be museum pieces, heavily researched and fiercely preserved. But in La Democracia they're just plonked in the town square like any other ornament and the locals use them as backrests to lean against while they eat ice cream. Not that much is even known about them – it's almost as if being non-Maya makes them less worthy in the nation's eyes. I go to La Democracia any chance I get and make sure to take visitors if we're ever in the area – the heads themselves are great, but it's the context that really makes the trip worthwhile.

THE GUIDE

THE PACIFIC SLOPE

 WHERE TO EAT IN LA DEMOCRACIA

Burger Chops
Just off the square, dishing up a range of snacks and set meals. The burgers are OK. **$**

Restaurante La Hacienda
The most formal restaurant in town, with a standard steak and seafood menu and a full bar. **$**

Asados El Jr
A simple neighborhood diner serving grilled meats and other standard Guatemalan fare. **$**

GETTING TO THE BEACH & HOTELS

Like many beach towns along this coast, Tulate is cut off from the mainland by an estuary. The bus pulls up right at the dock and from there you'll have to pay a boatman to take you across. Some brave souls walk/swim across, but that's a serious money-saving move. On arrival, you can walk the town's one paved street all the way down to the beach. If you're headed for La Iguana or Playa Paraíso, it's probably worth paying a bit more and getting the boatman to drop you off to avoid the long hot walk along the sand.

BARBARA ASH/SHUTTERSTOCK ©

Central plaza, La Democracia

held by the Museo Nacional de Arqueología y Etnología in Guatemala City, but should be home in La Democracia by the time you read this.

La Democracia is about half an hour by bus from Santa Lucía Cotzumalguapa.

Tulate

MELLOW IN EVERY WAY

Roughly midway between Retalhuleu and Santa Lucía, the little beach town of **Tulate** has a lot going for it. It's just out of the way enough to never really attract any serious crowds, but big enough to have decent transport connections.

 WHERE TO STAY IN TULATE

Hotel Playa Paraiso
Plain but spacious rooms with a good, if somewhat pricey, beachfront restaurant. **$$**

Hotel Shamma
A fairly basic setup with a good swimming pool and a wooden deck overlooking the waves. **$**

Bungalows La Iguana
Slightly ramshackle bungalows with basic kitchen facilities. Tell the boat driver you're coming here. **$**

The beach here is a lot kinder than most along this coast, too. There are fewer rip tides and the water gets deeper much more gradually than in other Pacific coast beaches, making it a good place to go for a paddle, especially if you've got kids along. The waves never really reach a surfable size outside of hurricane season, but they do come in regularly enough that bodysurfers should be able to catch a few quality rides.

There isn't much in the way of tourist infrastructure out here. Bring enough cash with you as there is no ATM. There are a couple of OK hotels along the beachfront – the rest are pretty basic and the ones on the mainland side are definitely worth avoiding. Little cook shops are set up along the beachfront, selling seafood dishes, snacks and cold drinks. You're free to swing in their hammocks as long as you like, but etiquette dictates that you should buy something every once in a while.

Tulate can be reached from Santa Lucía Cotzumalguapa or Retalhuleu in about two hours. You might need to change buses in Mazatenango.

Sipacate
GUATEMALA'S OTHER SURF SPOT

The first Pacific coast spot to really make it onto surfers' maps was **Sipacate**, a small fishing village pretty much directly south of Santa Lucía Cotzumalguapa.

The focus for surfers has since moved to El Paredón further down the coast – it has a better infrastructure for surfers and is more popular, mostly thanks to promotion, direct shuttle connections with Antigua and advertising. The waves at Sipacate remain consistently surfable, though, with three fast and hollow beach breaks within walking distance. El Paredón rarely suffers from crowds, but if you really want the waves to yourself, this might be the place for you.

For non-surfers it's a quiet little beach town much like many others along here – not a whole lot to do except work on your tan, swing in a hammock and sip on a freshly cut coconut.

Like many spots along the coast, the town itself is a bit ramshackle, and cut off from the ocean by an estuary that you need to cross via ferry. This separation actually works pretty well, leaving all the noise and hubbub on the mainland and keeping the beach and coastline fairly natural and tranquil.

Buses leave Santa Lucía regularly for Sipacate, passing through La Democracia on the way. The trip takes about an hour. You can also get here via a *tuk-tuk*/ferry combination from El Paredón.

CRUISING THE COAST

It would be great if you could meander up and down the coast, but the roads around here just aren't made for that – often getting to the next beach town is a question of going back out to the highway, waiting for another bus to come along and hoping that it goes all the way to your destination. Sipacate and El Paredón are almost connected by road – just one ferry crossing in the way. Monterrico and Hawaii are connected. For everywhere else, it's back out onto the highway. If you're planning on doing a lot of beach-hopping, consider renting a car or else plan for a lot of time spent making connections.

GETTING AROUND

Chicken buses connect all the major towns; *tuk-tuks* provide transportation within towns and are useful for short hops to nearby towns and destinations.

MONTERRICO

It's not quite accurate to say that Monterrico is Guatemala City's closest beach town – that title actually goes to Puerto San José, a place so overtaken by the excesses of day tourism that unless you're actively seeking crowds, you're advised to give it a wide berth.

Just down the road, though, Monterrico is another world. Effectively cut off from the mainland by a series of canals and mangrove swamps, this little town is developing relatively slowly – a road gets paved every now and then and the one ATM is mostly reliable – and there's plenty to like about the humble accommodations and simple seaside eateries that form the backbone of the tourist industry here.

Weekends can get busy and weekdays are very quiet. Visitors who end up staying for a while do so to brush up on their Spanish in the town's one Spanish school or volunteer at the local wildlife conservation projects.

⭐ Guatemala City

Monterrico ●

TOP TIP

There's no need for a car here, but if you have one it makes more sense to approach the town from Iztapa in the west to avoid the long, expensive ferry ride at La Avellana.

Chiquimulilla canal (p104)

Turtle Rescue

HELP SAVE MONTERRICO'S SEA TURTLES

The entire Pacific coast is a nesting and hatching ground for leatherback and olive ridley marine turtles. Despite spending most of their lives out at sea, these animals are amazingly regular in their arrival times for laying eggs. The peak period is around August and September, and unfortunately, this is also when they are at their most vulnerable. Turtle egg soup is considered a delicacy around these parts and egg hunters lay in wait for turtles to lay their eggs before bagging them, often selling them for as little as Q1 per egg.

Various *tortugarios* (turtle conservation projects) along the coast offer tours where you can accompany a ranger who will go out, collect the eggs and take them back to the *tortugario* before the egg hunters get their hands on them.

Fifty to 72 days later, possibly the cutest show in all of Guatemala commences. Having hatched and spent a few days in a holding pen, the baby turtles are released at sunrise or sunset and scamper across the sand and into the crashing waves (these little folks have about a 1% chance of making it to adulthood). In Monterrico, visitors can 'sponsor' a turtle from the

BEST PLACES TO EAT IN MONTERRICO

Osmosis
Right on the beachfront, overlooking the waves. Standard seafood, plus a few lobster dishes. $

Cafe del Sol
Another beachfront joint with palm-shaded tables on the terrace. A wide menu, good breakfasts and lovely pool area. $$

Las Hamacas
On the main street a couple of hundred meters from the beach. Good, home-cooked food and superb pizzas. $

Playa Saltamonte
The best beachfront setup, with hammocks. Doesn't stray far from the usual seafood and meat options. $$

 WHERE TO STAY IN MONTERRICO

Johnny's Place
This long-time backpacker favorite offers a range of rooms, good food and perfect beachfront amenities. $

Hotel Pez de Oro
Sweet little bungalows with great decorations arranged around a shady pool area. Worth the walk. $$

Hotel Cayo Coco
A block back from the beach, this rather formal hotel has lovely grounds and an excellent restaurant. $$

MATYAS REHAK/SHUTTERSTOCK ©

Monterrico

GETTING THE RIGHT GUIDE

Once you get to Monterrico (sometimes before you even step off the ferry) you'll no doubt get approached by someone offering a mangrove tour. Some of these folks have very official-looking credentials, some are very friendly, some speak great English. If you want to make sure that your money goes towards the conservation of the mangroves and their inhabitants, try to book your tour through the CECON-run Tortugario Monterrico. Tours tend to cost the same anyway, but booking through the *tortugario* means you know that your money is going to a good cause, and the boat driver is being paid fairly (plus the added bonus that *tortugario*-connected guides tend to be more professional and knowledgeable).

CECON-run Tortugario Monterrico for a nominal fee and if your racer is the first to the waterline, you win a prize at a local restaurant. The Biotopo Monterrico-Hawaii reserve in nearby Hawaii is more research-focused. If you'd like to get involved with them, it's better to inquire about volunteering.

Mangrove Tour

CRUISING THE LAGOONS

Once you're done with sun-baking, bar crawling and hammock swinging, you might be looking around for a little something to do. Horseback riding on the beach is an option, but if you're not that way inclined, the best thing to do is an early morning mangrove tour. You can go any time – these 'tours' pretty much just consist of jumping in a fishing boat and heading off around the canals. The reason why you want to be doing it in the morning (and the closer to sunrise, the better) is the abundance of birdlife that you'll see. Pelicans are commonplace. There are also large populations of herons, egrets, ibis, storks, kingfishers and plovers amongst others.

The route you take is very atmospheric, more so if you opt for the rowboat over motorboat option. You'll go through part of the Chiquimulilla canal, which was widened in 1895 to allow navigation through the lagoons, mangroves and inlets here – in some places the path narrows to a mere tunnel as thick vegetation surrounds you on all sides.

There are a couple of places where you can disembark and wander the boardwalks through the mangroves. The standard tour takes about two hours. Longer tours on request.

GETTING AROUND

Monterrico is supremely walkable, but *tuk-tuks* whizz around in case you ever get extremely lazy. If you're coming off the ferry from La Avellana it's about a kilometer from the dock to the beachfront where most of the hotels are.

Beyond Monterrico

The small towns scattered along this stretch of the coast offer more laid-back beach life.

The only other beach towns of note along this stretch of coast beyond Monterrico are El Paredón and Iztapa. They're a bit more developed than the others, but both have excellent surf hostels, and tours depart from Iztapa for those interested in sportfishing and whale-watching.

If you've got the kids along (or even if you don't) you might all get a kick out of the Auto Safari Chapín – a kind of open-air, drive-though zoo where nearly 100 species of animals roam freely and you drive through their enclosures. Visitors without cars can make the rounds of this safari park in mini-buses, which leave regularly.

Autosafari Chapín
Iztapa
El Paredón · Puerto Quetzal · · Monterrico
Barra El Jiote

TOP TIP

Bus terminals don't really exist here. If you see a bus coming, flag it down – it will stop, regardless of how full it is.

Monterrico Beach

SIMON DANNHAUER/SHUTTERSTOCK ©

BEST PLACES TO EAT IN & AROUND IZTAPA

Restaurante El Malecón
The most formal restaurant in Iztapa, with a great deck/pool area overlooking the estuary. Interesting seafood dishes and some good pasta options. $

La Cocina de Marielos
A much more gourmet experience than your standard fried fish joints. In El Garitón. $$

La Tasca de Papao
The ceviches are king here, plus there's a decent take on the Garifuna *tapado* casserole dish, all served up in a lovely Iztapa garden setting. $$

ANDREW GEIGER/GETTY IMAGES ©

Fishing, Iztapa

Iztapa

BIG FISH, WHALES AND WAVES

Iztapa once housed the main port on this coast, but that soon changed when the Puerto San José was built back in 1853. It also used to be the end of the line if you were on your way to Monterrico – from here it was a ferry across the river before moving on.

As a result, this little town got more visitors than it probably would have otherwise. There's very little to do here, which some claim is part of the charm.

The rather fancy (toll) bridge across the Río María Linda

 WHERE TO STAY IN IZTAPA

Surf Shack Iztapa
Rooms are basic but the staff is friendly and knowledgeable. Board rental available. $

Hotel Sol y Playa
Not much from the outside, but rooms here are clean and airy, set around a large swimming pool. $

El Majagual de Chicho
A resort-type setup on the beachfront. Rooms are spacious and there's a good restaurant. $$

that went in a few years ago made Iztapa even less of a stopping point, but there are three good reasons to be here. One is that right off this coast is some of the best sportfishing in the world.

These trips are usually organized well in advance as all-inclusive jaunts, but if you're in the area and fancy your luck, try dropping in to Buena Vista Fishing in nearby **Puerto Quetzal** to see if you can join a group.

Another is whale-watching – humpbacks and sperm whales migrate through this region between December and May, and there's a variety of sea life that can be spotted year-round.

Finally, little Iztapa is making a small name for itself as a surfing destination. It doesn't get as consistently good waves as El Paredón further up the coast, but it does have a great little surf hostel with boards and lessons available; while it never really gets crowded at El Paredón, the breaks around here quite often have no one on them.

Buses run regularly between Iztapa and Monterrico. The trip takes about an hour.

Barra El Jiote, Las Lisas

A REMOTE ISLAND GETAWAY

If you're looking for a remote beach getaway, **Barra El Jiote** near the El Salvador border ticks many boxes. It's difficult to get to and accessible only by boat (the Barra in the name refers to the fact that the entire island is in fact a sandbank), so you won't see any of the disco-banging crowds that you do further up the coast.

It's also fabulously underdeveloped – there's only one place to stay here, really: the wonderful Eco Hotel Playa Quilombo de Cucurumbé.

Constructed right on the beachfront, the feel is somewhere between backpacker hideaway and chic boho. Cabins are simple thatched hut affairs, but inside are delightful tile mosaics and artisanal furnishings. There are a variety of rooms available – the better ones in the main building have balconies with sea views, but there's no sign of air-conditioning anywhere, so if sea breezes and ceiling fans don't cut it for you, this isn't your kind of place.

Buildings are arranged around a lovely pool area. There are a few things to do here – tours of the mangroves at the rear of the property, visits to the nearby turtle sanctuary and other beachy type things, but mostly, it's just a wonderful place to relax, enjoy the sunsets and take a break from the otherwise hectic pace that Guatemala can sometimes throw at you.

GETTING TO BARRA EL JIOTE

If you're trying to get to Barra El Jiote by public transport, there are occasional departures to Las Lisas from Guatemala City's CentraSur terminal. If you're coming from Monterrico, you need to go to Escuintla and change buses there. You may not find a direct one, but you can catch any bus heading for the border and get off at the Texaco gas station at the turnoff. Taxis and *tuk-tuks* hang around the gas station and can take you to Las Lisas. If you have money but are short on time, a taxi or Uber is probably your best bet. Once at Las Lisas, a ferry crosses the canal to Barra El Jiote.

 WHERE TO STAY ALONG THE SOUTHERN HIGHWAY

Hostal Las Marias
In Taxisco; one of the region's top hotels. The restaurant serves the best food for miles. **$$**

Hotel Papagayo
Nothing fancy, but the large clean rooms will do for a night if you're passing through Guanagazapa. **$**

Hotel La Esperanza
In Chiquimulilla; lush grounds, multiple swimming pools and clean, spacious rooms. **$$**

BEST PLACES TO EAT IN EL PAREDÓN

Victor Myers found El Paredón by accident on a motorcycle trip 12 years ago and has called it his winter home ever since. @ corridor_surf_shop

El Paredón is a surf town for people who don't like overdeveloped surf tourism. If you like surfing beach break, friendly locals and black sand beaches that still have some magic left, you'll love it. The good wave season also happens to be when nearly all other Central American surf spots are flat. Best conditions are from October to March. Bring your own boards as rentals are limited and unreliable. Despite the abundance of bad DJs, partied-out backpackers and the general lack of infrastructure, the village is a wonderful Pacific hideout.

El Paredón

GUATEMALA'S SURF CAPITAL

In many ways your classic one-street Guatemalan beach town, **El Paredón** distinguishes itself by offering some of the consistently best surf on this stretch of the coast.

The infrastructure is growing accordingly – there's now a scattering of hostels and a few upmarket options, the road has been paved and not one but two phone towers connect the town to the outside world.

For now, the town has absorbed it well and doesn't feel touristy, despite tourism being an obvious focus.

Boards and surf classes can be arranged at any of the hostels. Even if you're not into surfing, El Paredón makes for a decent beach break if you're looking for a remote and otherwise sleepy town.

The food scene here has also dramatically improved over the years – most hostels offer decent meals and there are a couple of very good standalone restaurants, with more likely to be opened soon.

Mangrove tours, a turtle conservation project and traditional cooking classes might keep the non-surfers amused.

Transport connections aren't great, but daily shuttles run between Antigua and El Paredón, and weekly ones come from Lake Atitlán.

Coming from Monterrico, you'd need to catch a bus to Escuintla, then another to Sipacate, followed by a *tuk-tuk* to the river and a ferry across to El Paredón.

Autosafari Chapín

THE DRIVE-THROUGH ZOO

Guatemala is a pretty straight up and down place in many ways, but sometimes it throws you a curveball. One such place is this open-range zoo, Autosafari Chapín, a couple of hours from Monterrico.

Billing itself as 'an African Safari in Guatemala' (well, not quite), they do have nearly 100 species of animals on the grounds as well as a dazzling array of plant life.

The idea is simple enough – rock up in your car and drive through the 14 different enclosures, each of which is designed to replicate the natural habitat of the animals that live inside. All the big names are here – giraffes, rhinos, lions, crocodiles, and so on.

If you like seeing animals, but the small enclosures of traditional zoos make you squeamish, this is a pretty good com-

 WHERE TO STAY IN EL PAREDÓN

El Paredón Surf House
A mellow beachfront setup aimed at surfers, but catering to all. A good range of rooms. $

The Driftwood Surfer
This party hostel is still going strong, with cheap dorms, comfy rooms and a great rooftop bar. $

Swell
Stylish rooms and a restaurant that's worth coming for even if you're not a guest. $$

Crested caracara, Autosafari Chapín

GETTING TO EL SALVADOR

The border crossing at Ciudad Pedro de Alvarado/La Hachadura is pretty straightforward. Most nationalities do not require a visa in advance, but it's worth checking rree. gob.sv to see if you do. Some buses traveling down the southern highway go all the way to the border, but many run express and won't stop for you – you may have to catch a local bus to Chiquimulilla where there are plenty of departures to the border. The hotels on the Guatemalan side are pretty grim – if you do plan on staying the night before moving on, the options are much better on the Salvadoran side, or you could stay in Chiquimulilla and get an early start from there.

promise – the animals here seem at least vaguely happy, and they certainly have plenty of space to move around.

If you don't have a car, you can hop aboard the regular shuttle bus that makes the rounds of the park. If you arrive before midday, it is possible to feed the giraffes, which basically entails hanging some branches out your car window for them to munch on.

A fairly average fast-food restaurant operates at the entrance to the park, where there's also a swimming pool that guests are welcome to use.

GETTING AROUND

Transport between beach towns could be easier. There are plenty of long-distance buses cruising the main highway, but from there it's a question of pickups, shared taxis and local buses. Shuttle buses connect main destinations like El Paredón and Monterrico with Antigua. If you really want to explore the area, consider renting a car.

Templo I, Tikal (p116)

EL PETÉN

MAYA MYSTERIES, NATURAL WONDERS AND MORE

Tikal and other incredible ruins speak of the lost Maya civilization, and there's plenty to explore.

For many visitors to Guatemala, Tikal, arguably the greatest Maya city yet uncovered, and certainly the crown jewel of Guatemala's Maya patrimony, is simply a bucket list must-see. With its iconic temples rising so dramatically out of the surrounding verdant jungle, and the fact that so much about the Maya civilization is yet to be known: Tikal is the reason many tourists visit Guatemala in the first place.

Yet the Petén region is far more than just Tikal. In fact, there are so many ruins, each of them as unique and individual as modern cities today, that it's a shame so many people think they've 'seen it' when they leave Tikal. Tikal is

only the beginning, and to fully see the wealth of sites here would take more time than most travelers have, yet it's certainly worth exploring.

There's also far more than just ancient history to uncover: modern Maya traditions light up streets on colorful festival days, the thick jungles host a myriad of special animals and plants, and the Lago de Petén Itzá (pictured) region offers delightful, tranquil, relaxed lakeside living, whether on the island of Flores or El Remate area. South, the hills, valleys and lagoons of Sayaxché and Petexbatún lend themselves to leisurely river rides and hikes to ruins few tourists find the time for.

BYRON SAGASTUME/SHUTTERSTOCK ©

THE MAIN AREAS

TIKAL	**FLORES & SANTA ELENA**	**EL REMATE**	**SAYAXCHÉ**
Incredible Maya cities.	Quiet lakeside living.	Off-the-grid getaway.	River wonderland.
p116	**p136**	**p146**	**p152**

Find Your Way

El Petén is a vast place, much of it (thankfully) protected by amazing national parks. A 4x4 may take you only part of the way, however, with the rest on foot, horseback or by helicopter.

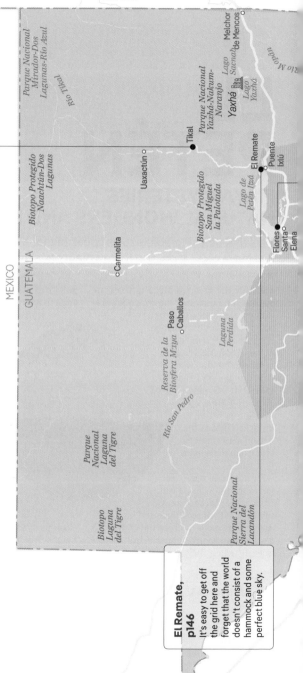

Tikal, p116

This majestic Maya ruin is a top spot not only for Guatemala, but for the entire Maya world.

El Remate, p146

It's easy to get off the grid here and forget that the world doesn't consist of a hammock and some perfect blue sky.

BELIZE

MEXICO

GUATEMALA

Parque Nacional Mirador-Dos Lagunas-Río Azul

Río Tikal

Parque Nacional Yaxhá-Nakum-Naranjo

Yaxhá

Lago Sacnab

Melchor de Mencos

Lago Yaxhá

Río Mopán

Biotopo Protegido Naachtún-Dos Lagunas

Tikal

Uaxactún

Biotopo Protegido San Miguel la Palotada

El Remate

Puente Ixlú

Lago de Petén Itzá

Carmelita

Flores

Santa Elena

Reserva de la Biosfera Maya

Paso Caballos

Laguna Perdida

Río San Pedro

Parque Nacional Laguna del Tigre

Biotopo Laguna del Tigre

Parque Nacional Sierra del Lacandón

BELIZE

MEXICO

Flores & Santa Elena, p136

These beautiful sister cities lie on either side of a thin bridge. Flores is the tourist hub; Santa Elena is cheaper and more local.

Sayaxché, p152

Winding rivers lead to exciting tourist hot spots and Maya ruins deep in the jungle.

Dolores

Poptún

San Luis

Santa Ana

La Libertad

Las Cruces

El Subin

El Ceibal

Sayaxché

Pipiles

Bethel

Río Usumacinta

Río de la Pasión

Río San Juan

Río Machaquilá

Crater Azul

Aguateca

CAR

No question, you'll be well-served if you can rent a vehicle. The freedom to roam where you want and when you want will allow you to make the most of your time here. Even so, certain regions may be out of reach.

BUS

Long-distance express buses serve all of the major parts of El Petén, and smaller microbuses zip (often at hair-raising, knuckle-whitening speeds) to nearly all the smaller towns and villages. To reach the more remote tourist spots requires a private vehicle.

BOAT

Believe it or not, to reach some of the popular tourist destinations, such as Aguateca or Crater Azul, you'll need a boat. They're usually easy to arrange either on the riverbank or in advance.

N

0   50 miles
0   100 km

Plan Your Time

El Petén will seduce you with its variety of things to do and see. You can hike through the jungle, laze on the shores of lakes, and follow rivers far upstream to swim or explore.

Lago de Petén Itzá (p137)

SIMON CROCKETT/GETTY IMAGES ©

If You Only Do One Thing

● It's **Tikal** (p116). As much as there are other things to see, including Maya ruins that compare to Tikal both in historical value and scale, if you visit El Petén and don't see Tikal, it's like going to Paris and not seeing the Eiffel Tower.

● The sunrise tour is particularly awe-inspiring, especially if you're lucky enough to see the sun. No joke, it's cloudy or raining up to 80% of the mornings, so keep that in mind. But regardless, you'll want to make sure that Tikal is on your list in some form.

Seasonal Highlights

You won't find a ski season here but there is a 'dry' and 'wet' season. Hikers should come when it's dry.

JANUARY

The colorful **Baile de la Chatona y el Caballito** is in early January, with outlandish costumes, dancing and parades.

FEBRUARY

Beginning of the dry season: hikers and deep jungle explorers, the 'Go!' light just turned green.

APRIL

By now, the **dry season is over**: hikers and deep jungle explorers, pack those bags before you're mired in mud.

3 Days to Travel Around

● After you've arranged for a visit to Tikal, you can plan the rest of your time here. Many will fly or bus to the quaint island town of **Flores** (p136) and use that as a base, going on a day trip either just to Tikal or to Tikal and other ruins, and arriving back at Flores after dark.

● The next day, take a boat tour of Lago de Petén Itzá, visiting the **El Mirador** (p132) lookout, then the often-flooded town of San Miguel (p142), and finally laze about at the rope swing or check out **ARCAS** (p142), an animal rehab center.

If You Have a Week

● Those with more time should plan trips to additional Maya ruins, such as **Yaxhá** (p129) – great for sunset viewing! – **Naranjo** (p131), and, for the truly intrepid, **El Mirador** (p132), which requires a multiday hike or a helicopter ride from Flores.

● **Uaxactún** (p121), nestled even deeper in the jungle than Tikal, is another possibility. Visitors to these lesser-seen sites will have a far more robust picture of the complex, majestic Maya world than those who just see Tikal.

● There are also volunteering opportunities to rescue wildlife at **ARCAS** (p142), or Spanish-language schools where you can really perfect your *español*.

MAY
The Enhiladera de Flores festival consists of bright garlands of flowers and palm leaves given to the Virgin Mary.

JULY
By some measures, the worst time to visit: heat over 30°C (85°F), **high humidity and rain.**

NOVEMBER
During the **Procesión de la Santa Calavera**, real human skulls are brought in procession to church and worshiped.

DECEMBER
Christmas: colorful decorations, trees, lights and even classic 1950s carols in plazas everywhere. Just don't expect snow.

115

TIKAL

Guatemala
City

Few people can see images of Tikal's majestic temples rising up out of verdant jungle without feeling their heart beat faster, and unlike so many tourist spots, Tikal is just as magical as the photos...if not more so. Catch the first rays of morning sun as howler monkeys clamor in the treetops, or meander mazelike passages of a lost and once-forgotten world. Yes, other tourists – even busloads of them – will join you, but the ruin is so vast that it's easy to duck away and find a part that feels like you might just be the only person to be here for centuries. Mossy steps beckon, ancient glyphs tell stories of conquests and kings, and astronomical structures still point to the stars as they did so many centuries ago. Though it's a challenge to get here, nobody leaves thinking it wasn't worth the time.

TOP TIP

Be sure to buy your tickets (even for sunrise and sunset tours, as well as for Uaxactun, if you're going) before you enter the park. No tickets are sold inside, meaning a sunrise tour ticket must be chosen – and paid for – in advance.

Gran Plaza with the North Acropolis and Templo I

WITR/SHUTTERSTOCK ©

Sunrise in Tikal

STAR WARS FANS...

...anything look familiar? Are you having a strange sense of déjà vu? If so, it could be because this view you're looking out at was used in the filming of the first Star Wars movie, *A New Hope*. It's towards the end, where the rebel base is getting ready for the final attack. A helmeted rebel stands looking out at the jungle as the *Millennium Falcon* comes in for a landing and as it approaches the base, the shot (from behind the rebel) reveals the unmistakable vista of Templo III and Templo II that you'll see at sunrise. In fact, it was filmed from the very same spot.

Sunrise in Tikal

MYSTICAL, MAGICAL JUNGLE EXPERIENCE

Even jaded ruin-hunters who have done and seen it all agree that few experiences top that of sitting on Tikal's Templo IV, shrouded in mist, listening to the demonic roars of howler monkeys as they wake up to a new day's sunlight piercing through the tattered clouds. Ahead of you lie not one, not two, but four other temples just peeking out of the jungle. There's a palpable hush among the other visitors, a shared understanding that whatever your background, story or politics, what you're seeing is a spiritual, precious thing. It's spine-tingling to think that perhaps – centuries ago – the Maya who built these incredible structures also welcomed the day much as we do now (without the human sacrifice, of course).

Part of the wonder of experiencing this is that it's not easy to see: clouds cover the sunrise up to 80% of the time. It's also common that tourists arrive not realizing that the sunrise tour tickets they'd expected to buy for the next day are not sold inside the park. And to buy them, they have to get to the gate office, which opens at 8am. So people wanting to experience the sunrise tour need to plan ahead and have all their ducks – or jaguars, as the case may be – in a row.

Spider monkey

 TIKAL HOTELS INSIDE THE PARK

The Jungle Lodge
A classy option closest to the ruin gate, and where the archaeologists first uncovering Tikal's ruins stayed. **$$**

The Jaguar Inn
The most fancy of the three Tikal options, but don't expect air-conditioning. **$$$**

The Tikal Inn
Rooms and bungalows; some surround a large pool and others face the jungle. **$$**

TIKAL

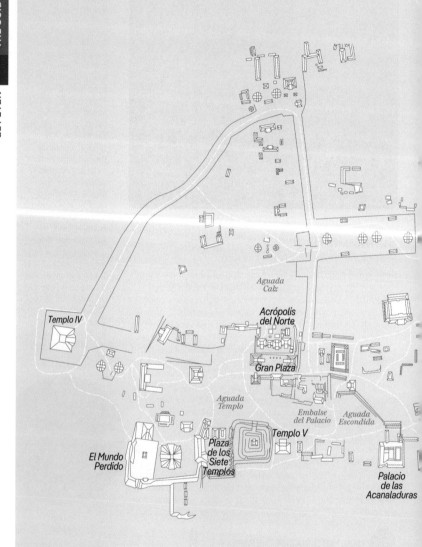

Uaxactún
(24km)

Templo IV

Aguada
Calz

Acrópolis
del Norte

Gran Plaza

Aguada
Templo

Embalse
del Palacio

Aguada
Escondida

Templo V

El Mundo
Perdido

Plaza
de los
Siete
Templos

Palacio
de las
Acanaladuras

N
0 — 200 m
0 — 0.1 miles

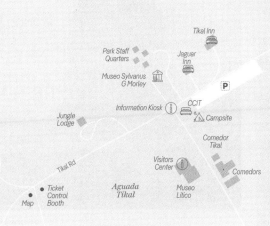

Carretera a Uaxactún

Tikal Inn

Park Staff
Quarters

Jaguar
Inn

Museo Sylvanus
G Morley

P

Information Kiosk (i)   CCIT

Jungle
Lodge

Campsite

Comedor
Tikal

Tikal Rd

Visitors
Center (i)

Comedors

Ticket
Control
Booth

Aguada
Tikal

Museo
Lítico

Map

Templo VI

Yaxhá
(67km)

SUNSET, SUNRISE; WHICH IS RIGHT FOR YOU?

Sunrise Tour
Get up at 3:30am and be at the ruin well before sunrise, seeing nothing until the sun begins to rise. You must have a guide.

Main Entry
Gates open at 6am and close at 5:10pm (officially it's 6pm, but they want you out sooner). For many, this is all the time you'll need.

Sunset
No guide needed, but you must leave by 8pm. Great for anyone who wants dramatic light without the agony of an early morning wake-up call.

Sunrise in Tikal

Sunset in Tikal

CATCH THE PARK'S LAST RAYS

Ocelot

Staying until sunset in Tikal is another popular option and offers ticket holders the chance to remain past six o'clock, taking sunset photos until well after golden hour and allowing you to leave in dusk's dark shadows. It's a nice time to be at the park because there are far fewer people, though there's a bit of confusion about the purpose: by 6pm, the park's normal closing time, sun has often set much of the year.

A sunset tour allows you to have a far better chance of seeing wildlife, animals and birds that show themselves after most of the park visitors have left. It's also a great way for photographers to not have to be looking at the clock while they film. Possible finds include agoutis, *pizotes* (also known as coatis, a ring-tailed critter that's often seen begging for

 BIRDS TO LOOK FOR IN TIKAL

Trogons
These colorful dove-sized birds are popular with birders.

Great Tinamou
This chicken-like bird is shy and rarely seen, and was once nearly hunted to extinction.

Aracari Toucans
Delightfully colorful, aracaris have a dark bill with a serrated edge.

food in the Tikal parking lot), foxes and, though chances are slim of seeing one, wild cats like the margay or ocelot could make a brief appearance. A number of species of parrots make Tikal their home. You may also see trogons, which come in the evening to feed on nuts and berries. And if you've spent all day in Tikal and *haven't* seen a monkey or two, you're not looking hard enough. If you do see – or are lucky enough to approach – wildlife, please be respectful and keep a safe distance at all times.

Uaxactún

A MYSTERIOUS, RARELY VISITED RUIN

Visiting **Uaxactún** isn't easy, and you have to get special permission at Tikal prior to embarking, but for those who like checking off ruins on their list, Uaxactún is a delight. To get here, you'll take a bumpy dirt road that leads past Tikal for nearly an hour, finally reaching a town by the same name. There, you'll either wander or ask and find a number of different groups to visit. A and B are roughly northwest of the small airfield; E, the astronomical observatory, is on the other side. The ruins are secluded and beautiful, with rich moss covering the quiet, solemn structures. Most are fine to clamber around on, too. A number of thatched shelters cover artefacts and stelae, some of which are in good condition (though some are replicas). To fully explore the entire site requires several hours, so be sure to allow for enough time – the round-trip drive takes two hours.

One might assume that the city, with such close proximity to Tikal, was an ally, but it was defeated by the latter in 378 CE by the Tikal ruler, Siyaj K'ak'. It continued – perhaps under the watchful eye of its neighbor – to erect monuments and perform rituals, and shared a similar period of 'silence' when Tikal was defeated in the mid-500s to early 700s CE. Despite a brief resurgence after that, as with so many Maya cities, Uaxactún was abandoned by 900 CE.

WHY I LOVE TIKAL

Ray Bartlett, writer

I lug a DSLR and 400mm zoom lens with me, hoping for great photos of the toucans, woodpeckers, trogons, howler monkeys or elusive foxes that live here. But I'll also stop and marvel at the side of a lone tree, its myriad vines that wrap around, connecting the ground to the sky. I think about the orchids and bromeliads hosted by just this *one* tree, the insects, the birds. I love that here in Tikal one has that sense of this still being the jungle, and I never forget that underneath those forested sections lie many other fascinating secrets to be found.

GETTING AROUND

Arranged tours to and from Tikal can be found all over the country, but if you want to see the sunrise, you'll need to arrive the night before and stay overnight inside the park. Otherwise, it may be just as good to stay in Flores and use a group tour to visit the park. You'll also need comfortable walking shoes, as many of the structures are far from each other. There's no shuttle or transport inside the park, so plan on lots of walking.

Tikal

SURVEYING THE CLASSIC MAYA KINGDOM

Constructed in successive waves over a period of at least 800 years, Tikal is a vast, complicated site with hundreds of temples, pyramids and stelae. There's no way you'll get to it all in a day, but by following this itinerary, you'll see many of the highlights. Before setting out, be sure to stop by the visitors center and examine the scale model of the site. The small ❶ **Museo Sylvanus G Morley** houses a wealth of artefacts, including some superb ceramic pieces. The elaborately carved Stela 31 and the simulated tomb of King Moon Double Comb are two of the museum's most highly prized items. Present your ticket at the nearby ticket booth and when you reach the posted map, take a left. It's a 20-minute walk to the solitary ❷ **Templo VI**. From here it's a blissful stroll up the broad Calzada Méndez to the ❸ **Gran Plaza**, Tikal's ceremonial core, where you may examine the ancient precinct of the ❹ **Acrópolis del Norte**. Exit the plaza west, and take the first left, along a winding path, to ❺ **Templo V**. Round the rear to the right, a trail encircles the largely unexcavated Acrópolis del Sur to ❻ **Plaza de los Siete Templos**. Immediately west stands the great pyramid of the ❼ **El Mundo Perdido**. From here it's a quick stroll and a rather strenuous climb to the summit of ❽ **Templo IV**, Tikal's tallest structure.

TOP TIPS

- Bring food and water.
- All tickets, including sunrise/sunset, must be purchased in advance or at the entry gate. No tickets are sold inside the park.
- If you enter after 3pm, your ticket is good for the next day.
- Stay at one of the on-site hotels to catch the sunset/sunrise.
- To watch the sunset/sunrise from Templo IV, you'll need to purchase an additional ticket (Q100).
- Bring mosquito repellent.

ZAI ARAGON/SHUTTERSTOCK ©

Templo IV
Arrive in the late afternoon to get magically tinted photos of Templos I, II and III poking through the jungle canopy. Sunrise tours offer mystical mists that lift as the sun finally appears.

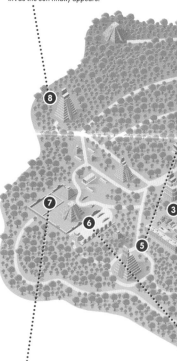

El Mundo Perdido
This 'Lost World' features two impressive pyramids and some smaller structures, and the talud-tablero design hints at influences from distant Teotihuacán.

RALF BROSKVAR/GETTY IMAGES ©

KOBBY DAGAN/SHUTTERSTOCK ©

MICHAEL ZYSMAN/SHUTTERSTOCK ©

MATYAS REHAK/SHUTTERSTOCK ©

FRANCISCO SANDOVAL GUATE/

Templo V

As steep as it is massive, Tikal's second-tallest temple (52m) has unusual rounded corners. Tempting as it may seem to climb, the broad front staircase is off-limits.

Gran Plaza

Though the surreally tall Templo I, a mausoleum to the late Classic ruler Ah Cacao, is off-limits to climbers, you're welcome to ascend the almost-as-tall Templo II across the plaza.

Acrópolis del Norte

Amid the stack of smaller and much older temples that rise up the hillside north of the plaza, take a peek beneath the two thatched shelters on a ledge to find a pair of fearsome masks.

④

Ticket Booth ①

Posted Map

Visitor Center

CCIT

Museo Sylvanus G Morley

Volumes have been written about the remarkably preserved Stela 31, a portrait of the ruler Stormy Sky crowning himself, flanked by spear-toting warriors in the attire of (ally or overlord?) Teotihuacán.

Templo VI

The secluded temple has a lengthy set of glyphs inscribed on the back of its lofty roofcomb, recording the lineage of successive kingdoms. Be patient: the contents of the weathered slab may take some effort to discern.

②

Plaza de los Siete Templos

Seven miniature temples line up along the east side of this grassy courtyard. Climb the larger 'palace' at the south end to get a sightline along the septet.

PATRICIA HAMILTON/GETTY IMAGES ©

PRACTICALITIES

Scan this QR code for prices and opening hours.

TOP SIGHT

Tikal

Guatemala's most impressive ruin is iconic, a place where archaeology continues to reveal fascinating discoveries even today. The massive temples honored rulers who governed a feared, powerful capital for centuries. Like so many cities, it was eventually burned and abandoned, covered by the jungle until relatively recently. Excavations began in 1956, uncovering hundreds of structures, ballcourts, temples and residences.

DON'T MISS

Templo IV

Gran Plaza

Acrópolis del Norte

El Mundo Perdido

Templo V

Palacio de las Acanaladuras

Templo VI

Plaza de los Siete Templos

Planning & Arrival

Visiting Tikal can be overwhelming even if you're on a tour, so plan to give yourself plenty of time and, if possible, see your personal top spots first while you're not too hot or too tired. Be sure to have pre-purchased your tickets prior to entering the park, as you cannot buy them at the gate. Though maps make it look compact, the site is huge and many of the top spots are ten, twenty or even thirty minutes' walk from each other. Sunrise ticket holders have the luxury of early morning coolness; once the sun comes up, the park can be very hot. Take your time, bring plenty of water and rest if you need to. Many visitors arrive planning to see Tikal in a quick two hours and realize they need to budget an entire day.

Templo IV

One of the ruin's most impressive temples and – thrillingly – one of the few you can ascend, Temple IV looks out across the rest of the site with a commanding view that is both pic-

WIRESTOCK CREATORS/SHUTTERSTOCK ©

Templo IV

ture-worthy and breathtaking. Whether you're here for the sunrise tour or later in the day, it's a thrill to climb up above the treetops and stare across at the temples poking out of the jungle the way mountains poke out above the clouds. Star Wars fans will enjoy seeing a spot used in *A New Hope*, and if you're lucky, you'll hear or see monkeys cavorting in the treetops.

Gran Plaza

If there's one place you need to be sure to visit, it's the Gran Plaza,where the incredible Templo I and Templo II stand facing each other. If you've got a brochure image of Tikal in your head, chances are it was taken here. You cannot climb Templo I, but across the plaza, wooden walkways lead you up Templo II, where you can take fantastic photos, that must-have selfie, strike a yoga pose (while those around you roll their eyes), and so on. In the center, near where the ceremonial offerings are burned, you can clap your hands and hear a quetzal-like sound in the echo. It's not too far off to imagine that just like today, much of the action and focus of the ancient Maya revolved around this sacred plaza.

Built by the son of Tikal's ruler Jasaw Chan K'awiil I to honor his memory, Templo I,also known as Temple of the Great Jaguar, rises 41m vertically; a stately,commanding presence that spoke to the ruler's greatness even after death. It is not possible to climb this one, but the nearly-as-impressive Templo II faces it, and has stairs to a viewing area that overlooks the entire plaza.

Templo II, 38m high, looks across at Temple I and was built by Jasaw Chan K'awiil to honor his wife, and the construction was completed after both of their deaths by their son.

Birders, take note: The *ramón* trees attract both aracari toucans and slaty-tailed trogons. Keep your zoom lenses at the ready!

DECIPHERING MAYA SCRIPT

The glyphs left behind by the Maya astonished western explorers Stephens & Catherwood (p39). They suspected it was a form of writing. But it wasn't until a sharp-eyed scholar Tatiana Proskouriakoff connected glyphs to dates,such as births and deaths of rulers, that scholars could begin deciphering them fully. From there it gradually became possible to not only understand, but to read these texts. Tragically, though the Maya had highly developed writing and thousands of books, only four escaped the destruction of the Spanish. Of those, the Dresden Codex is the most famous.

TOP SIGHT
Tikal

A BRIEF TIKAL TIMELINE

100 CE Tikal's rich culture flourishes and Maya dominate the area.

200 CE Teotihuacán's regional influence shows in Tikal's El Mundo Perdido.

562 CE Tikal is defeated by nearby Caracol, beginning the 'Tikal Hiatus'.

700 CE Tikal is in rivalry with Calakmul to the north.

950 CE Tikal is abandoned.

Acrópolis del Norte (North Acropolis)

The plaza isn't the only spot where you can make cool discoveries: peek under the *palapa* (palm thatch) shelters and you'll find gruesome masks. The maze like structures are interesting to explore. This area was used as a necropolis for centuries, with over fifteen structures and many substructures, as it was not built once and left as is, but built, rebuilt, buried, rebuilt, and so on. Looting at the site may have begun as early as the 10th century, 500 years before Spanish contact, as evidence shows some tombs were robbed of precious stones such as jade.

El Mundo Perdido (the Lost World)

El Mundo Perdido is one of the most fascinating areas of Tikal, as it was used as an astronomical observatory and still functions today. Perhaps more interestingly, it shows many links to Teotihuacán, the famous ruin outside of Mexico City: its stepped *talud-tablero*-style structures clearly show the influence of the latter. *Talud-tablero* is a style of architecture that begins with an inward slope, then has a front-facing 'table,' which is followed by another inward-facing slope. Like the Acrópolis del Norte, it's believed that for a time, El Mun-

Gran Plaza

MATYAS REHAK/SHUTTERSTOCK ©

Temple I

do Perdido also served as a funerary and possible necropolis, in addition to its astronomical value. Surprisingly, even when parts of the grand city were going into decline in the Terminal Classic period, El Mundo Perdido continued to be used. Some believe that was due to it being close to one of Tikal's great reservoirs.

Templo V

Also known as Temple of the Inscriptions, this temple is tucked at the end of a long path that's a great place to spot wildlife and birds. Along the way, look for Palacio de las Acanaladuras, if you're interested. The front side of this temple looks similar to others, but if you go behind it, you'll be able to see the namesake: a large panel of carvings and glyphs detailing the history of the dynasty.

Plaza de los Siete Templos

Near El Mundo Perdido, this group is known for its seven temples that surround and enclose a central plaza. Among other highlights is a covered stucco relief that depicts a skull and bones.

Beyond Tikal

A wealth of fantastic journeys begin where Tikal ends. Any ruin lover will find plenty to explore here.

The vast region around Tikal makes any Maya aficionado swoon, as there are dozens of well-known sites and dozens more that have yet to be excavated. Some – but for their remoteness – supersede even Tikal in grandeur, but even in the Maya world, it's still the same adage: location, location, location. And if getting to a ruin requires a five-day hike on foot through the jungle or a helicopter ride, it's not going to get the bus tour visits. At some of these ruins you may be the only people there, looking from the top of a structure at an unbroken jungle that stretches to the horizon.

TOP TIP

Do your deep jungle exploring in the dry season, as roads become impossible to pass otherwise, except by horseback or on foot.

El Mirador

Carmelita

Tikal • *Nakum*

Topoxte •• *Naranjo*
Yaxhá

Jungle canopy, Yaxhá

VLADISLAV T JIROUSEK/SHUTTERSTOCK ©

Yaxhá

Yaxhá

PERFECT SUNSET SPOT AND MORE

This delightful ruin sits off to the southeast of Tikal, due east of El Remate, on the eastern bank of the Laguna Yaxhá, giving it a near perfect location for sunset viewing, which is the primary reason it's often included in Tikal tours. Many people visit Tikal during the day and – timed right – catch an incredible sunset in **Yaxhá**, looking west from the top of the ruin's Templo 216. High enough to be above the jungle canopy, the pyramid lets viewers look out at eye level with parrots and monkeys as they wait for the dusk to deepen and the sky to turn from blue to gold. Like sunrise in Tikal, sunset at Yaxhá is a time for quiet, tranquil contemplation, and staff will remind the loud and boisterous there on the viewing platform to zip it once the sun dips low. A hush of expectation falls on the crowd, the selfies stop, thoughts turn inward, and the sun seems to muster a final defiant glow before sinking into, as the Maya viewed it, the realm of the jaguar.

But as special as the sunset is here, the site has much more for people to discover. The excavated part of the ruin is shaped roughly in a large letter 'L,' and the parking lot is close to the sunset-viewing pyramid. Because of this, many visitors overlook its numerous unique features and just go

HOLTUN

So close to Yaxhá that the two cities surely faced each other is the relatively unknown ruin of Holtun, a great site to visit if you're looking for something unexcavated and have some time on your hands. Its giant twin pyramids today look like natural hills, but if the leaf litter and soil were to be removed, they would be impressive equals to any other ruins nearby. Sadly, many of the structures here have already been looted: the deep tunnels into the mounds look like scars. There's little chance you'll be sharing this spot with anyone other than your guide, so it's a refreshing change from the more popular ruins.

Ruin detail, Yaxhá

 BEST THINGS TO SEE IN YAXHÁ

Grupo Malher
Temples and structures at the far end; this area is also known as the Plaza de las Sombras (the square of shadows).

Causeways
These wide, raised roads connect plazas and other parts of the site.

Ballcourt
Yaxhá has a very nicely restored ballcourt.

Boat trip, Topoxte

A TALE OF THREE TROGONS

Birders will find it hard to remain calm when so many amazing birds are so easily seen. Among them are several species of trogon, so get that Life List ready:

Slaty-Tailed Trogon
The males are bright green and red, females are a matte gray with a red belly.

Black-Headed Trogon
A black-and-yellow trogon, easily confused with the gartered trogon.

Gartered Trogon
Check the underside of the tail to distinguish between this and the similar black-headed trogon.

directly from the parking lot to the pyramid, missing the beautiful wide causeways linking parts of the ruin, perfectly graded and rising several meters above the jungle floor. These made it easy for inhabitants to access areas such as the lake shore or other palaces and residences. Interestingly, as with its neighbor Tikal, Yaxhá too has architectural and historical connections to Teotihuacán, both in its *talud-tablero*-style structures and stelae that depict the Mesoamerican north's Venus-Tlaloc warriors, who were not Maya. As with Tikal, Yaxhá was overlooked by explorers Stephens and Catherwood, and thus not brought to the attention of archaeologists until 1904, when it was described by Teoberto Maler. Mapping was done in the 1930s and again in the 1970s, but excavations are ongoing and some of the key structures, like the Acrópolis Sur (South Acropolis), were restored as recently as 2007.

The ruin's shaded causeways are a great place to look for wildlife and birds, especially if you allow for some time before the sunset. Parrots land in the treetops, both howler and spider monkeys dance around in the branches, and if you're lucky, you may startle a lizard or snake as you explore. A word to the wise though: try not to stand directly underneath a band of monkeys. When they gotta go, they gotta go.

Topoxte

BOAT TRIP TO SEE UNRESTORED RUINS

A delightful day trip for anyone who enjoys a bit of time on the water, the infrequently visited ruin of **Topoxte** is reached by boat from the shores of Laguna Yaxhá. From there, the

 NOT TO MISS IN NARANJO

The Palace of Lady Six Sky
The expansive palace of Naranjo's iconic female ruler.

Tlaloc Masks
Structures bearing the distinctive Tlaloc motif show the influence of Teotihuacán.

Chultuns
Cavities in the earth used for food storage. Watch your step!

boat takes you to a small series of islands, passing the iconic Templo 216 of Yaxhá on the way. The structures of Topoxte are mostly unrestored, but a series of wooden stairs and walkways make touring a bit easier, and there's a chance to see crocodiles, egrets and monkeys as you meander about the site. The largest structures are impressive, reaching several stories high and with intricate decorations. Other structures are still completely unexcavated.

Naranjo

A KINGDOM SWALLOWED BY JUNGLE

There are ruins that take some getting to and then there's **Naranjo**, which – when the road is passable at all – requires a high-clearance 4x4 and a good two to three hours each way...to go just 17km. Yes, the road is that bad. But reaching the ruin, even if you have to abandon your vehicle and hike the rest of the way, is usually possible except in the wettest parts of the year. It's like that advertising meme: priceless.

The reward is experiencing a ruin that at its height may have been grander and even more important than Tikal; one that was governed for many years by the fabled, and feared, Lady Six Sky. She was the daughter of a Dos Pilas ruler who – allied with the Snake Kingdom of Calakmul to the north – attacked and defeated Tikal, the city's main rival in 695 CE. (That attack did not go unavenged, however, as Tikal attacked and defeated Naranjo in the mid-700s CE.) The tit for tat would not last much longer, however: just over 50 years later, Naranjo would fall for good, abandoned like the rest of the Maya world shortly after 810 CE, and Tikal shortly thereafter.

The city lay buried in the jungle until the 1920s, when it was 'discovered' and then promptly decimated by repeated looting, though there is heated debate whether this pejorative word should be used when others feel it was merely locals – rather than PhD-holding archaeologists – who benefited from the site and its treasures. Regardless of which side of this debate you agree with, Naranjo's pottery and sculptures were mostly gone by the mid-1950s, and a survey done by archaeologists found over 250 looter tunnels inside the various structures. It's hard to comprehend how quickly the history and artefacts of Naranjo vanished into the hands of private collections, their information lost forever.

The structures, which include an observatory, pyramids and a stunning palace that was the residence of Lady Six Sky, all remain in varying stages of restoration. They rise up dramatically out of the jungle, and some show the Tlaloc warrior motif (look for the walls that have 'googley eyes' on them).

THE JUNGLE'S BIG CATS

Jaguar
Look for tracks but don't expect to see one unless you're lottery-winner lucky.

Jaguarundi
An unusual dark-colored cat much smaller than its namesake.

Ocelot
A reclusive, strikingly patterned cat about the size of a fox.

Helicopter tour (p135)

NOT TO MISS IN NARANJO

Astronomical Observatory (E-group)
TUsed to calculate calendar dates and observe rituals.

Maler's Cave
Maler lived in a small cave on-site while excavating.

Structure B-18
Inside is a hieroglyphic stairway, though the entry is closed to prevent looting.

**BEST
DAY-TRIP RUINS**

If you want to combine
ease-of-access with
worth-the-trip and
rate for value, here are
some top spots that
you'll still need a 4x4
to reach:

San Clemente
A beautiful ruin with
multiple stories set
deep in lush jungle,
plus vampire bats and
whip scorpions.

La Blanca
A long drive over a
series of hills will put
your 4x4 to the test,
but it's worth it in the
end.

Holtun
An impressive ruin
that lies mostly
unexcavated, with
views of nearby Yaxhá
from its still-covered
pyramids.

This indicates Teotihuacán links, though its rivalry with Tikal implies otherwise, so it's one of the many enigmas that artefacts left in place might have solved. Of the items that remained at the site were several important stelae depicting the city's historical events, pottery, and a hieroglyphic stairway not unlike the one in Copán, Honduras.

Visiting Naranjo is not for the casual tourist and requires careful planning, preparation and a bit of good luck. But it's a delightful, near-forgotten spot that deserves its place in the fascinating legacy the Maya left to the world.

Nakum

LIKE NARANJO ON STEROIDS

If you've been to Naranjo and liked it, well, you may just be ready to add **Nakum** to your list. It's everything Naranjo is... turned up to 11. Instead of two to three hours of off-roading, a visit to Nakum requires most of a day, possibly more, and for much of the year the road there is simply impassable. Some have had to camp en route going and coming back. The cause? The Holmul river basin floods for much of the year, turning roads that are (at their best!) just passable and muddy into a deep, impossible, impassable swamp. If you're game to give this a try, the best time to go is the dry season, between February and the end of March.

You will be the only one at the site, which sports one of the best-preserved roof combs in the Maya world, second only to its neighbor, Tikal. It is remarkable for a number of things; among them, it shows evidence of being inhabited from approximately 1500 to 1000 BCE, the Middle Preclassic period. It remained inhabited all the way to the end, the Terminal Classic, about 900 CE, when the city fell, as did nearly all the Maya cities, to factors that still remain shrouded in mystery. Disease, famine, drought and the Maya calendar are all thought to have played a part in the abandonment. At its zenith, the city benefited from its prime location next to the Holmul river, and thrived between 600 CE and 800 CE.

El Mirador

THE TALLEST PYRAMID IN GUATEMALA

Getting to **El Mirador** is arguably the hardest (or easiest) of all the jungle ruins. You can either hike here – a trek that takes five or six days – or you can travel by helicopter. The latter is as easy as it is beautiful, but it's not cheap, and your time at the ruin is limited. Hikers will enjoy not only the chance to see El Mirador and camp, but also several other exciting ru-

 RUINS ALONG THE TREK TO EL MIRADOR

El Tintal	La Florida	Nakbe
Named for its tinted water and known for its irrigation canals.	A small ruin with several distinct restored structures.	A large ruin with several above-the-canopy views, once important for its limestone.

RAJH.PHOTOGRAPHY/SHUTTERSTOCK ©

Black-headed trogon (p130)

ins as well. Regardless of which method you take to reach it, El Mirador is a crown jewel: mention you've been and people know you're more than just a casual tourist.

Once only known to *chicle* harvesters journeying into the jungle to collect rubber sap, El Mirador ('The Lookout') was eventually put on the archaeology map in 1962, making it a relatively recent 'discovery' and one where new finds are still happening. Among the curious facts, much of the site was not built at the same time as Tikal and Uaxactún, but much earlier, despite the proximity to its neighbors. Despite a general lack of good soil for growing crops, the El Mirador farmers devised an advanced system of agriculture that depended on bringing mud from nearby swampy lowlands and using the fertile soil for their terraced fields. They could even control the pH to maximize crop growth. For a culture that existed mostly before the Common Era, this showed incredible agrarian skill and may have allowed the site to sustain a population far larger than what might have otherwise been possible given the resources.

Climbing La Danta is the main purpose of a visit to El Mirador, though there are other exciting things to see here. La Danta (the Tapir) is the highest pyramid in all of Guatemala,

GETTING TO NARANJO & NAKUM

Naranjo and its 'neighbor' Nakum are decidedly off the beaten track, requiring not only time and a high-clearance 4x4 to reach, but also a bit of luck as well. The latter is only reachable in the driest of the dry season, as a nearby river floods its banks much of the year, turning the road into a swampy, muddy mess. Naranjo is more doable but can also require a hefty bit of off-roading know-how, and you can expect axle- or floorpan-deep mud at times. As is often the case, there's no cell service in these areas, so if you get stuck, getting unstuck is up to you and the fates to figure out.

GUIDES TO THE TIKAL-AREA RUINS

Marlon Diaz
Offers excellent English or Spanish-language tours, birding, and history. Visit gemtrips.com.

Victor Lopez
Knowledgeable guide to Naranjo and Nakum as well as others. WhatsApp: +502-4696-9949.

Mauricio Herrarte
Expert birder and guide fluent in Spanish and basic English. WhatsApp: +502-3278-5023.

Moss on ruins, Tikal (p116)

XIBALBA

Xibalba was the Maya underworld, a dark afterlife that was entered through the Yucatán's many cenotes, as well as important grottoes and caves. According to the *Popol Vuh*, a Maya scripture, two 'hero twins,' Hunahpú and Xbalanqué, descended into Xibalba and restored order in the world by defeating the underworld gods through a series of cunning tricks and ruses. Many of the water scenes depicted in stucco friezes, such as the ones in El Mirador, show these twins in various scenes of their battles. The belief in Xibalba being entered via cenotes is why so many offerings have been found in their depths, including in the cenote at Chichén Itzá.

ascending to a height of 72m, so tall that when you reach the top you'll be looking down at the jungle canopy. It's second only to Toniná, in Chiapas, Mexico. The structure is made of several base platforms that you must climb before the final pyramid appears, so plan on breaking a sweat if you want to reach the top. It's worth it, though, to make it to the 'Everest' of the Maya world and see nothing but jungle in all directions.

Other notable structures include El Tigre (the Tiger), a slightly smaller pyramid that has three peaks atop a flat base, and a beautiful stucco frieze that adorns a cistern. The perfectly preserved stucco depicts scenes from Xibalba, the Maya underworld; in particular it shows how the 'hero twins' succeeded in returning victorious from Xibalba. Incredible *sacbe* (white path) roads connected El Mirador to a number of other nearby sites, with walkways that were anywhere from two to six meters higher than the jungle floor.

 EL MIRADOR AREA TOUR OPERATORS

Cooperativa Carmelita
With an office in Flores, this Carmelita coop has five- and six-day tours.

Rony Rodriguez
Rony makes a few El Mirador treks each season. @rony_rodriguez.g

Antonio Centeno
A long-time guide based in Carmelita. expedicion.mirador@gmail.com

Ruin Trekking

GET OFF THE GRID COMPLETELY

Most of the ruins mentioned in this book can be visited (if you time it right) with the trusty help of a 4x4, or even a helicopter in the case of El Mirador. But for those who want to experience the jungle the way the Maya did, there's only one way: a multiday trekking tour.

You'll start where the road ends, in tiny **Carmelita**, loading your gear onto your back or a helpful mule and heading north, following trails through the jungle that have existed for centuries, perhaps even since the Maya themselves. Hiking through the jungle is alternately magical and horrible. One moment you're mesmerized by the emerald flash of a hummingbird, the next you're swatting mosquitoes that seem about as big. It's not for the faint of heart, nor for people unused to jungles, mud, and insects.

But the reward is seeing jungle in its pristine state, and visiting ruins known only to archaeologists and those who've done the trek before. The chance to bond with fellow hikers, the chance to see – if you're incredibly lucky – one of the rare big cats that silently glide past. Though tours vary, a popular perk is spending a full day in El Mirador, where you can view sunrise from one pyramid and sunset from the other, before camping there overnight. There are stops at different ruins on the return. It's not for everyone, but those who've done it find it sobering, fascinating, beautiful, and wellworth it. Fun? Maybe not. But if you have the chance, you won't be disappointed.

Helicopter Tours

SKY-HIGH FUN

For those who don't envision a multiday hike to see El Mirador, there's another option: a helicopter. These tours leave out of Flores airport, though you can even book them from Guatemala City. You'll need to have purchased your park ticket in advance. Once airborne, you'll have a fantastic bird's-eye view of Lago de Petén Itzá, then see farms gradually vanish into virgin jungle, out of which the peak of La Danta finally appears. It's thrilling to swoop low over the treetops and land, even more to explore the ruin and get a sense of how majestic this spot is. On the return, the pilot may circle the site so you can get good photos.

EXPLORING RISKS & SAFETY

Ascending many structures at the popular ruins is either prohibited entirely, or done via easy-to-use walkways and stairs. But when you're on your own at ruins that haven't been visited for months, it's easy to think of them as a playground and forget how dangerous climbing these structures can be. One fall can bring your vacation to a sudden halt. Go up and down in a zigzag pattern, which directs a fall horizontally, rather than up or down. Have plenty of water, and stop and rest if you're winded or getting a cramp. Rain on stones or moss can make surfaces remarkably slippery, and insects or plants such as chichicaste can leave stings and rashes.

GETTING AROUND

To reach most of these ruins, a good 4x4 with high clearance is recommended, and in some cases required. Even then, access depends on road conditions, and that changes dramatically based on the weather and other factors. Your best plan will be to coordinate carefully with your local guide to ensure that you're arriving with the best chance of getting where you want to go. In some cases, horses, a helicopter, ATVs (all-terrain vehicles), motorcycles or hiking may be the only option.

FLORES & SANTA ELENA

Flores &
Santa Elena

Guatemala
City

Tiny island Flores and its nearby 'sister' city, Santa Elena, are a delightful gem in the Petén region, with excellent restaurants, a lively night scene, great bars and a host of activities. Yes, you'll almost certainly visit Tikal, but the town is a great base for all sorts of day excursions to other parts of the region. Evenings can be spent calmly with a glass of wine, watching the sunset, or in a bar filled with boisterous dancers. The entire island takes less than 10 minutes to circle by car and less than 30 by foot, unless you're distracted by the shops, cafés or restaurants that beckon. Access to a hospital and airport is a plus, but most people won't need the former and will be sad when they have to use the latter, since it's likely you won't want to leave.

TOP TIP

In Flores, choose a hotel that's on either the east side (sunrise) or the west side (sunset), as the views will be spectacular. And if Flores is full, look for vastly cheaper, non-touristy hotels in Santa Elena.

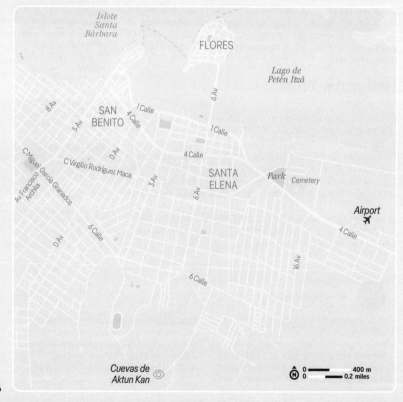

Flores

LAKE LEVELS

Geology has cursed Lago de Petén Itzá in some ways, for it is essentially a vast flat plain that eventually flooded when runoff from surrounding land had no exit. At its deepest spot, a cenote goes several hundred feet, but most of the lake is quite shallow. Water levels rise and fall at the mercy of evaporation and rainfall. In the rainy season, streets that might be otherwise walkable can be several feet under water. In the dry season, it seems unthinkable that a shoreline so dry could flood to that extent. The traffic patterns may change at times to account for flooded streets, but it's all part of what makes this island so unique. Go (pun intended) with the flow.

Sunrise & Sunset

BEAUTIFUL EAST OR BEAUTIFUL WEST

There are those who like waking up before the sun rises and those who are thrilled to see the dusk deepen at the end of the day. Whether you're one, the other, or somewhere in between, Flores is perfectly positioned for serene sun appreciation. In fact, most of the west-facing restaurants bank on that, as their tables fill with diners and patrons who want to sip or dine while watching the performance outside. It's almost a ritual for some visitors, and certainly it's the rare tourist who doesn't appreciate just how calming, peaceful and beautiful it is. In light of this, it's not impossible to envision this may have been what the Maya felt too, a sense of reverence and solemn gratitude for the day. The truly intrepid will opt to hail a water taxi and get a different perspective. For those on land, it's easy to let the sunset turn into stargazing as one glass of wine turns into two, then three, as you chat with friends.

On a small island such as Flores, it's hard to find a restaurant that doesn't have some kind of water view, but those on the west side are particularly nice. The changing water levels make it a challenge sometimes to reach certain spots, but most put out temporary walkways to guide you to their establishment despite the flooding.

 GREAT LAKE VIEWS

Sky Bar
No doubt, Flores' Sky Bar has dibs: a lovely open-air terrace lets you take in everything above you. $$

San Telmo
This cute, west-facing Flores restaurant is right on the water. $$

Casa Blanca
It's hard to beat the lovely scene from this Flores lakeside restaurant. $$

BEST BITES

Flores is a gourmand's playground and there are dozens of delicious spots to satiate your hunger and slake your thirst. Here are a few top spots to keep in view:

Maracuya
This delightful multistory restaurant has traditional Guatemalan food and tasty cocktails overlooking the lake's east side.

Il Terazzo
Italian fare with a view that won't disappoint, looking west and (thus) perfect for sunset watching.

Maple y Tocino
A tasty breakfast and lunch spot with freshly made donuts, avocado toasts, and yes, bacon.

Lago de Petén Itzá

Flores Nightlife

LOTS GOING ON AFTER DARK

This island has a bit of a Dr Jekyll, Mr Hyde thing going on between its sleepy, easy, relaxed days and its pumped-up, frenetic nights, and there's no place but Flores for nightlife in all of Petén. Things start shortly after the stars come out, generally with people seeking spots on the west side of the island to drink, chat and mingle. Walk along the main circle (mostly Calle Union and 30), and listen for music you like. Then follow your ears, sometimes up stairways or down narrow alleys, or even across flooded foot bridges, and find the place that's right for you. It could be quiet karaoke in a dive bar, a hopping scene at a second-story terrace, or even drinks and new friends at a youth hostel or hotel bar. Later, after 10pm, expect to hear the nightclubs and see lines, sometimes long

 WHERE TO STAY IN FLORES

Casa Ramona
A bright, spanking-clean spot with a nice cafe on the first floor. $

Casa Azul
Blue is the theme here at this west-facing hotel with a pool. $$

Los Amigos Hostel
It's all happening here at centrally located Los Amigos, with dorms, private rooms and a great restaurant/bar. $

ones, to get in on Fridays and weekends. Put in earplugs if you have them and plan on quite the party.

There's a bar for just about every lifestyle and most are within easy walking distance from each other. Your best bet is to start the night and wander, letting whatever happens happen. Don't expect the party to last all night though: things wrap up and shut down by 1am, and once revelers have stumbled back to their bunks, beds or homes, the island is quiet as a tomb until morning.

Life on the Lake

WATER BY DAY OR NIGHT

It's impossible to spend time in Flores and not end up getting out on the lake, even if you hate boats. The water is mostly calm and glassy, and even a ten-minute zip out and back lifts the spirits: who could resist feeling happy when the sun is tickling the lake's surface, turning the entire vastness into glitter and sparkles like a ballerina's gown. It's delightful. There's little chance of feeling queasy when the lake surface is so placid.

Even those not actively on the water can't help but take the lake into account in their daily life. The edges rise and fall not with the tides but with the seasons, and the island slowly relinquishes curbs, cobbles, and walkways and even whole streets to the frogs and tadpoles, the herons, and the darting fish that claim – if only temporarily – the stones and pavement as their own.

At night, the party boats depart for cruises through the darkness, with neon strobes and music. Crowds of mostly tourists get to see the lake as a backdrop for socializing or more. Crowds gathering in rooftop bars to watch the dark, still water blend as the sun vanishes into the darkness of the sky.

Cuevas de Aktun Kan

SOMETHING DIFFERENT UNDERGROUND

Most of the time you'll be outside or indoors, but if you feel up for something a little different, try heading to Cuevas de Aktun Kan. This large cave is on the opposite side of Santa Elena from Flores, so you'll get to cross the city if you go, but it's a quick trip of only 10 minutes (less if there's no traffic). When you arrive, you can hire a guide to lead you through the series of passages or opt for a short, self-guided tour. You'll need to rent a helmet and flashlight at the entrance; while the pathways are lit, it can get dark and gloomy at times. Watch your head, as the ceiling gets low

BEST PLACES FOR COFFEE

Maple y Tocino
Delightful spot on the west side of Lago de Petén Itzá with seating that overlooks the lakeside. Great coffee and plenty of menu options if you need more than just a cup of joe.

Casa Ramona
Great lattes and other espresso drinks served with a cheery smile at this spot on the lake's southeast side.

Maracuya
A delightful dinner and coffee spot, with airy balconies and vine-entwined terraces. Great for morning sunshine over the lake's east shore.

Whip scorpion (p140)

WHERE TO DRINK IN FLORES

Remolino
A bar and nightclub that can get wonderfully wild on weekends.

Al Fogon
This west-facing bar has fun karaoke and cocktails.

Los Amigos
Yep, this hostel has a happening bar scene, too.

Flores (p138)

WHAT'S A WHIP SCORPION?

A whip scorpion is an arachnid that's related to spiders and (yes) scorpions, but – despite the name and fearsome appearance – they will *not* harm you. They fall pretty solidly into the list of creepy crawly things though, so if you're averse to those, maybe consider if you really want to be exploring Maya ruins or dark cave passages in the first place. If you're interested in cool critters, get closer: you'll notice that it has no stinger, and the pincers, though deadly to its insect prey, can't harm you. They're actually kind of mellow, and move slowly across walls or ceilings, eventually finding a spot to hide if you shine enough light on them.

sometimes and if you're doing the longer route you'll find a few passageways get tight. Suck in that gut a bit and you'll squeeze or squiggle through. Keep in mind that the long tour will dump you out at a different entrance than the one you came through, so you'll either need to hire a taxi or return back through the cave the way you came. Along the way you're sure to see bats, and if you look closely you might find cool arachnids, like whip scorpions.

It's a relatively wet cave, so you'll hear water dripping, and this is what – over millions of years – creates the intricate waxy-looking stalactites and stalagmites, as well as the other cave features. Tiny pieces of sediment carried in the water solidify, drop by drop. You'd be wise to wear clothes that can get dirty. Consider yourself warned.

MORE ABOUT THE MAYA

If you're keen to learn more about the incredible culture of the Maya and the rise and mysterious demise of its civilization around 900 CE, check out our full story on page 244.

GETTING AROUND

Flores and Santa Elena are small, bustling spots where it's easy to flag a taxi or a *tuk-tuk*, which may even be easier than parking and re-parking a vehicle, if you have one.

Beyond Flores & Santa Elena

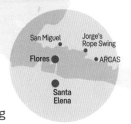

San Miguel
Jorge's Rope Swing
Flores ● ● ARCAS
Santa Elena

Quiet and quirky, with spots to relax, interesting activities, and educational opportunities if the Flores scene starts to tire.

The region around Flores and Santa Elena is in many ways markedly different from the packed, busy towns, with lots of pastureland, forest and jungle. Or water, if you're on the lakeside. For tourists it mostly means day trips to places that give depth and diversion, a yin to the yang, so to speak, of busy Flores or dusty Santa Elena which mostly offers hotels, restaurants and tourist-friendly bars. Zip across the Lago de Petén Itzá to experience Maya ruins that are only just being excavated, learn about endangered wildlife and its awful trade, or laze about on the lakeshore, catching up on your vitamin D. Wherever you choose, you'll surely have a great time.

TOP TIP

Make sure you've got bug repellent handy, as some spots (such as the ruins) can be intense without it.

Jaguar (p131)

HENNER DAMKE/SHUTTERSTOCK ©

Tayasal

MEGA MAYA RUIN NEARBY

Thanks to a renewed interest in Maya and other indigenous cultures, both tourists and researchers are starting to understand the value of ruins far beyond Tikal. The ruin of Tayasal, behind the lakeside village of **San Miguel**, is far vaster than many thought and is currently being excavated. You can take a quick ten-minute boat ride across to the site (be sure to look for giant iguanas at the shoreline!) and then hike up to a beautiful *mirador* (lookout). Flores appears small and quaint and far below you, with the rest of the lake stretching out in all directions. The lookout is atop one of the ruin's tallest structures, but if you walk for another ten minutes, you'll find yourself surrounded by a number of mounds and hills. Like so many other sites, Tayasal had residences, pyramids, observatories and ball courts, and it supported a population of tens of thousands, making it a heavyweight among the lakeside civilizations. One of the many highlights is a broken stel, currently protected by a small awning and wooden frame. The city's location likely meant that – like Ixlú – it controlled lake-to-lagoon trade.

Plans are underway to make this area far more accessible and to excavate and restore many of the structures. Though it will never rival the grandeur of Tikal, it will be a fascinating ruin experience that's right in Flores' backyard. Stay tuned!

THE ITZÁ MAYA'S FALL

The Spanish arrived in Yucatán in the 1500s, forever reshaping the history of the Americas. Slowly, inexorably, Maya city-states fell or were subjugated, and many collapsed due to introduced disease. The final stronghold of the Maya was right here on the island of Flores, known as Nojpetén. Though the Spanish tried numerous times to defeat the city, the Maya repelled them, often lying in wait in the reedy shallows, then flanking the invaders and decapitating them. The strategy worked until almost 1700: in 1697, with the help of a galleon built on the opposite shores, Martín de Ursúa y Arizmendi and his men conquered the city, and the last Maya kingdom fell.

ARCAS

WILDLIFE RESCUE AND REHABILITATION

A visit to ARCAS might be your easiest way to view some of the region's most endangered wildlife, including the big cats: jaguars, pumas, ocelots and jaguarundis. There are also dozens of beautiful macaws, parrots and other trafficked birds. Sadly, the reason these animals are here is that they're unable to be released back into the wild due to a variety of reasons, but the common theme is that they were all involved in the illegal wildlife trade. Demand for wildlife – whether it's live animals and birds, or parts of, or products made from dead ones – unfortunately drives these beautiful animals to be hunted, and in many cases, they are on the brink of extinction. Jaguars, once ranging throughout South and Central America and as far north as New Mexico and Arizona, now exist in only a few protected regions, and threats such as poaching continue. Birds like the resplendent quetzal, Guatemala's national bird, are nearly extinct and ironically more easily seen in Costa Rica than here. ARCAS provides visitors

WHERE TO EAT IN SAN MIGUEL

Raices del Lago
Popular waterside restaurant that offers a free boat shuttle from its Flores location. **$$**

Playa La Punta
'The Point' has simple fish plates, snacks, sandwiches and beers. **$**

Veamar
Pretty lakeside tables with tacos and Guatemalan food. **$**

WIRESTOCK/GETTY IMAGES ©

Rope swing, Lago de Petén Itzá

EL MORZILLO: HOW CORTES' HORSE BECAME A GOD

Legend has it that colonizer Hernán Cortés, on his way through Guatemala, left his ailing horse Morzilla with the Maya inhabitants of Tayasal. However, the natives were unfamiliar with horses and had little experience caring even for healthy ones, let alone ones that were ill. Despite the Maya's best intentions, Morzilla died. To honor him, the Itzá carved a stone statue, naming him Tziunchan. One hundred years later, when missionary priests visited the island, they found the statue being idolized, and festooned with flowers and offerings. Cortés' horse had become a god. The original statue was destroyed but a monument to this tale can be seen on the lakeshore in San Miguel.

with a sense of the depth and scope of illegal wildlife trafficking, though recovered and rescued animals aren't kept at the facility on Lago de Petén Itzá. If you are interested in supporting ARCAS or volunteering with them, check out their website or ask at the center for more information. Though not exactly a zoo, a self-guided trail leads through their various informational cages and is a nice, all-age-level-appropriate way to gain more information and see animals and birds you wouldn't otherwise see.

Jorge's Rope Swing

SIMPLE LAKESIDE PLEASURES

For many, Flores might seem so idyllic that there wouldn't be a need to 'get away from it all,' but for those who do, there's **Jorge's Rope Swing**, a rickety series of platforms on the Tayasal/San Miguel side that – you guessed it – has a rope swing. It drops you into one of the deepest parts of the lake,

 WHERE TO STAY IN SAN MIGUEL

Hostal Casa de Grethel
A colorful ochre building with a dock and iconic heart for selfies. $

Zapote Tree Inn
Views of the lake, a pool, and a terrace make this a top option. $$

Hotel San Miguel
A long-time mainstay, with affordable rooms right on the water's edge. $

SWEET SAN MIGUEL

Though Flores gets all the fame, credit and a lot of the fortune, there's another lakeside town that's worth checking out on the Tayasal side: San Miguel. It was historically a fishing village and the modern remnants of the Maya's Tayasal settlement, but today it's a tourist spot, with hotels, a few restaurants and a statue of Morzilla, colonizer Hernán Cortés' horse. If you're looking to unplug for a while, it's a great option if Flores just has too much going on. Come for a day, a night, or a week or two. Like Flores, it's got easy water access to all the lake's activities, but is quieter and more relaxed than its across-the-pond neighbor. Lake levels rise and fall, so be prepared.

Sunset, Lago de Petén Itzá

a flooded cenote, so there's no worry about plopping into the muck on a particularly direct dive. You'd have to go down hundreds of feet to reach the bottom. It's a simple childhood pleasure that's perfect even for adults. Just wait your turn, holler like Tarzan, swing out over the water...and let go. Families will find it may be tough to coax youngsters away from the swing. For adults, it's usually a thrill that wears off after the first couple of selfies get taken. After that, just perch yourself on one of the hammocks or string up your own, check social media on your phone, sunbathe or open a bottle of wine and

 WHERE TO STAY ON THE FAR SIDE OF LAGO DE PETÉN ITZÁ

Hotel Bahia Taitza
A San José option with lake views, clean rooms and a lovely pool. **$**

La Lancha
A Coppola-owned option between San Pedro and San Román with private dock, Jacuzzis and a library. **$$$**

Gucumatz Lakeside Inn
Right on the lakeside west of San Pedro, this colorful spot is a relaxed, if simple, getaway. **$$**

chat with friends. Reptile lovers will want to look for the giant orange and green iguanas that often frequent the tops of the palms, enjoying the sunshine much like you are. For those who simply can't get far enough away from civilization, it's even possible to camp overnight here in Jorge's precarious wooden platforms.

Circumnavigating Lago de Petén Itzá

A BEAUTIFUL JOURNEY

Those with their own transportation or even those who just want to hire a vehicle for an afternoon will enjoy taking a trip around the lake. Most people go clockwise, starting after breakfast and passing the airport and military installation. The road between Santa Elena and El Remate is pockmarked and has a few of the dreaded *tumulos* (speed bumps), so keep your eyes open. You'll pass a combination of pastures, fields, farms and forest, and eventually reach Ixlú. You may want to stop in nearby El Remate for a peek at the marshy lakeshore (you may even see a crocodile or two sunning itself in the shallows). Perhaps plan a bite to eat or a beverage before continuing. From El Remate, you'll hug the lakeshore on a paved road that birders will enjoy. This road once was a pothole-strewn disaster, but at the moment it's a delight. The Cerro Cahuí is a great place to stretch your legs if you need to. Or just keep going, eventually reaching the towns of San José and San Andrés de Petén on the northwest shore. If you time it right, you can be heading into the sunset; stop for a great photo at the lake's westernmost point, where the Sacpuy bridge crosses a little marshy finger that's popular with fishers and birders. From there, you'll head east again, reaching Santa Elena in about twenty minutes or so.

RADIO PETÉN

You may zip right past it in a *lancha* (small motorboat) without realizing that the area's first – and only – radio station is on a tiny island to the west of Flores. It's easily seen: just look for the big radio tower. It's a popular stop for those doing a lake tour as there's interesting memorabilia of the bygone days of radio, plus a small museum of curios and artefacts from the Tayasal and surrounding Maya sites. It's humble and what little documentation exists is mostly in Spanish, but it's a fun spot to detour to if you're coming back from a day on the water.

GETTING AROUND

Buses circumnavigate Lago de Petén Itzá and hit the major towns, though a boat may be faster. *Tuk-tuks* are the prime way to get around in places like Flores, Santa Elena and San José.

EL REMATE

El Remate, located at the far eastern end of Lago de Petén Itzá, is often overlooked as people zip from Flores to Tikal and back. That's a shame, because this quiet, relaxed lakeshore spot has a lot to offer, especially if you're looking to get away from it all and don't need the nightlife scene of Flores. There's a decent selection of hotels and restaurants, and a vibe of easy camaraderie that will mean anyone who stays will find friends quickly. Though many will be here just as a way to get closer to Tikal, some will hang out for days, weeks, even years – diving off the docks, kayaking and watching birds, day-drinking by the water in a hammock, watching the sunset, or checking out the birdlife that teems around the reedy shores or finds its way to the feeders that folks put up for their feathered friends.

Guatemala City

TOP TIP

Birders will want to seek out the 'Toucan Express' – a beverage-carrying contraption that shuttles drinks out to the deck at La Casa de Don David. Dave's a big birder, with tips on spotting all the species you're hoping to see.

El Remate

Kayaking

A BEAUTIFUL LAKESHORE AWAITS

The narrow finger of Lago de Petén Itzá that forms the El Remate area is perfect for kayaking, stand-up paddleboarding (SUP), and even swimming (though please be aware, this part of the lake does have crocodiles!). The calm waters – especially in the morning as the sun comes up – are sometimes mirror, smooth, and the shorelines are filled with birds and other wildlife. *Pizotes* (coatis) come down to lap or search for crustacean prey, herons and egrets stalk through the reeds and rushes, and coots and jacanas run frenetically over the lily pads. Each time the paddle hits the water, you'll likely feel energized. Sometimes the water temperatures – warmer than the surrounding air – make for ghostly, ethereal mists and add to the mood. Be sure to bring a camera, and if possible – for anyone wanting wildlife shots – a good high-powered telephoto lens. Lago de Petén Itzá isn't deep until you head further out, so if the light is right you'll be able to see fish lurking down in the shallows as well. If fishing is your thing, be sure to check first, as a license may be required.

Most of the shoreline hotels have a kayak or two available for guests to rent or use, so if this is a key reason for you to come, be sure to make sure these are available.

BEST PLACES TO EAT IN EL REMATE

Casa de Don David
Standard Guatemalan and Western food in an open-air deck setting that's great for birders, as the owner has multiple feeders set up, which attract orioles, hummingbirds, and tanagers. **$$**

Mon Ami
The area's best French cuisine in a lakeshore restaurant that's tucked on the northeast corner of the Remate side of the lake. **$$**

Las Orquideas
Pizzas and pastas beneath a *palapa* surrounded by flowers. If you're lucky, you'll spot some hummingbirds dancing about in the ginger blooms and orchids as you dine. **$**

 WHERE TO STAY IN EL REMATE

Casa de Don David
Birders will delight in staying here, but its prime location and restaurant are other reasons to stay. **$$**

Alice Guesthouse
A hostel-type atmosphere at this forested site up the hill. **$**

El Sotz Campground
Basic sites and spots for RVs convenient to the highway and the water. **$**

LAURA KATHLEEN LEWIS/SHUTTERSTOCK ©

Sunset, Lago de Petén Itzá

IXLÚ

There's only a small bit remaining of what once was a key Maya city that controlled the lucrative trade between the vast Lago de Petén Itzá to the west and the smaller Laguna Salpetén on the east. Ixlú, as the city was known, was perfectly situated to regulate this route, and may have been part of the Maya city of Tayasal, behind what is now San Miguel. Today, it's mostly just a highway intersection: north to Tikal, east to Belize, or south to return to Flores and other parts of Guatemala. But if you're curious, inside the triangle intersection there's a small park, and a structure – the only one remaining – that marks Ixlú.

Lago de Petén Itzá Sunset

A SUNSET-WATCHER'S HEAVEN

Sunset-watching is taken very seriously at Lago de Petén Itzá, and a number of spots offer lakeside viewing. Some places, like La Casa de Don David, have even taken things to the next level with a handmade contraption known as the Toucan Express that lets you order drinks and cocktails from the cozy comfort of their pavilion at the other end of the property. You order and when the drinks are ready, the server places them onto the pully-system cart and shuttles them off, off, and away...while you wait in the gazebo. But whether you're appreciating the setting sun in a kayak on the water, floating in a swimming pool, or if you have simply pulled your car over at exactly the right time, you'll be presented with a scene of unparalleled beauty. The changing colors in the sky as it reflects off the water. The shifting light that deepens the shadows of the shoreline and reeds. The blues and purples in the clouds that blossom into spectacular pinks, yellows and golds. Few people can catch a sunset here without understanding how truly special it is. Thoughts turn inward. There's a moment of silence that lasts until the final rays of light have sunk below the horizon. Dusk deepens. Shorebirds find spots to sleep. Night creatures begin to prowl. And it may just be time to finish whatever you're sipping...and order another one.

GETTING AROUND

El Remate is a convenient stop for those not wanting to stay inside Tikal's park bounds. It's accessible by bus, and frequent transport takes people to and from the ruins. Those wanting to circle the lake can also use public transport. Those heading east to Belize will need to change buses in Ixlú, just to the south, and head to Melchor de Mencos at the border.

Beyond El Remate

The area around El Remate is quiet, tranquil, serene and perfect for getting off the grid for a while.

Most people visit areas outside of El Remate as a day trip, for sights or vistas they won't find elsewhere, or for festivals such as the *Procesión de la Santa Calavera,* which only happen once a year. Some people will find, however, that staying for a while in a small village is exactly the medicine they're looking for. On the north side of Lago de Petén Itzá there are some excellent hotels that are worth seeking out, though little in the way of restaurants other than what's there at the hotel. Far to the north of the lake's western side is the road to Carmelita, where El Mirador trekking begins.

TOP TIP

The road around the lake's northern perimeter is now paved, meaning you can circle it in under four hours.

Collared aracari (p150)

MICHEL GASSER/ALAMY STOCK PHOTO ©

PLAYAS YAXJABÍN

The infrequently visited **Playas Yaxjabín** lie on the north side of the odd, thick isthmus that extends out to the north of Flores, forming the south side of Lago de Petén Itzá at that point. Easiest to reach by boat as a day trip, this swampy 'playa' is less beach and more marsh, with great expanses of reeds and scrub, as well as forests further back from the waterline, and a dock or two. It's still relatively free of people and thus a great spot for wildlife and birding. Depending on the time of year and rainfall, this can be dry or completely underwater, so ask around before heading out.

Biotopo Cerro Cahuí

Procesión de la Santa Calavera

FASCINATING AND MACABRE

Though the Día de los Muertos festivities are world-famous in Mexico, they are also marked throughout Guatemala in a variety of ways. Usually, this involves making an altar, lots of decorations and offerings, painted faces, and such. There are often treats for youngsters, colorful costumes, partying, fireworks and alcohol. But there are a few places where Day of the Dead is honored in a different fashion. In the small town of **San José**, on the northwestern side of Lago de Petén Itzá, November 1st sees a curious procession: real human skulls are used in a blend of pagan and Catholic tradition, and they are thought to be from Itzá Maya ancestors. The procession is done for the entire night, starting at the church, where the

 THREE TOUCANS TO SPOT AROUND EL REMATE

Keel-Billed Toucan
This beautiful, striking bird has a black body with yellow on its face and beak.

Collared Aracari
With a rust-colored stripe on their light yellow breast, and a serrated beak that's dark on the underside.

Emerald Toucanette
A beautiful bright green and blue bird with a smaller, sickle-shaped beak that's yellow on top.

sacred skulls are kept. The skulls 'visit' various community members who receive blessings.

Unlike many of Guatemala's festivals, this is a somber affair done with respect and solemnity, and is a tradition that likely has persisted here since the Maya. While fascinating, it's important to understand that it's not a time for tourists to be in the way. If you're in the area, be considerate of any requests festivalgoers or authorities may have.

Biotopo Cerro Cahuí

GREAT RAINFOREST HIKING

Most of the activities in the Lago de Petén Itzá region involve the lake in some way, but people often overlook the Biotopo Cerro Cahuí, a vast expanse of protected forest on the lake's north shore. Hiking trails here are accessed through a small booth which charges a modest entry fee, but once inside you'll have a shorter and longer route through dense forested jungle. It can be muddy at certain times of year, and of course, the ever-present mosquitoes can be a nuisance, but those are minor. The Cerro (hill) offers a chance to see orchids, bromeliads, vines and a variety of jungle plants, as well as – though luck always plays a part – *tepezcuintles* (agoutis), *pizotes*, foxes, squirrels, and possibly even a larger mammal or two. You're likely to see as much when you look up as what's on the ground: spider and howler monkeys, parrots and toucans. Several small, unrestored Maya ruin sites are also there, both of them on the longer of the two trails. Though you're unlikely to see one, the Cerro Cahuí is still listed in the current range for that prize mammal, the jaguar. You probably won't get a glimpse, but who knows. For many hikers, however, the most rewarding aspect of the trails are the delightful vistas that one can see from the *miradores* (lookouts) at the summits of the various hills. Seeing the lake spread out before you gives a sense of scale.

FLAAR-MESOAMERICA

For those looking to get a more in-depth peek at park plants or animals, a series of digital publications in both English and Spanish are available online thanks to FLAAR-MesoAmerica (flaar-mesoamerica.org). These mostly focus on plant species but one guide by Nicholas Hellmuth describes Cerro Cahuí in detail, discussing among other things the park's numerous edible plants. More than 25 species are edible, including breadfruit and the orchid that produces vanilla. Other guides and blog entries offer insight on flora and fauna around Guatemala, often with excellent photography to accompany the research. Check back frequently; the site may be updated as new publications are released or become available.

GETTING AROUND

You'll have the most flexibility if you have your own vehicle, but there are inexpensive local buses that circle Lago de Petén Itzá. You can also hire a taxi by the hour or by the day if you just want to get out of Flores for a while. The quickest way to reach the opposite side of the lake is by water taxi.

SAYAXCHÉ

● Sayaxché

⊕ Guatemala
City

This gritty river town doesn't hold a lot for tourists, though it's a nice spot to watch the sunset, and the ferries crossing the river (worked by four outboard motors at each corner of the boat) are interesting and full of character. The town has a few riverside motels and some restaurants that serve local food, so for many, Sayaxché itself isn't the reason to come here, but rather the wealth of activities surrounding it. Crater Azul is a stunning spring-fed gem at the end of a crystalline tributary and a great day-trip. Be sure to bring a bathing suit and snorkel. Another popular spot is Aguateca, up a different tributary and beyond Laguna Petexbatún. Perched high on a well-defended ridge, Aguateca came to a quick, violent end, with much of it preserved for archaeologists. On either voyage you're sure to see a host of river birds, and maybe a croc or two.

TOP TIP

Check the weather carefully and – if possible – time your trip for certain sunshine, as neither of these river journeys are very fun in the driving rain, and Crater Azul isn't nearly as *azul* (blue) when it's overcast.

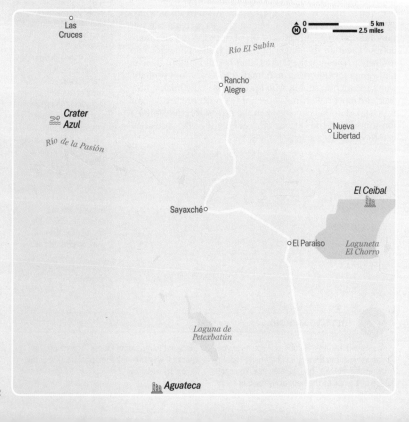

Crater Azul

Crater Azul

CRYSTAL CLEAR SWIMMING HOLE

In the dry season (February and March) it's possible to get to **Crater Azul** (Blue Crater) by 4x4, but this gorgeous swimming hole is more dependably reached by boat up the river from Sayaxché. And that's often half the fun, as there are loads of birds like kingfishers and swallows to see, plus the rarer glimpse of a sunning crocodile.

Once there, what happens next depends a bit on the water level. Some years, it's low enough to leap and frolic off the (albeit rickety!) dock that's there. Other years the dock is submerged in three feet of water.

What's a constant is that the water is just gorgeous: visibility of up to 100ft and the mangrove hammocks are ringed with gorgeous green, maroon and purple water lilies. Wading birds like jacanas poke about in the shallows. Herons and egrets perch in the branches above. You may need to change into your swimsuit in the boat and jump off the bow, but for young and old alike, that's all part of the attraction. If you tire of swimming or get too chilly (the water can be quite 'refreshing' depending on the time of year!) then sit in the boat and toss crumbs to the thousands of minnows that swarm about. If you've packed a lunch, you can make a day out of it, but most tours last under four, fun-filled hours.

MORELET'S CROCODILE

Spend time around Guatemala's rivers or lagoons and you're likely to spot a Morelet's crocodile. Or two. Or ten. Big or small, they're exciting to see and it's nice that – for now anyway – they're listed as a species of least concern.

But whether or not you think crocs are cute and cuddly, they're worthy of respect: they leap out of murky water with surprising speed and have been known to eat whatever they can drag underwater. Though attacks on humans are extremely rare, they're not unheard of. So use caution when approaching water and if you're with a guide, ask if you need to consider whether crocs are in the region.

WHERE TO STAY AROUND SAYAXCHÉ

Chiminos Island
A perfect base for Aguateca and beyond, with howler monkeys and its own on-site ruins. **$$$**

Hotel Casa Grande
Basic, clean accommodations at this central Sayaxché hotel. **$**

Hotel Villa Aquazul
A nice spot with a pool and two stories of rooms around the central, off-street parking. **$$**

MILTON-SOSA/SHUTTERSTOCK ©

El Ceibal

BEST SAYAXCHÉ AREA RUINS

Sayaxché has a number of important Maya ruins to see other than Aguateca, but visiting them may require river rides, hikes or a 4x4:

Dos Pilas
A regional Maya powerhouse believed to have Aguateca ties.

El Ceibal
Another famous ruin set beside a river with long trails that beg to be explored.

Chiminos Island
Fascinating location used by archaeologists, with ruins as well.

Tamarindito
A remote, smaller site with stelae and glyph stones.

El Ceibal

A RIVERSIDE RIVAL OF DOS PILAS

El Ceibal, poised as it was on the banks of the Río de la Pasión, was a commanding force in the region, but like many Maya cities, it was threatened by nearby rivals, and fell, catastrophically, to the nearby Dos Pilas kingdom in 735 CE. Much of its history was destroyed by the conquerors, including its monuments, some of which had the glyphs chiseled away. Interestingly, when Dos Pilas finally fell, El Ceibal rose again and thrived after many Maya cities collapsed. It was finally abandoned in the 10th century CE. As many as 10,000 people may have lived here before the city's final fall.

Hikers will love the site for its long jungle paths and extended causeways, made even longer if one arrives by boat from the river, following the footsteps of the Maya traders who would have arrived the same way. A unique structure shows evidence of influence from Mexico, in that it is circular rather than square, has jaguar carvings still visible, and is believed to connect to the north's god of the wind, Ehecatl. Due to the proximity to the Río de la Pasión, the thick jungle setting and depending on the time of year, this ruin's mosquitoes are impressive, but so too are the chances to see other wildlife, such as reptiles, amphibians and birds. Do yourself a favor, though, and be sure to bring repellent.

GETTING AROUND

Getting to many of the sites mentioned requires not a bus, not a car, but a boat. You can find captains by asking at the ferry crossing. Some spots, like El Ceibal, can be reached by road.

Beyond Sayaxché

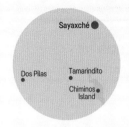

If you're lucky enough to have the luxury of time on your hands, the area around Sayaxché has a lot to explore.

Most people zip from Flores and Tikal south to the other Guatemala hot spots, such as Semuc Champey, Atitlán, Antigua or Guatemala City. But those who stop and smell the flowers will find quiet, stately ruins, small towns, delightful river trips, and a tranquil rural lifestyle that hasn't changed dramatically in decades, maybe centuries. Stop for a night or two in a remote island reached only by a river ride, or get deep into the jungle with a trip to a ruin most people never get to see. Along the way, you'll meet friendly locals and make discoveries those on the beaten path will always miss. Lucky you to be on the path less traveled.

TOP TIP

No question about it: bring good mosquito repellent if you don't want to be the main thing on the menu.

Dos Pilas (p156)

REALLY EASY STAR/ALAMY STOCK PHOTO ©

Chiminos Island

A SECLUDED ISLAND PARADISE

If taking a boat ride that seems like something out of the *The African Queen* is your cup of tea, then **Chiminos Island** is for you. Getting here is usually done by boat out of Sayaxché, and can take a good two to three hours. But when you arrive, the delightful jungle lodge is all you could possibly ask for: delicious meals, relaxing hammocks, incredible views and monkeys frolicking in the treetops. It's so easy to arrive and then forget that somewhere out there is real life, and you'll have to return to it...someday.

On-site is a Maya ruin, which, though in poor condition and mostly unexcavated, is interesting because Chiminos Island was once a peninsula, but the Maya settled here and then dug away the connector for defensive reasons. This is where archaeologists excavating the ruins of Aguateca stayed, so there is additional historical value. Even if you're not much of an archaeologist yourself, it's still a fun, interesting and restful place to kick back for a while. Birders will find themselves unable to put down the binoculars.

The only nightlife is the chirping or crawling kind, so don't expect to stay up late into the night partying. If you're coming to relax, or to day-trip to other nearby ruins, then this is the place to be.

Aguateca

A HIGHLY DEFENDED MAYA RUIN

The ruins of Aguateca are not easy to get to, but for the Maya, this was the whole idea. This city was well-defended, not only by its remote access via Laguna Petexbatún, but also because it was built on top of a ridge with a deep ravine on most of its sides. It is believed that this site was connected to nearby Dos Pilas, and that both were linked to faraway Tikal. Today, you need to take a boat ride up a gorgeous tributary into the lagoon to reach the site. Then you disembark and hike up to the site, eventually reaching an overlook where you can see a commanding view of the entire region. It would have been easy to spot any advancing rival army long before they arrived.

Based on the discovery of quickly made walls and other key signs, archaeologists can tell that this site was almost certainly trying to defend itself against attacks. And despite its defenses, around 800 CE, the city was abandoned in great haste, then invaded and burned. Yet because of this sudden end, it's a valuable spot for its many artefacts and items that were left behind so quickly that there wasn't time to do much

HOWLER MONKEYS

You'll likely see both spider monkeys and howler monkeys during your trip, but it's easy to to tell which is a howler if you know what to look (or listen!) for:
If you're listening to an angry, demonic howl that seems louder than a jet engine, that's just a little ole howler monkey doing its thing. The howler monkey is the loudest land animal on the planet, and is second only to whales, with calls that reverberate through the forest for miles. Entirely black and usually more sedentary than spider monkeys, the howlers are particularly loud at daybreak, sometimes seeming to fill the jungle with their calls.

 WHERE TO EAT AROUND SAYAXCHÉ

Cafe Maya
This Sayaxché standby is a good spot for tasty Guatemalan food. **$**

Antojitos The Country Girl
A Sayaxché spot with snacks, *antojitos* (snacks from food stalls) and sit-down meals. **$**

Food & Market
Don't knock it just because it's at a gas station; there's tasty food and a pretty view. **$**

THE GUIDE

EL PETÉN

RAPHAEL R VEST/SHUTTERSTOCK ©

Spider monkey

SPIDER MONKEYS

The irony of spider monkeys is that they're the ones you're more likely to see leaping acrobatically from treetop to treetop, often with heart-stopping, death-defying falls before they cling to a branch and keep going. They're as noisy moving through the foliage as the howlers are loud. So if you look up because you heard branches rustling, those are likely spider monkeys. They're more gangly than their howling cousins: look for long, thin arms, and fur that's a bit more unkempt, giving them the look (the origin of the name) of a spider's hair-covered legs. If you've got binoculars or a high-powered zoom lens, look carefully: often there's a baby clinging to the mother, and both may be looking right at you.

than leave them in place. Interestingly though, it was not abandoned entirely, but rather seems to have been a quick coup or defeat of the rulers; other residences were not under the same kind of haste.

Aguateca has thus been a place where we've learned about not only warfare and the destruction of the city, but ironically, due to its quick destruction, its life and habits in a way that's not usually preserved. As such, it's a valuable feather to add to the cap of anyone with more than a passing interest in the Maya.

 WHERE TO EAT AROUND SAYAXCHÉ

Restaurante La Jungla
A *palapa*-roofed spot tucked away from Sayaxché's center. **$$**

Los Gemelos
A restaurant (and hotel) on Sayaxché's south side. **$$**

Mercado Municipal
Super cheap produce, fresh meats and street food. **$**

BLOQUEOS

The road from Sayaxché south is a major – and the only – thoroughfare, and thus it's a prime spot for the dreaded *bloqueos*.
If you don't know what these are, consider yourself lucky: they're roadblocks, and they're a prime way that local communities protest. Against the government, against corruption, against injustices, against having their electricity cut off, whatever. It may sound ineffectual, but at times, *bloqueos* have brought Guatemala to a standstill and they remain one of the only ways the 'little guy' can make his or her voice heard in a country that all too often only listens to those with the *quetzales*.
Unfortunately an ill-timed *bloqueo* can mean that a journey of a few hours turns into an overnight.

JUDITH LIENERT/SHUTTERSTOCK ©

Aguateca (156)

Dos Pilas

A FEARSOME POWERHOUSE

Dos Pilas, with deep ties to Tikal, is located along the Río de la Pasión. It not only controlled the waterway's traffic, but also had heated rivalries with other regional cities such as El Ceibal, which it defeated, destroyed and humiliated in 736 CE. Chillingly similar to the way the Spanish would erase the history of the Maya by burning their books, so too did Dos Pilas remove the writing on El Ceibal's stelae, at an incalculable loss to archaeology. It also enslaved the El Ceibal ruler, further humiliating him.

Though its existence seems to have been mostly a state of constant warfare, thanks to detailed historical artefacts and writings from Dos Pilas as well as other sites like Aguateca,

 SAYAXCHÉ PARKS

Los Chorritos
Riverside spot with hyacinths and waterbirds.

Parque Nacional El Rosario
A mix of mowed fields, jungle and waterways.

Petexbatún
Vast protected area with Maya sites, rivers and lagoons.

the chronology of this site is remarkably well-recorded, giving researchers detailed insight and access to the life and lifestyle of this city's inhabitants. The city switched allegiances between Tikal and Calakmul, it attacked and defended against other nearby cities, and was a fearsome power in the Sayaxché region. Not surprisingly, the city that ruled by the sword also died by it: in the mid 800s CE, nearby cities such as Tamarindo rose up and defeated Dos Pilas, and some scholars believe the ruling elites fled to Aguateca, which also fell not long after.

A relatively small site, one of its most popular structures is the Bat Palace (no, don't look for Bruce Wayne), which featured temples and a fascinating entrance to a cave. Archaeologists found a destroyed throne inside, a possible indication that the Dos Pilas elites met a violent end.

Tamarindito

AN EARLY CAPITAL GETS REVENGE

The early capital of the Petexbatún region, expansive **Tamarindito** was superseded by nearby Dos Pilas, but had its eventual revenge in the mid 800s CE, defeating a weakened Dos Pilas and possibly driving the latter's ruling elite to the hilltop site of Aguateca. The victory was short-lived, however, as the entire region descended into warfare and collapsed shortly after, part of the Maya collapse that saw the entire civilization vanish.

Like many of its neighbors, Tamarindito features a number of impressive structures, pyramids, residences and a ballcourt. Even more interestingly, it has three hieroglyphic staircases. It was also a leader in agriculture, and possibly the most fertile, productive city in the entire region. Despite many attempts by looters, several important tombs were found still intact in some form at the site, including a rich burial of a ruler believed to be Chanal Balam, the same ruler who vanquished Dos Pilas and exacted revenge.

Getting here is a challenge, as with many of the area's ruins. It's often combined with a visit to Dos Pilas and/or Aguateca, as these other sites factored into the same history. Chiminos Island is a good spot from which to plan trips to this site as well as other surrounding ruins.

AMAZING LEAF-CUTTER ANTS

As you walk around many of these ruins, you'll notice some odd trails that are far too narrow to belong to an animal, at only 4in to 6in wide. They belong to leaf-cutter ants, which if you're lucky you'll see in action. These amazing insects cut and carry vast amounts of leaf litter back to their nest, where the leaf pieces are used to farm fungus that's harvested to help the colony survive. The farming analogy even extends to their protecting the precious crop from pests or non-useful molds. Their trails, made by millions of ants over years, even decades, are a common fixture on the jungle floor. Some colonies are nearly the size of a football field.

GETTING AROUND

Buses and smaller collective vans will get you to the majority of the larger towns and some smaller villages, but to reach most ruins you'll need some form of private transportation, often in the form of a boat.

THE HIGHLANDS

CULTURAL GEMS AND NATURAL WONDERS

Defying easy definition as a region, the highlands offer a vast variety of authentic cultural opportunities, incredible scenery, and quirky natural and man-made wonders.

The highlands region stretches over a vast and fascinating patchwork, and much of its diversity is due to geography that still separates its different parts today. Steep mountains, sharp valleys and dense jungle prevented easy communication between communities that developed independently for hundreds, even thousands, of years. Even with today's modern gizmos like cellphones and that thing called the internet, Guatemala's highlands remain steeped in local customs and cultures. Places like the Nebaj region – decimated by the Guatemalan civil war – still proudly wear the crimson red skirts of their ancestors, while next door cities like Xela (aka Quetzaltenango) seem as modern as can be. Quirky architecture, stunning landscapes, and a friendly, off-the-map vibe make the highlands delightful. You'll likely find Spanish used as a second, not a primary language. Most Highlanders grow up speaking an indigenous Maya language, though even those vary from region to region or – in some cases – town to town. Crowded markets, vibrant fabrics and textiles, and regional dress are a visual feast for artists and photographers, though you'll find most locals are shy or fearful of cameras – refrain or ask before taking photos, and you may be asked to pay if they agree. Even though they're nowhere near the majesty of Tikal or other Petén-area sites, the highlands have some notable Maya ruins.

DAVESIMON/SHUTTERSTOCK ©

THE MAIN AREAS

ANTIGUA	PANAJACHEL	LAGO DE ATITLÁN	SANTIAGO ATITLÁN
Heart-melting historic capital.	Beautiful lakeside town.	Caldera-created lake.	Authentic textile town.
p166	p177	p183	p190

Lago de Atitlán (p183)

HUEHUETENANGO	**QUETZALTENANGO**	**NEBAJ**
Historic transit town.	Lovely colonial city.	Authentic and oft-forgotten.
p197	**p203**	**p209**

Find Your Way

The highlands beg to be explored for months or lifetimes, and we've picked the top spots where you'll find history, nature and culture. Spend as much time as possible here, and plan to return.

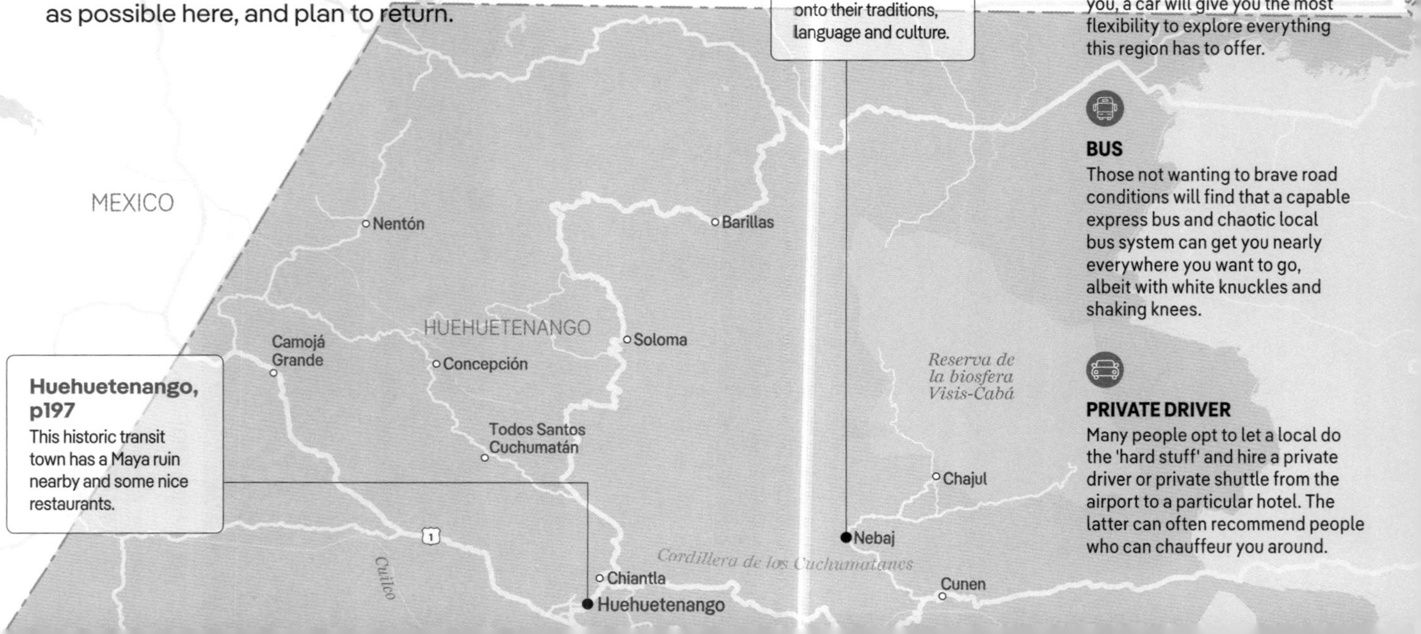

CAR

If you're up for the surprises the road can have in store for you, a car will give you the most flexibility to explore everything this region has to offer.

BUS

Those not wanting to brave road conditions will find that a capable express bus and chaotic local bus system can get you nearly everywhere you want to go, albeit with white knuckles and shaking knees.

PRIVATE DRIVER

Many people opt to let a local do the 'hard stuff' and hire a private driver or private shuttle from the airport to a particular hotel. The latter can often recommend people who can chauffeur you around.

Nebaj, p209

Often overlooked by tourists, Nebaj and its 'Ixil Triangle' are defiantly holding onto their traditions, language and culture.

Huehuetenango, p197

This historic transit town has a Maya ruin nearby and some nice restaurants.

MEXICO

Nentón

Camojá Grande

Concepción

HUEHUETENANGO

Soloma

Barillas

Todos Santos Cuchumatán

Cuilco

Chiantla

Huehuetenango

Cordillera de los Cuchumatanes

Reserva de la biosfera Visis-Cabá

Chajul

Nebaj

Cunen

Antigua, p166

The historic capital (one of the country's four!), Antigua has ruined cathedrals next to hipster coffee shops, with cobbled streets and a pulsing energy.

GUATEMALA

Lago de Amatitlán

Escuintla

Antigua

Ciudad Vieja

Alotenango

Comalapa

Chimaltenango Market

Chimaltenango

CHIMALTENANGO

Tecpán

Patzún

1

Canilla

Chinique

Chichicastenango

Santa Cruz del Quiché

Panajachel, p177

Beautiful town by Lago de Atitlán, with plenty of spots for tourists. It serves as a hub for much of the lake's transit.

Sololá

SOLOLÁ

Panajachel

Lago de Atitlán

Santiago Atitlán

Volcán Atitlán (3537m)

Santiago Atitlán, p190

A rugged textile town on Lago de Atitlán's far southeast side.

Momostenango

Totonicapán

San Cristóbal Totonicapán

TOTONICAPÁN

Quetzaltenango

QUETZALTENANGO

Volcán Cerro Quemado

Quetzaltenango, p203

High up in the mountains, lovely Quetzaltenango is a large colonial city with a delightful, vibrant center.

Lago de Atitlán, p183

This lake sits within view of eight spectacular volcanoes, and serves as a highway between lakeside towns.

San Sebastián

Volcán Tajumulco (4220m)

Volcán Tacaná (4100m)

Sibinal

0   50 miles

0   100 km

Plan Your Time

The highlands are a delight, a place to come, stop, and stay awhile, whether you're lazing around on the shores of Lago de Atitlán, or studying Spanish or an indigenous dialect high in the mountains.

Lago de Atitlán (p183)

If You Only Do One Thing

● **Antigua** (p166). It's got to be Antigua. It's an enchanting city with magic and wonder on every street corner. Whether it's a snapshot tiled roof full of sunflowers, wandering through the mazelike ruins of a destroyed monastery, the sight of Volcán Fuego puffing, a course that wraps you hands-on into a part of Guatemalan culture, or a tooth-dislodging *tuk-tuk* ride through the cobbled streets, Antigua just has a way of capturing hearts. There's great food, absorbing culture, and day-trip and overnight activities for any type of traveler, from backpackers to luxury honeymooners.

Seasonal Highlights

Winters are chilly, especially in higher elevations; temps can dip below freezing at night. Summers are warm but not tropical.

JANUARY

Dance of the Venado brings costumed 'deers' and 'monkeys' into the streets, with maracas and fireworks.

FEBRUARY

Mid-February's tasty **Festival del Café** celebrates the coffee harvest in Atitlán and other coffee-growing areas.

APRIL

Semana Santa is observed across Guatemala during Easter, with processions and decorations in the streets.

3 Days to Travel Around

● Start with a visit to Antigua and maybe learn the ins and outs of Maya chocolate, then hop over to **Lago de Atitlán** (p183), take a course in weaving from a women's collective in one of the shoreline towns such as **San Pedro La Laguna** (p187) or **San Juan La Laguna** (p191), and be sure to catch a spectacular sunrise hike or morning at the **Rostro Maya** (p188).

● From there, cruise over to **Quetzaltenango** (p183) to enjoy the colonial architecture and great food, maybe with a day trip to a quirky church or two.

If You Have a Week

● If you have more than a few days, really take the time to explore: from Antigua, dive deep into Lago de Atitlán's lakeside towns, with some time spent in **Panajachel** (p177), San Pedro La Laguna, San Juan La Laguna and **Santiago Atitlán** (p190).

● Shift your focus to a bigger city, visiting the incredible market at **Chichicastenango** (p210), and Huehuetenango's interesting ruin at **Zaculeu** (p198).

● Then venture out to sweet, far away **Nebaj** (p209), seeing a region that has recovered from, but not forgotten, the horrors of the Guatemalan civil war. Finish up in the beautiful city of Quetzaltenango before returning home.

JULY
Festival of Santiago in Antigua is the city's grand annual fiesta, with dancing, fireworks, street food, vendors and rides.

AUGUST
People cheer effigies of the Virgin paraded through town at the **Fiesta de la Virgen de la Asunción.**

NOVEMBER
Held on 1 November, **Día de Todos los Santos** is linked to the spirits and Day of the Dead.

DECEMBER
Chichicastenango's **Fiesta de Santo Tomás** is a festive bacchanal, with drinking and dancing connected to the city's 500-year-old church.

ANTIGUA

Antigua continually melts visitors' hearts, and is one of the top spots that people who come here from abroad retire to. For some, the magic is in the quaint cobblestone streets, the painted walls, the tiled rooftops or the contrast of the alleys with the blueness of the sky. For others, it's the ruined cathedrals, churches and convents; their testament to nature's power and the flimsy human endeavors it can so easily destroy. Still others come and are seduced by the flavors: the wealth of different foods from around the world, the delicious salsas, the sensual bliss of freshly made chocolate, the rich coffee, the flavors at every turn. And for some it's the chance to meet cosmopolitan people from all over the world in coffee shops and cute cafes.

TOP TIP

Highland cities – especially Antigua, Quetzaltenango and those in the Atitlán region – are extremely popular, so at times finding a hotel can be a challenge despite the apparent plethora of options. Make reservations well in advance.

Ruined cathedral (p168)

K. BOONNITROD/SHUTTERSTOCK ©

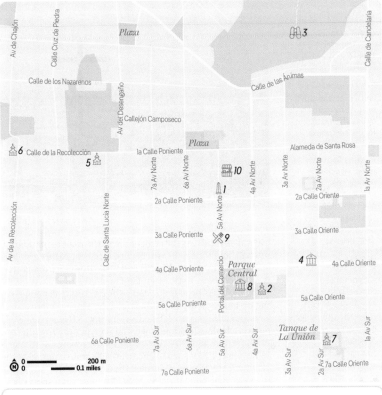

SIGHTS	5 Colegio de San	de Santa Clara	SHOPPING
1 Arco de Santa Catalina	Jerónimo	8 Parque Central	10 Nim Po't
2 Catedral de San José	6 Iglesia y Convento		
3 Cerro de la Cruz	de la Recolección	EATING	
4 Choco Museo	7 Iglesia y Convento	9 Casa Troccoli	

Cerro de la Cruz

BIRD'S-EYE VIEW OF ANTIGUA

Cerro de la Cruz (Hill of the Cross) is one of the (many!) iconic 'to-dos' in Antigua, offering a sweeping bird's-eye view of the entire city, with the incredible, immense Volcán Agua as a backdrop - so perfect it could be the opening scene in a movie. But the view is only part of the whole experience of getting here, especially if you choose to hike from your spot in town. Morning offers the best light, and you'll surely spot photo- and selfie-worthy walls, buildings, rooftops, and so on, as you make your way

WHERE TO EAT IN ANTIGUA

Casa de las Sopas
A surprisingly tasty spot dedicated to the perfect bowl of soup. **$**

El Viejo Café
Popular cafe in the center with food, coffees, pastries, desserts and more. **$$**

Romeo y Julieta
Great Italian food in a quaint restaurant that feels like you're in Italy. **$$$**

BEST RUINS

Bring your camera, and if possible, arrive in the early morning or late afternoon for the best, most atmospheric lighting.

Iglesia y Convento de la Recolección
A large, spectacular monastery ruin with giant pieces of wall and masonry left in place since it fell centuries ago.

Iglesia y Convento de Santa Clara
A long-disused convent with evocative stairways, chambers and baths.

Colegio de San Jerónimo
This ruin features a star-shaped fountain and numerous gardens, walls, alcoves and passageways.

MILOSZ MASLANKA/SHUTTERSTOCK ©

Cerro de la Cruz (p167)

towards the hill. At the edge of town, the road turns slightly upward, and the *cerro* (hill) begins. A cement pathway guides you in a series of switchbacks and turns through a delightfully shaded forest, until you finally reach the top.

The park has been renovated as of 2023, with cement seating arranged in an amphitheater style. The *cruz* (cross) has a commanding view of the city, standing as if a person, arms outstretched, is looking down and blessing the town below. Look for the photo-worthy set of quetzal wings and take a selfie, make friends with other travelers or just marvel at the view. One small note of caution: the area is remote so it's wise to ask at your hotel if there are safety concerns, especially in the early morning or late in the day when you might be the only one up there.

Magnificent Destruction

RUINS ARE A TOP DRAW

One of Antigua's many charms is its multitude of ruined churches, cathedrals, convents and monasteries. Ironically, the terrible tragedies that befell these buildings is what make these spots so popular today. Even shortly after Spanish colonization, the city was a nexus for Catholicism, with dozens of different denominations setting up 'shop' here over the span of just a few centuries. Soon the entire city was filled with beautiful structures, each sporting delicate decorative work and European-style, lofty vaults and arches. That all came crashing down – literally – in a series of earthquakes in the

 THE BEST PLACES TO LEARN SPANISH IN ANTIGUA

Antigüeña Spanish Academy
Highly rated classes taught in a lush garden setting at a level that matches your needs.

Ixchel Spanish School
Excellent instruction and can arrange for homestays with local families as well.

Don Pedro de Alvarado
This school believes in high teacher-to-student ratios and offers online as well as in-person classes.

1700s and 1800s, and the disasters were so severe the government fled from Antigua to Guatemala City. Thousands of people lost their lives, and thousands more were maimed and wounded. The structures lay in ruins: a testament to the destructive force of Mother Nature. Many of these buildings were never rebuilt, and many were not even cleared away. Today, they are tourist attractions, and there's an undeniable majesty about them...something poignant and telling in the giant pieces of brick and stone, the ornate decorations split and fragmented.

Several of these are free to enter; most require a nominal fee. Some have Spanish- or English-speaking guides who can explain some of the key features, often shedding light on structures or rooms that would be oddly mysterious otherwise. Visiting and exploring these structures is one of Antigua's most unique activities.

Learn Spanish in a Stunning City

SURROUND YOURSELF WITH THE LANGUAGE

It's hard to argue that learning a language – any language – is best done by immersing yourself in it, and where better to do that than in beautiful, iconic Antigua? Its many language schools offer the chance to stay, eat, speak and even dream in Spanish, letting you maximize your education...all while experiencing this artsy, stunning city. Interestingly, unlike Mexico's part of the Yucatán Peninsula, here in Antigua locals will continue speaking Spanish with you even long after you've made it obvious that English is the faster, easier way to get points across. Guatemalans seem to understand that if you're speaking Spanish, that's the language they should reply with, even if their English is just as good as yours. What this means is that you can deeply and fully immerse yourself in Spanish, without having the frustration of being spoken to in English all the time just because you're a foreigner. Yet unlike more remote parts of Guatemala, Antigua is a spot where you can still find that cup of familiar latte that you crave, or other expats to commune with if you start pining for the comforts of home. You can immerse yourself, but still retreat to the familiar when you need to. (There's even a Burger King.)

Look for language schools that fit your budget, offer the level of instruction you need, and ideally, offer homestay programs where you can spend time being part of a local Guatemalan family. This will deepen the cultural bond, help your language skill, and who knows, perhaps lead to lifelong friendships as well.

NOT JUST SPANISH

Spanish is the official language of Guatemala, but it's by no means the only one and, in some parts of the country, it's not even the primary language. You may spend a month or two brushing up on Spanish only to travel around Guatemala and realize you're not able to understand anything people are saying because it's all Greek – or no, make that K'iche', Q'eqchi', Kachiquel or Mam – to you. In addition to Spanish, the country has an astonishing 23 other languages that are actively spoken, 21 Maya dialects and two non-Maya ones. So in case you get bored with learning Spanish, you can dive into learning the other languages as well.

WHERE TO EAT IN ANTIGUA

El Refectorio
A fancy, atmosphere-laden delight in the heart of the Hotel Santo Domingo. **$$$**

Osteria di Francesco
A nice Italian spot tucked away on the south side of the city, with alfresco seating. **$$**

El Garden Antigua
Lots of vegan and vegetarian options, with meat dishes cooked using separate utensils. **$$**

Make Your Own Chocolate

EAT, PLAY, LOVE

Chocolate was a sacred food for the Maya and their complicated process has been handed down through the centuries, making its production a key staple of Guatemala's export trade. But stop and smell the...cacao for a moment and you'll start realizing how complex, interesting and (yes!) delicious this whole process is. Chocolate addicts will want to tie on an apron and get their hands dirty in a class about all things chocolate. Learn the history, how the pods are harvested, what the different types are. Open pods and extract the beans. Some classes (the longer ones) will even show you how to roast your own, and while the fermentation isn't possible in a few hours, you'll have a sense of how that happens as well. Once the beans have been extracted from the pods and roasted, the fun part happens: grind them, either with a *molcajete* (mortar) or machine (the easy way) until a paste forms. This paste, though bitter, is what is used to make chocolate bars or – in the case of the Maya – a sacred drink called *chocol-ha*.

At **ChocoMuseo** in the plaza, classes usually run for one or two hours, and can be taken in Spanish or English. In both the short and long classes, you'll get to learn, play, laugh and eat. Best of all, you'll go home with a bar or two of tasty chocolate that you made yourself.

CHOCOL-HA

The word 'chocolate' comes from the Maya word *'chocol-ha'*: a bitter, chocolate-based drink often spiced with chili and black pepper. First the roasted beans were crushed into a dry paste, with water and spices added until it was the right consistency to drink. Residue has been found in vessels that are hundreds, even thousands of years old. The concoction was originally reserved only for the ruling elites who could afford the luxury. (Though modern recreations of the original *chocol-ha* don't particularly appeal to a modern palate – it's pretty nasty, bitter stuff!) Over time, this liquid got sweetened, first with honey and then – as today – with sugar. And the name slowly morphed into the word 'chocolate' that we all recognize.

The Plaza, Personified

LOVELY BY DAY OR NIGHT

Part of why people fall in love with Antigua is its beautiful main plaza, **Parque Central** – not only a central city location, but also the integral 'heart' of what it means to be here. It's a delightful, relaxing and exciting place, and care has been taken to maintain the park's historical value: for example, the buxom mermaids in the central fountain are a reconstruction of the original 1738 version, which was trashed early in the 20th century. The brilliant white facade of the Catedral de San José, dating back to 1545, rises benevolently over a foreground of cobblestones, people and pushcarts. The park benches are full: octogenarian couples toss grain for the sparrows as their toddler grandchildren chase after pigeons. Tourists line up for selfies. Vendors mill through the crowds selling everything: hats, jewelry, chewing gum, waterproof cellphone cases and charging cables. The calm emptiness of the plaza at daybreak gives way to traffic jams by morning's rush hour. If you're a people-watcher, you could

WHERE TO STAY IN ANTIGUA

Hotel Casa Santo Domingo
Pricey but worth it, the Santo Domingo is in a restored ruined convent filled with antiquities. **$$$**

Porta Hotel Antigua
A luxury spot, with a stunning pool, fine restaurant, and easy access to many city attractions. **$$$**

Hotel Las Faroles
A mid-range hotel with a nice garden restaurant and simple, clean rooms. **$$**

Parque Central

BEST SPOTS FOR PHOTOGRAPHS

Okay, so maybe your goal is to post a selfie with the hashtag #Antigua. Here are some great spots to say 'cheese':

Arco de Santa Catalina
No doubt, this spot wins the popularity contest, with a beautiful arch and Volcán Agua behind.

Catedral de San José
This brilliant white cathedral facade overlooks the main square.

Cerro de la Cruz
The Hill of the Cross overlooks the city, giving selfie-takers a nice way to put all of Antigua in the background.

spend a whole day here, watching artists set up on corners, street vendors hawking food or souvenirs, and tourists from across the world taking it all in. Volcán Fuego, looming in the background, may erupt, sending billows of ash high up into the sky. Late morning and afternoon, some cafes are open for alfresco dining. By evening, there's music and the lights have come on to illuminate the cathedral. The crowds have changed a bit; there are fewer grandparents and more teens. A vibrant electricity hangs in the air long after the sun goes down, but by midnight expect the plaza to be quiet, if not empty, and if you're here later, you may only find a cat or two, stalking through the shadows.

Antigua After Dark

VIBRANT, WELCOMING AND FUN

There's all sorts of things to do during the day here, but nights are just as fun. A night on the town can be anything from quietly enjoying wine or an aperitif with friends, to hitting a dance club and meeting rowdy strangers. One of the best aspects of nightlife here, whether it's a bar or club, is just how international it is. Pick five people at random and they're likely all from different countries, possibly different continents. So Antigua's a delightful spot to plan for some nights out, especially if you've been in the smaller highlands

Making chocolate

 WHERE TO STAY IN ANTIGUA

Tzunun Hostel
A friendly, small hostel with rooms along a long central courtyard. **$**

The Purpose Hostel
Views from the open-air terrace can't be beat, and the staff are welcoming and kind. **$**

Tropicana Hostel
Known for its rooftop bar, this is a party hostel, so come here for new friends, not sleep. **$**

POYNTON27/SHUTTERSTOCK ©

Antigua after dark

CASA TROCCOLI

This liquor store, restaurant and wine bar sits in a fascinating storefront that was started by the Troccoli family in 1903. The walls of Casa Troccoli are now lined with hundreds of bottles of tempting liquor, most of it higher end, so if you're searching for a bottle of something special to take home, this is the place. But it's worth a browse just to see the delightful bygone-era memorabilia, such as old scales, cabinets and a cash register. Dusty barrels top the liquor shelves. There's a lovely sense that you've stepped back in time the moment you cross the threshold.

areas where things are as dead as a door nail when dinner's done. There's a lot happening in and around the plaza, and some may just enjoy the view with a glass of wine in hand. The section just south of the plaza on **5th Avenida** is a nice spot to start, with several options right there to hop to...or from. Then from there, turn west and check out options on **6 Calle Poniente** (6th Street). West of the plaza, dance clubs will have you up until 1am, possibly later on weekends, but you won't find things open all night the way you do in places like Guatemala City. LBGTIQ+ travelers will find that while some spots specifically mention they are friendly, there's a general acceptance of all types and it's unlikely any Antigua bars or clubs would make you feel unwelcome.

Nim Po't Market

A GREAT PLACE TO PICK UP SOUVENIRS

If you're looking for souvenirs, you'd be hard-pressed to do better than Nim Po't: a sprawling warehouse near the Arco de Santa Catalina. It has a vast array of traditional Maya clothing, as well as hundreds of masks, wood carvings, kites, refrigerator magnets, assorted Maya deity Maximón figurines and edible gifts, such as locally roasted coffee and (of course!) chocolate. The *huipiles* (tunics), *cortes* (skirts) and other traditional garments are arranged by region, so it makes for a fascinating visit whether you're buying or not. If getting to Nim Po't is too much of a challenge, there's a smaller market on the town plaza that's also got – most likely – anything you're looking for. (Except Maximón, that is.)

GETTING AROUND

Antigua is a central nexus for transport to almost everywhere. The colorful, often crazily decorated buses leave from several spots in the city, or you can flag one down and hop on.

Beyond Antigua

Antigua is a delightful base for day trips and overnights to surrounding countryside towns, and for outdoor activities.

The city is cradled between several beautiful volcanoes, one of which, Fuego, is active and puffs out billows of ash several times a day. Hikers will thrill to ascend the peak of nearby Volcán Acatenango, where an overnight camp allows you to see the lava glowing bright against the darkness. However, there are lots of more sedentary thrills to be had for those who don't think summiting a 9000ft peak is quite their cup of tea. Quaint villages have delightful markets, there are rich historical landmarks and structures to visit, plus plant and animal life that you might not otherwise get to see.

TOP TIP

Most tours in Antigua will happen through a 'middleperson'. You can usually save quetzals by arranging things directly with the guides.

Volcán Fuego

BARGAIN ETHICALLY

When it comes to bargaining, some tourists may worry that they're being cheated or overcharged, and may haggle tooth-and-nail with a vendor who's spent a month hand-crafting an item that they're selling for mere pennies – a trade that's taken decades, or even generations, to learn. It's fine to check prices and to stay within your budget, but don't bargain just for the sake of it, and always be kind, respectful and ultimately ethical. Remember that for the person who's selling the item, it may be their only sale of the day and something that puts food on the table.

Ciudad Vieja

AMAZING, MESMERIZING AND COLORFUL

Just a 20-minute car ride from Antigua is the quaint, quiet town of **Ciudad Vieja**. It's a nice day trip out of its larger neighbor, and has a lovely main plaza overlooked by the brilliant white Parroquia Purísima Concepción, founded in 1534, with ornate decoration on the exterior and a simple interior that's worthy of a peek. The town was flooded in 1541 when Volcán Agua's lake burst through the crater and emptied in a deluge, destroying everything below. Behind the church you'll enjoy checking out a lively produce market, refreshingly aimed at locals rather than tourists – you may feel almost as if you're in the way. Find fresh corn, grab chilies picked hours before and get a bag of crispy green beans, but don't expect to find T-shirts with cutesy slogans on them or magnets saying 'I Love Antigua.'

While there, check out the combination museum, market and workshop that is the **Casa del Tejido Antiguo**, where you can find demonstrations of backstrap loom weaving techniques and learn about the designs woven into the fabrics. (They'll even pick you up in Antigua if you make a reservation!)

Not too far away, between San Antonio Aguas Calientes and Ciudad Vieja, is **Valhalla Macadamia Farm**, where you can tour the tree farm and learn everything you want to know about the world's most luxurious nut. Over 300 species are grown here, and the shop sells oils, cosmetics, and of course nuts.

Exploring the World of Coffee

COFFEE, AVOCADOS AND MORE

Visiting a coffee *finca* (plantation) is a unique way to see everything that happens behind the scenes when you sip that delicious cup of morning latte. It's a surprisingly complex process that begins long before the cherries (the name for ripe coffee beans) are picked. Coffee grows best in a mix of sun and shade, so the farms often use both shade trees such as avocados or citrus, and leafy trees that will still let some light reach the coffee plants below. If you tour one of these places, you'll learn the differences between the Robusta and Arabica varieties (hint, Robusta is more hardy, as in more *robust*), and then you'll get to see the various processes used to ferment the harvested beans and get them ready for roasting. Those processes vary depending on the flavor profile, but they all involve drying out the beans in some fashion. Finally, they are roasted, and this is what determines the final strength

 BEST ARTISAN MARKETS

Mercado de Artesanías Antigua
This Antigua market has locally made crafts and textiles.

Mercado de Artesanías San Antonio Aguas Calientes
Featuring mostly locally made backstrap loom textiles in San Antonio Aguas Calientes.

El Mercadito Antigua
On the main plaza, this densely packed 'mini market' has a vast range of textiles and other souvenirs.

Parroquia Purísima Concepción

AVOCADO, AVOCADO...

If coffee's not your cup of tea, well, perhaps avocados are? A tour of a nearby avocado farm such as **Earth Lodge** will begin with some discussion of the farm's specific ownership, founding and harvesting, and then you'll likely get to hike a bit and see the trees, forests and fields. If they're ripe, you might even get to harvest an avocado yourself. Regardless, you'll learn all about this incredible fruit (Yes! It's a fruit, not a vegetable!) and perhaps sample some tasty avocado recipes when the tour ends. Avocados almost never grow naturally anymore because their natural propagation was via the digestive tract of the now-extinct giant ground sloth, which roamed all over the Americas about 13,000 years ago.

of the coffee: how bitter and dark versus smooth and mellow it is. Tours will include a variety of tastings and, of course, a shop where you can buy some for yourself or as a tasty souvenir for that coffee-lover in your life back home.

Hiking Pacaya

ROAST MARSHMALLOWS ON LAVA

If you've made s'mores at a campfire after a long day of hiking before, you'll love the chance to roast marshmallows over hot lava rocks atop **Volcán Pacaya**. This volcano erupted spectacularly in March of 2020, sending rivers of molten rock pouring down its sides; rock that's still warm today, several years later. It's a delightful hike, though the less active can rent mules or horses for the journey, and at the top your guide will pull out the sticks and confections, and you get to hunt around

 WHERE TO STAY AT A FINCA

Finca San Cayetano
A delightful spot to stay, with stunning views of the volcanoes. **$$$**

Finca Filadelfia
North of Antigua, this is a coffee finca with tasty breakfast and a tour. **$$$**

Finca El Pilar
Also known as Antigua Mountain Trail. Camping with good trails and great birding opportunities. **$**

Volcán Pacaya

SAY 'NO' TO FUEGO

If you hike the very popular (and well-worth it!) Volcán Acatenango and camp overnight, chances are you'll be offered an option to cross the ridge and get closer to Volcán Fuego. It's tempting, as social media is full of incredible photos of lava erupting, and who wants to miss out on that? What the guides do not say is that the area you'll visit can be hit with lava bombs as large as a small car. The area is *not* safe and access is *not* approved, yet people keep going. Know if you go that this is extremely dangerous and no scientist would recommend getting that close.

for a spot still hot enough to toast them. It's a delightful entertainment, especially with kids. If you feel like something a little more substantial, there's even a pizza oven up there, where you can purchase what might be the world's most expensive pizza for the low, low price of just US$35 for a small pie, $55 for a larger one. Ouch.

The only other painful aspect of the hike is that this lava is sharp, and you do not want to fall. Make sure you have good, sturdy footwear and take your time walking across the lava flow. After roasting marshmallows and/or eating a slice of pizza, most will continue hiking and summit the nearby peak of **Cerro Hoja de Queso**, which overlooks the lovely valley below. After that, it's a steep and somewhat manure-strewn descent. Those mules just don't know any better.

GETTING AROUND

Getting to some of the farther spots around Antigua in a *tuk-tuk* might be a stretch, but then again, it's doable in a pinch. A taxi or bus might be just as good.

PANAJACHEL

This quirky town has a reputation as a hippie hangout but there's a lot more to do and see than just smell the patchouli. For starters, it's one of the few areas in Guatemala where men still wear the traditional *traje* (outfit) of the region: a pair of simple, backstrap-loom-woven pants, a shirt, a cowboy hat of some kind and, almost always, a man-bag slung over the shoulder. It's unmistakable, unforgettable and endearing. The town was visited by explorers Stephens & Catherwood as they journeyed through Guatemala, and there's a lovely church they mention that's worth a visit. Thanks to tourism, there's a host of coffee spots and restaurants, and one can grab *lanchas* (small motorboats) across the lake to the other shoreline cities. One thing you *won't* be is alone: it's a tourist town that's very much on the map, so plan accordingly.

Panajachel ● ✪ Guatemala City

TOP TIP

You'll pay about four times the cost of a public shared boat ride to get a private one, but the trade-off is time: private boats take 20 to 30 minutes to your destination versus up to two hours for a shared boat to go from port to port.

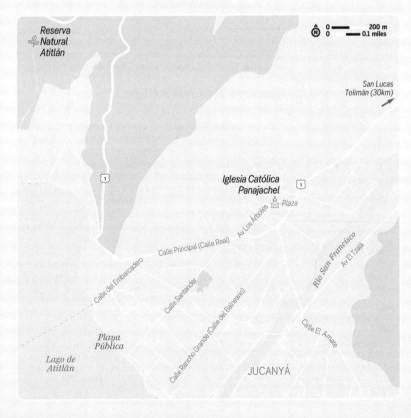

Reserva Natural Atitlán

San Lucas Tolimán (30km)

Iglesia Católica Panajachel

🏛 Plaza

Av Los Árboles

Calle Principal (Calle Real)

Río San Francisco

Av El Tzalá

Calle del Embarcadero

Calle Santander

Calle Rancho Grande (Calle del Balneario)

Calle El Amate

Playa Pública

Lago de Atitlán

JUCANYÁ

0 — 200 m
0 — 0.1 miles

Life by the Lake

SIMPLE PLEASURES AT THEIR BEST

Whether or not you subscribe to Lago de Atitlán's spiritual or rejuvenating powers, there's something undeniably refreshing about living in a place that wows you from morning until night with its beauty. **Panajachel** is one of those spots, and the simple luxury of being able to sip a cup of freshly ground coffee while looking out at morning sunlight sparkling on the lake's surface, with the cinder cones of the volcanoes all around, makes your heart leap, and not just from the jolt of caffeine.

As busy and bustling as the town is, there's something calming and tranquil here too, so what you find here will depend on who you are. Some like to wake early, as the first fingers of dawn are stretching themselves across the sky, and walk to the water's edge, perhaps accompanied by a friendly street dog or two. There you'll surprise ducks as you wait for the first rays of the sun to shine. Or perhaps you're a day person, finding time to bask by the shoreline or chat with newfound friends over a cup of steaming latte. Perhaps you need to be on the water, not just next to it, in a kayak or canoe, or stand-up paddleboard. Perhaps you're here to peruse the many bustling street markets in hopes of finding souvenirs. Or perhaps for you, the best time is sunset, as the stars start to pop out above an ever-darkening lake that's swallowed up by lavender, then purple, then midnight blue. Sip coffee or grab a cocktail, chat with friends and feel a part of something big and vast and beautiful. That's the experience of lakeside life in Panajachel.

Reserva Natural Atitlán

OUTDOOR HIKING AND ACTIVITIES

You can stay overnight at the **Reserva Natural Atitlán**, but many visitors come just for the day. The park turned hotel has a number of different activities and if you get bored with the lake, why not hop into the jungle for an hour or two? Hiking trails run throughout the park, some going down to the beach and others crisscrossing over a ravine via suspension bridges. Hikes offer the chance to see wildlife that people who've come here by bus directly from Guatemala City might miss otherwise: spider monkeys, *pisotes* (coatis) and a variety of birds. Some of the trails wind through a coffee grove.

The most popular activity, however, is the zipline: two different levels of speed allow for both timid beginners and adrenaline junkies to have fun, and they can even make special arrangements for people who are mobility-impaired. For those

SUNRISE AT PANAJACHEL

Of all Panajachel's pleasures, seeing sunrise may be the best, and one of the nicest spots is right by the lakeshore and at the public boat landing. The streets are empty except for the dogs, and the contrast with the bustle of the evening or day is striking. But even more striking is the sight of Volcán Fuego, far in the distance to the east, puffing up an ash cloud with a backdrop of fiery yellow or gold as the sun comes up. Sights like this make it easy to see why the Maya were such sun worshippers. And you may become one too, after seeing sunrise at Panajachel.

 WHERE TO STAY IN PANAJACHEL

Hotel Jabel Tinamit
Not on the water, but the quiet garden and rooftop terrace make for a lovely getaway. **$$**

Hostel Jardin
A well-situated youth hostel with dorms and private rooms near the water. **$**

Porta Hotel del Lago
Right on the water, this hotel has a pool and great views of the volcanoes. **$$$**

Panajachel

STEPHENS & CATHERWOOD IN PANAJACHEL

Stephens and Catherwood (p39) stayed for a time at a convent near the **Iglesia Católica Panajachel**, waiting for a friend of theirs to visit them from across the lake. He never arrived, so at one point the two men tried to cross the lake themselves in a small canoe and recount getting nearly stranded by some strong winds that picked up and carried them far from shore. This area did not have Maya ruins, but the church is beautiful and worth a visit if you're a fan. For more of their incredible journey, pick up a copy of *Incidents of Travel in Central America, Chiapas and Yucatán*.

who aren't comfortable ziplining on their own, a two-person zip can be done with an experienced instructor. And as if that weren't enough, there are even curious cable bikes, which will let you ride through the jungle canopy suspended on a bicycle. Just don't look down.

Those who aren't up for the in-the-air experience above the canopy may find that the butterfly garden is more their speed. This walk-in dome allows for hundreds of butterflies to live within the enclosure, and you'll be able to get close-up views of several prized species, such as orange monarchs and the bright iridescent blue morphos.

VOLCANO TOURS

If you want to learn about the area, look for Matt Purvis, aka Matt the Geologist of Geo Travel Guatemala (p188), and take one of his geology-based hiking tours.

GETTING AROUND

You'll likely be using a *lancha* (small motorboat) to get around most of the time if you're heading to lakeside villages. For those driving, be aware that the roads here are very steep and have multiple hairpin turns. Use the engine to brake, and it's common (and polite) to beep the horn before going around blind corners. If you circle the lake, be aware that a portion of the road between San Pedro La

Laguna and Santiago Atitlán has issues with masked, armed bandits; ask in the former for a free (tips are appreciated) police escort to avoid problems. New road construction may help to eliminate that but it's best not to take chances; ask at the police station for current, up-to-date info, and decide from there what feels right to you.

Beyond Panajachel

- Sololá
- Mirador del Lago Atitlán
- Panajachel
- San Antonio Palopó

Cornfields and cows, fields and farmland; there's not a lot here for tourists, but it sure is beautiful.

The rural beauty of this area can't be overstated, but it isn't usually a place where tourists stop except to snap a photo of the landscape. The nearby town of Sololá is your biggest 'metropolis' and can feel like one after spending time in the quiet, quaint lakeside villages. It's mostly a working-class town, but if you find the tourist-heavy towns at the lake are getting tiresome, you can return here to remember you're in Guatemala, and perhaps you'll again be the only foreigner in the crowd. There are cathedrals to look at, colorful buses zip by and coffee 'cherries' ripen into crimson on the trees.

TOP TIP

Use the engine brake to slow your car on the steep hills, and beep before going around the hairpin turns.

Maya cemetery, Sololá

IMAGEBROKER/ALAMY STOCK PHOTO ©

Sololá Market

Take in Sololá

WORKING-CLASS CITY WITH GREAT VIEWS

Sololá is often overlooked by the vast scores of tourists (usually on tour buses) who zip past it to get to the shoreline towns like Panajachel, but you'll pay far less staying here, and guess what? It's got a great view and some nice sights. The town also has a fun, vibrant authenticity that makes it worth stopping at, if only for the afternoon or a night. Its location at the top of the caldera makes it a better spot to do driving trips from, as you don't have to start and end with a hair-raising, knuckle-whitening slope into Panajachel. In **Parque Centro America**, the town's main square, the beautiful town hall lends itself to great photographs, or visit the delightful **Parroquia Nuestra Señora de la Asunción**. Sololá Market is a bustling spot to get fresh produce and watch the buses' organized chaos as they stop, shouting for passengers, and then rumble off in clouds of dust and exhaust. If you've got time, check out the **Museo Sololá**, where you'll find photos and memorabilia commemorating Sololá founders and history.

Though there are exceptions, most locals speak Kaqchiquel. If you want to learn one of the 23 non-Spanish languages spoken in Guatemala, doing a homestay or spending time in Sololá is an excellent place to start.

Visit a Pottery Studio

ATITLÁN'S DELIGHTFUL POTTERY

All over Guatemala you'll likely notice Atitlán-style pottery in the markets and shops. The delightful ware is easy to spot: it's

MIRADOR DEL LAGO DE ATITLÁN

Drivers coming into Panajachel will find that it's hard to see the lake until suddenly – wow! – it's looming vastly there in front of you. At a particularly scenic hairpin turn there's a pullout, **Mirador del Lago Atitlán**, for a few cars and a nice vista from the steep hilltop of that beautiful Atitlán blue. There's even that all-important thing, the *baño*, for those in 'need.' You can enjoy other views as you head down, but keep in mind that pulling off to the side at random places can be a serious hazard to the traffic ahead and behind you, so do so with extreme care.

 WHERE TO EAT AROUND PANAJACHEL

Chero's Bar Pupusería
A dive bar, offering delicious *pupusas*, a filled tortilla that's a Central American specialty. $

The Little Spoon
A delightful breakfast/lunch stop that's got a beautiful third-floor terrace with rooftop views. $$

Hana
Longtime Japanese restaurant serving sushi, gyoza and noodles in a relaxed setting. $$

MAYAN KE

Of the studios around the lakeshore, the most famous is Mayan KE, the one that started it all. The 'KE' stands for Ken Edwards, who arrived in Lago de Atitlán decades ago and began a small pottery studio in **San Antonio Palopó**. As business grew, he began teaching others in the town how to do the craft, and as is the case with many arts, these apprentices started their own studios once they'd mastered the techniques. The distinctive pottery is so common that many visitors assume it was a traditional art passed down through the centuries. Not so.

Pottery studio

hand-painted, often with blues and greens. While some pottery is made elsewhere, even as far away as Mexico's Puebla, chances are this area's work will be from an Atitlán studio.

You can visit the studios, and depending on what's going on at the time, you'll see all aspects of the work that's done to craft these bowls, cups, mugs, salt shakers and figurines. If you're lucky, you'll even see them adding the hand-painted designs before glazing. It's a painstaking process that involves a lot of skill. Artists start by learning the process on small, simple pieces, then as they develop their brushwork, they move on to tackling the larger items such as plates or bowls. You'll notice that the glazes often look nothing like they do after firing: when wet, they often appear more like colored mud, opaque and dull, and often completely different colors than how they'll be once they come out of the kiln. For example, a bright blue cobalt might start out looking more like a pink goo. The magic happens as the ware is heated to 900°C. Purchasing items at the studio itself can often mean lower prices, and you can ask if they have a seconds rack for even more of a discount.

GETTING AROUND

Unless you're planning to circle the lake, a *tuk-tuk* or *lancha* (small motorboat) may be your best options if you don't have your own

vehicle. For a *lancha*, be sure to leave plenty of time if you're using the shared public ones.

LAGO DE ATITLÁN

Lago de Atitlán

Guatemala City

The bluest of blue water rimmed by volcanoes that seem tall enough to touch the sky, Lago de Atitlán is more than just a body of water or a part of a geography quiz. It's an experience, a purpose, a goal, a destination. It's a world all its own, and whether you're there looking down from mountain vistas or speeding over its surface toward a shoreline town, the lake has the power to inspire, awe and thrill that few places in the world can match. Simultaneously a barrier and a method for transportation, it is the first thing most people here think of when they arrive and the last thing they see when they leave. And it's what they miss, when they've left and returned home.

TOP TIP

Even if you're not an early riser, force yourself to see at least one sunrise, whether on a hike or from the shoreline. The sun rises behind Volcán Fuego, which often erupts fully backlit by the yellow glow of dawn. It's a spectacular sight you won't regret waking up for.

ATITLÁN YOGA RETREATS

Doron Yoga
This center in Tzununa offers retreats and yoga teacher training.

The Yoga Forest
A yoga *shala* that sits on a hillside, surrounded by trees but with views of Atitlán.

Eagle's Nest
A hotel dedicated to yoga and forms of dance.
Villa Sumaya Close to the lake shore, offering yoga studios, outdoor meditation areas, a dock and pool.

Hostel del Lago
A yoga-oriented hostel with inspiring views from its studio.

KESTERHU/SHUTTERSTOCK ©

Sunset, Lago de Atitlán

Yoga by the Shore

YOU'LL NEVER FEEL MORE CONNECTED

Yoga is, for many, far more than a form of exercise. It's a religion, a philosophy, a way to experience the world in a positive, life-affirming way.

Whether you've only just taken your first yoga class or you've been practicing poses for decades and are as flexible as a rubber band, yoga in the dazzling arena of **Lago de Atitlán** will delight, inspire and ground you. If you're the type who doesn't mind eyeballs, try bringing your mat to a flat area near the shoreline at sunrise or sunset, whichever best suits your personality.

Find a place where you can relax your mind and look out at the restorative energy of the volcanoes. Their symmetry, the way their curves drop smoothly into the lake. Make your poses mirror the landscape around you. Inhale. Exhale. Breathe deeply.

 GREAT SPOTS FOR COFFEE AROUND LAGO DE ATITLÁN

Café Loco Coffee Roasters
A Panajachel spot that delights with rich espressos and creamy lattes. **$**

Cafe Chuasinayi`
A small shop that roasts their own beans in San Pedro La Laguna. **$**

Coffee Eiffel Le Crepe
Get your crepes and cup of joe at this colorful Santiago Atitlán mainstay. **$**

If all that sounds too easy or humdrum, then take it to the next level by doing your poses on a stand-up paddleboard; just don't blame this writer if you fall in.

If public exercise isn't your cup of tea, try finding a hotel terrace or rooftop and you'll be able to get nearly the same vista as being right on the shore. Another option is a hotel with a dedicated yoga retreat, where you'll be able to devote much of your visit to mindfulness and your personal journey.

Atitlán Fishing

PRETEND YOU'RE HEMINGWAY

Okay, so maybe you *won't* pretend you're Ernest Hemingway, since there are no marlin in this landlocked, freshwater lake. No need to go all *Old Man and the Sea*.

But if you're the kind of person who longs to have a rod and reel in your hand when you're near the water, this is a beautiful place to while away a few hours while you cast.

Largemouth bass were introduced into the lake in hopes of promoting a sportfishing industry; however, that failed to happen and unfortunately, the ever-voracious bass promptly ate most of the indigenous fish. What this means is you can feel at ease removing a few of these predators from the waters.

Fishing is challenging not only because of the depth of the lake, estimated at over 1000ft, but because several parts of the lake benefit from volcanic warming, and allow bass that would normally only flourish near the surface to remain well below most anglers' ideal range.

It's still quite possible to catch up to five pounders using regular tackle. Popular times include sunrise and sunset, though this may be partly due to the lake being jaw-droppingly beautiful during those hours.

If you really want the local experience, see if you can get a local fisher to take you out in a dugout canoe so you can handline. Who knows, you may end up catching one so big that you can write a short story about it just like Hemingway did.

TO SWIM OR NOT TO SWIM...

Swimming is a popular activity in Lago de Atitlán, and you'll see plenty of locals enjoying a dip, or waist deep in the water washing their clothes. But before you take the plunge, remember that you just walked through a minefield of street dog droppings to get here, and those get washed into the lake with every single rain. That runoff isn't the only thing to consider since several towns allow their farmers and industries to bypass local water treatment and dump the effluent directly into the lake. If you do decide to swim, you'd be wise to keep your head above water and take a shower after you get out.

GETTING AROUND

Getting around, especially from village to village or onto the lake for some watersports or activities, will be all about a boat. You can use the public *lanchas* or opt for a private one, depending on your needs.

Lago de Atitlán

Rostro Maya

San Pedro
La Laguna

Beyond Lago de Atitlán

A string of interesting towns and villages dot Lago de Atitlán's shores like a string of pearls.

You might expect that it's a 'seen one, seen them all' experience when you hop from spot to spot across the lake. After all, they're only a 20-minute ride as the crow flies from each other. But no, Lago de Atitlán's communities are as different from each other as people on a commuter bus. Take the time to explore and you'll find many of them consider their birthplace more important to their identity than being Guatemalan. What this means for the tourist is that you can enjoy the sense of excitement and discovery in each of these towns, despite the fact that they're all a quick boat ride from your hotel.

TOP TIP

If time is of the essence, it's worth opting for a private boat to your destination.

View from Rostro Maya (p188)

INGO BARTUSSEK/SHUTTERSTOCK ©

MILOSZ MASLANKA/SHUTTERSTOCK ©

San Pedro La Laguna

San Pedro La Laguna

VIBRANT, HIPSTER AND HIPPIE

San Pedro La Laguna (aka San Pedro) is located at about the 7pm mark if you think of Atitlán as a clock (albeit a rather squished clock). It's in the shadow of the beautiful Volcán San Pedro and one of the most picturesque of Atitlán's towns. As such, it's a tourist mecca, filled with tattoo parlors and tourist-oriented stores selling items that cost half as much in an authentic market. But the trade-off is a delightful range of restaurants and coffee houses where everything from Israeli food to Japanese sushi can be found.

There are delightfully narrow streets, all of them one way, making for frustrated drivers. Tucked as it is on the west side, the town isn't as optimal for sunsets as you might think, but it has a great view of sunrise, especially if you're atop the Rostro Maya at 5am. **Playa Xetawall**, where the last finger of land pokes into the lake, is an interesting spot to poke around and beachcomb while walking your dog. People do swim, though the trash on the shoreline gives one pause, and there are other things to consider if you plan to wade or dip (p185). Many people come to San Pedro expecting to spend a day or two here, and find themselves coming back frequently...or nev-

DRIVING, TUK-TUKS & PARKING...OH, MY!

No question about it, whether you've driven all over Guatemala for decades or just arrived, driving in San Pedro is a challenge. Many streets are one-way, some are mislabeled and some begin as roads and narrow into pedestrian-only passageways. Not to mention the cobbles and steep slopes. Your best bet is to park on the outskirts of town and then hire a *tuk-tuk*, which will zip you from spot to spot far more easily than if you try to navigate on your own. Those arriving by boat will find a squadron of colorful *tuk-tuks* waiting at the dock. If you're staying at a hotel, be sure to ask in advance about the parking.

 WHERE TO EAT IN SAN PEDRO LA LAGUNA

Sababa
Hip and trendy, this Israeli brunch spot is great for shakshuka and other specialties. **$$**

Café 'Las Cristalinas'
Get excellent coffee, fruit bowls and sandwiches at this popular spot. **$$**

El Clover
It looks like an Irish bar, but actually has a wide range of local and foreign options. **$**

I LIVE HERE: THE ROSTRO MAYA

Matt Purvis, founder of Geo Travel Guatemala, (Geo TravelGuatemala. com) shares his thoughts about hiking the Rostro Maya.

The sunrise over Lago de Atitlán from the Rostro Maya is usually glorious, but immediately after sunrise, the glare becomes a bit harsh. Most tour groups head straight back to town as soon as the sun is up, but if you'd like to spend a bit more time enjoying the view (and getting better photos!), opt for a later start. Beginning the hike after breakfast means you avoid the crowds and reduce the glare, but don't leave too late, as clouds may start to form. An 8am departure from San Pedro is ideal, returning around lunchtime.

Women's weaving collective

er leaving at all. Some opt for Spanish lessons as an excuse to stay, others find yoga studios and still others learn about weaving from one of the delightful women's collectives here.

Hiking the Rostro Maya

AMAZING ANY TIME OF DAY

If you spend time in San Pedro, at some point you really must find yourself atop a peak looking down at the lake below you. The **Rostro Maya** (aka Indian's Nose, which is now regarded as being an offensive term) is one of the most popular. You ascend one of the chins, you look out from the upper lip, and finally arrive on the 'nose,' often at sunrise, for a breathtaking view of the lake below and the volcanoes all around. If you're lucky, Volcán Fuego will burp or puff in the distance, sending out a billow of ash as the sun makes its appearance above the horizon and a new day begins. But come here later and the view is just as lovely, the water bluer and more dazzling without the glare.

WHERE TO STAY IN SAN PEDRO LA LAGUNA

Mikaso
At the end of a long walkway, this quiet spot is right on the lake and has beautiful views from the terrace. **$$**

Hotel Adulam
Inexpensive and clean, this hotel is close to the center, yet far enough away for quiet. **$$**

Mr. Mullet's Party Hostel
If you want to be up until 4am and get plastered, you'll do just fine here. **$**

Be aware that hikers will be on private land and that trails have been made by farmers or landowners – they have a right to ask for a fee to let you pass. Some visitors mistake this for banditry, which while not impossible, is usually not the case. The best way to experience Rostro Maya is to go with a guide, someone known to locals who already pays them a usage fee. It is also a great way to learn more about the plants, animals and landscape; things you might miss if you hike it alone.

Women's Weaving Collectives

FASCINATING FABRICS

One of the best, most-rewarding experiences you can have in the Atitlán area is to see – or even participate in – one of the many women's weaving collectives. These are wonderful organizations that often offer work to single mothers and women with little or no education, teaching them a trade that helps them provide for themselves and their families.

The process is fascinating, involving a bewildering number of steps that start with harvesting the cotton at the right time of year. It's spun by hand into thread; the threads are then dyed using over 40 natural ingredients – barks, leaves and so on – to produce a rainbow of stunning colors.

The threads are tied into loose skeins, and then colors are selected and the warp is wound out onto a rack. The most challenging part is when the threads are separated. Finally the weft thread is wound onto a spindle, and then the whole thing is strapped around the back, and weaving begins.

It often takes an experienced weaver a month to make a length of cloth - more if the pattern is intricate or challenging.

Demonstrations are available and making your own scarf may take a full two days. If that's too much of a time commitment, stop in, chat with the weavers and feast your eyes on the textures, colors and clothes.

MORE ON TEXTILES

To learn more about Guatemalan fabrics and types of dress, and to find out where to get more information on textiles, see page 248.

BEST NATURAL DYES

Say natural dye and most people think of bland beige, greens or yellows. But some surprisingly vivid colors come from nature as well.

Cochineal
Made from parasitic cactus insects, this dye produces a bright crimson prized for centuries.

Indigo
A plant known throughout the world for its deep blue.

Hibiscus
The flowers of the hibiscus plant make a beautiful purple-pink.

Logwood
A dark black dye comes from this tree.

Achiote
The seeds of this plant produce a vivid red.

GETTING AROUND

Tuk-tuks are the way to go, but San Pedro is small enough that even that seems excessive at times: walking will do just fine.

SANTIAGO ATITLÁN

On the southeastern side of Lago de Atitlán and tucked beside a cove that was created when Volcán San Pedro erupted, Santiago Atitlán is perhaps the most authentic of all the lakeshore towns. It has a quirky mix of gritty Guatemala, touristy shops and traditional ways that span centuries. There's beautiful architecture, lovely lakeside views, and some mountains, fields and forests that you won't see elsewhere. Its proud people are fiercely independent, and were persecuted during the Guatemalan civil war. Among the incidents, government troops from Guatemala City fired on an unarmed crowd, killing several people and straining the already bad relationships between the revolutionaries and the establishment. If you've spent time across the lake studiously building up your knowledge of Kaqchiquel, guess what? Here they speak Tz'utujil, so you're back to square one.

Santiago
Atitlán ● ✪ Guatemala
City

TOP TIP

You've got to visit the famous smoking god, Maximón, or you're missing out. You can hop on a *tuk-tuk* and take a 30-60 minute tour that will (be sure to ask!) include a visit to this quirky character, as well as other tourist spots such as ones listed below.

THE RUIN OF CHUITINAMIT

Just a short boat ride across the quiet inlet of Santiago Atitlán is an unexcavated Maya ruin known as 'Chuitinamit, Sololá' (not to be confused with the Quiché ruin). The site is situated on a hillside and features a variety of structures, such as a ball court, stelae and residences. If you ascend to the top of the site, you'll have some nice views of Santiago Atitlán from across the water. It's a small ruin, certainly no Tikal, but it's a pleasant way to spend an afternoon if you're looking for some outdoor fun that gets you out of town.

Maximón, the Smoking God

HAVE A BEER WITH A GOD

Of all Guatemala's traditions, the one that strikes visitors as the most unusual is that of Maximón, the smoking god. Festooned with scarves, sunglasses, a cowboy hat and of course a cigarette, he resides for a year in a particular house with alcohol and cigarettes nearby.

On either side, caretakers (his *cofradía*) sit, smoking and drinking themselves, and in the evenings, Maximón 'sleeps' in a protected area, such as a closet or attic. Only then can the attendants leave.

Visit Cofradía Maximón by first getting a *tuk-tuk* ride to the current abode. It changes yearly. You'll find that many drivers will want to up their fee and take you on a tour of the town as well, so be aware of that. If you just want to see Maximón, make that clear at the beginning and bargain for a there-and-back fee that isn't inclusive of the other spots on the tour. When you reach the smoking god, you'll need to wait outside while the driver checks to see if you have permission. You'll also be asked to pay a small fee for the privilege of entry. Some visitors bring cigarettes or alcohol as well, so you can impress the minders if you're prepared.

And then, you are ushered in to see Maximón. No description will fully express how unusual and odd this effigy is; astonishing, wonderful and bizarre. It's a reminder of how rich and varied traditions can be and how important it is that the world be protected from ubiquity.

If you pray to Maximón for anything, pray that he remains as he is; always revered, cigarette in his mouth and bottles of liquor at his feet, with vassals at his sides.

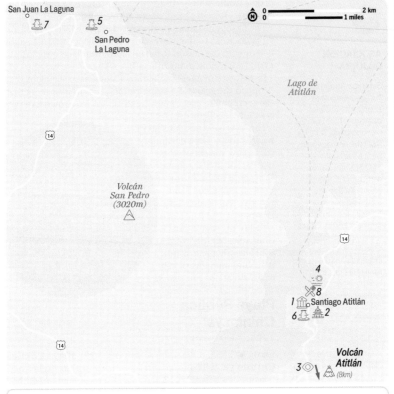

SIGHTS
1 Asociación Cojolya
2 Cofradía Maximón
3 Parque de Paz
4 Playa Pública Chinim ya'

ACTIVITIES, COURSES & TOURS
5 Atitlán Women Weavers
6 Batz – Tejidos y Bordados
7 Casa Flor Ixcaco

EATING
8 Restaurante Café Arte

Parque de Paz

REMEMBERING THE WAR

During the civil war, Santiago Atitlán became the first village in the country to succeed in expelling the army, following the horrific massacre of 13 villagers on December 2, 1990. The events leading up to it and the causes and consequences of the war are far too complex to detail in a short paragraph. But the situation in Guatemala was dire, and here in Santiago Atitlán, as in other parts of the country, it was routine that

 BEST ATITLÁN-AREA WEAVING COLLECTIVES

Atitlán Women Weavers
This San Pedro collective was started by Anita Cortez, a teacher who runs a Maya cooking school next door.

Casa Flor Ixcaco
Located in San Juan La Laguna, this collective has demonstrations and a nice storefront.

Batz – Tejidos y Bordados
A Santiago Atitlán cooperative with textiles and gifts.

ASOCIACIÓN COJOLYA

Santiago Atitlán is (yet another!) spot to enjoy incredible backstrap loom woven workmanship. Coming from the docks, you'll pass a vast gauntlet of shops and stores displaying a panoply of colorful fabrics, including shirts, pants, table runners, blankets and more. It's worth spending time here if you have any interest in textiles, but for a more in-depth look, seek out the Asociación Cojolya, a collective of women weavers where you can learn weaving techniques and see a variety of types of clothing, as well as purchase items and support the collective. There's nothing wrong with buying from a roadside shop, but knowing a little about the person who made the item adds value to the souvenir.

people would simply 'disappear' at the hands of the encamped army, often in places where ethnic tensions were high.

The flashpoint came when a crowd of peacefully protesting villagers went to the army with their grievances. Instead of listening to the mayor, the army fired into the crowd, killing 13 and wounding many others.

It was a key moment in the war, a moment so atrocious that it tipped the scales. So many people rose up in protest that the army had to leave, marking the first time a town had successfully rebelled.

The site of this massacre, where troops were encamped, is now the small, somber Parque de Paz, about 1km south of the Parque Central along the road toward San Pedro La Laguna.

Today it seems unthinkable that this event could have happened, but it's a vital reminder of how easily situations can change.

MORE ON THE CIVIL WAR

The Guatemalan civil war tore the country apart, hitting rural villages especially hard. Santiago Atitlán was the first to successfully resist. For more about the civil war, see page 238.

Playa Pública Chinim ya'

A PUBLIC BEACH AND MORE

Chances are – unless you're driving – the **Playa Pública Chinim ya'** will be your first Santiago Atitlán experience, because it's where the *lanchas* and ferries land. You'll hop off the boat onto creaky docks and then be surrounded with one of the most unique spots in town.

You may see people washing clothes in the shallows. Fishermen tend to nets or shoot the breeze with one another. Tourists amble about as they wait for a boat. All with the beautiful volcano backdrop behind.

If there's a festival, you may see families out in the public grilling area fixing lunch or snacks, aromas wafting your way from the sizzling meats and veggies.

The pavilion, with murals on the stairs, is another unique view spot. It's not particularly high but gives a bit more of a commanding view of the lake below or the city behind.

If you're hungry, consider a quick bite at **Restaurante Café Arte**, steps away from the water.

 PLACES TO EAT IN SANTIAGO ATITLÁN

Cetcafe	**La Antigua**	**Restaurante Café Arte**
Casual cafe with great coffee, surprising sandwiches and entrée options, and fresh-made donuts. **$**	Burgers, wraps and breakfast items in a clean cafe near the main plaza. **$$**	Tasty spot near the docks with eclectic decor and a variety of fusion food. **$$**

Maximón (p190)

For many, the best part of arrival in sweet Santiago Atitlán is passing through the narrow market street, lined on both sides with a rainbow of colorful textiles. It's hard not to find something that simply has to come home with you. There's everything from handmade backstrap loom work, *huipiles* and *cortes,* to souvenir T-shirts with slogans that will either make you smile or groan. Ceramics, woodenware and, of course, sun hats in a variety of styles are all on display.

SAINT JAMES THE APOSTLE CHURCH

In Santiago Atitlán's central square is one of the oldest churches in the region, built in 1547 in honor of Saint James the Apostle. The exterior facade is bright white and not particularly ornate compared with many others, but is worthy of a peek...or a selfie. Inside, you'll find a plain church with simple wooden pews, but a few of the altar relics are quite decorative, and there is some impressive woodwork. Along the walls are wooden statues of the saints, each of which has new clothes made by local women every year. At the front there are three colonial altarpieces that symbolize the three volcanoes around Santiago, which are believed to protect the town.

GETTING AROUND

Drivers will want to be cautious (p179) - this area is known to have bandits, but as road improvement continues, it's possible this problem may vanish in the near future. Before continuing, consider a (free) police escort, available by inquiring at the San Pedro police station. They will know the current situation and can advise you if an escort is necessary. Decide from there what feels right to you.

Beyond Santiago Atitlán

A quiet, beautiful and proud region with farmland and forests, where many live a lifestyle that's been the same for centuries.

There's a lot to see in the southeastern region that surrounds Santiago Atitlán, but it's often overlooked by tourists who stay in the more popular towns on the lakeshore. Getting out into the surrounding country can be a surprise for many – go just a few minutes and it's a bit like turning back time. You'll see farmers tilling fields using oxen and hoes, women carrying water on their heads and beautiful fields and farmland that provide only enough for these people to live. Further away, the volcano slopes begin and the climate changes, allowing for excellent hikes, coffee *fincas* and even reserves where the rare resplendent quetzal can be seen.

TOP TIP

This area is very infrequently visited by tourists, so be mindful that this may be some people's first chance to interact with foreigners.

Volcán Atitlán

BYRON ORTIZ/SHUTTERSTOCK ©

Resplendent quetzal

See a Resplendent Quetzal

GUATEMALA'S ELUSIVE NATIONAL BIRD

The resplendent quetzal is a reclusive, quiet relative of the trogon that was once found all over Guatemala and many other parts of Central America. It's one of the world's most spectacular birds, and one that many birders pine to add to their Life List. Hunting and habitat loss have reduced its range to just a few places, but one of them is up here on the slopes of **Volcán Atitlán**.

Seeing one is for many birders a true (pun intended) feather in their cap. Quetzals are not easy to find, but if you are lucky enough to see one, they're hard to miss: a large bird with brilliant green feathers and a red breast.

Birders may want to familiarize themselves with the three distinctive calls the bird makes, too. The males have spectacular tail feathers that are up to 3ft long and are used for impressing females during mating season.

Hikers will likely want to have a guide, as guides know exactly what to look for and can pick out a bird far faster than even the sharpest-eyed visitor.

Despite their bright plumage, quetzals blend in magically with the surroundings, so it's easy to miss them if you don't know precisely what you're looking for. In flight, however, they're unmistakable. The best time to see them is in the early morning when they come to feed on the fruits of certain cloud forest trees.

BEST VOLCANO HIKES ON THE SOUTH SIDE

Volcán Atitlán
The tallest, biggest and baddest volcano, with a peak at 11,598ft, and great birding.

Volcán San Pedro
This is a kinder, gentler volcano that separates San Pedro La Laguna and Santiago; it is 9,908ft high.

Volcán Tolimán
A middleweight volcano of 10,361ft between Volcán Atitlán to the south and Lago de Atitlán to the north.

 WHERE TO STAY BEYOND SANTIAGO ATITLÁN

Los Tarrales Nature Reserve
A beautiful hotel set in the midst of forested hills, with walking trails and a lovely pool. $$$

Los Andes Nature Reserve
Spectacular birding spot, with resplendent quetzal and azure-rumped tananger sightings possible. $$$

Finca San Agustin
A basic campground, convenient to the volcanoes, for those not needing a hotel. $

Rostro Maya (p188)

SAMABAJ

Volcanic activity wasn't just a problem millions of years ago. In 1998, a diver in Lago de Atitlán made a fascinating discovery: a Maya 'Atlantis' of sorts – an abandoned city, Samabaj, that now lies 50ft or so below the surface of the lake. Initially, this was discounted, but new excavation has shown it is an important archaeological discovery, and while you won't be able to get there (not without diving gear, anyway!) it's still fascinating to know that some of the area's history is there in the lake itself. It's believed that when the nearby Volcán San Pedro erupted around 300 BCE, it cut off the lake's outflow, causing the levels to rise precipitously. Eventually, the island had to be abandoned and has remained there, forgotten until now.

The Big Bang

A MASSIVE EXPLOSION

It may look like the fury of Volcán Fuego is far away and sometimes it's hard to imagine these placid lakeshores could ever be anything but peaceful, but geologists know otherwise. Stand on the peak of the Rostro Maya (p188) and look out around you. It's breathtaking, beautiful, serene. Now count the volcanoes: you'll see not one, not two, not even three...but eight near-perfect cinder cones looming up around you. Squint and take a moment to think of this in geologic time and you'll see it not as a serene spot but as a turmoil of ever-burbling tectonic forces.

Lago de Atitlán was formed not – as many incorrectly think – by a volcano erupting, but by a series of massive eruptions, ones so large they make Mount St. Helens look like a baby's breath. Some estimates claim the quantity of ash released was on the order of two hundred times what the largest volcano in recorded history, Krakatoa, put into the atmosphere. It happened quickly, either as a series of eruptions or as one catastrophic event, and the crust of the earth collapsed into the hollow space below. And if you think this is all a thing of the past, think again: geology shows that this has happened at least three separate times in this region.

One last tip: look at the lake and find San Pedro. You'll see a smaller 'bump' coming off the smooth cone of the larger volcano: that's known as a parasitic cone. It forms off the side of a larger, sometimes dormant volcano.

GETTING AROUND

At the time of writing, there are still reports of bandits operating on the road between San Pedro La Laguna and Santiago Atitlán. They wait at a section of road that is as yet unpaved, and are masked and armed. No joking around. To avoid trouble, it's best to arrange for a police escort in San Pedro. It's free (though tipping is customary), and a motorcycle policeman will lead you down through to Santiago Atitlán. If you're driving in other parts of this area it's worth asking at police stations if there are any reports so you can decide what feels right to you, as this may happen in other areas as well.

HUEHUETENANGO

This is a bustling, working-class city that is often overlooked by tourists, yet there's a lot more here than initially meets the eye. The Parque Central is a fun, vibrant place, especially at festivals, with colonial-style architecture, throngs of people and tasty food stalls. The Catedral Templo de La Inmaculada Concepción sits on the park's southeast corner, with a lovely exterior and some interesting altars inside. The park also hosts a daily market, with food stalls, produce, piñatas and plasticware. (Need a set of nesting bowls in bright fluorescent colors? You'll find them here.)

Nearby, the enigmatic ruins of Zaculeu, just outside the city, are a quirky place to spend an afternoon, and there's a small museum on the ruin grounds as well. The town isn't going to be where you'll spend weeks or months, but it's not a bad spot to overnight as you go between places like Quetzaltenango and Nebaj.

Huehuetenango

Guatemala City

TOP TIP

Find a spot to stay near the plaza to make the most of your time here. You'll have your pick of restaurants, cafes, hotels and things to see and do. It's not a huge tourist town, so what's here is authentic Huehue. Enjoy!

9N

○ Chiantla

Zaculeu   Archaeological Park Zaculeu

7W

Reserva Natural

Cueva del Mamut

● Huehuetenango

9N

0 ———————— 4 km
0 ———————— 2 miles
Ⓝ

○ Malacatancito

MUSEO ZACULEU

If you get tired of walking around, check out the ruin's small museum, which has artefacts on display such as pottery and figurines, as well as a somewhat macabre cutaway showing a funerary vase burial. Though a replica, it shows clearly how the dead were placed in a fetal position and buried within large pots.

You'll also see – don't get confused and think they're excavation photos! – many black and white images showing scenes from when the ruin was used in a Tarzan movie. Modest might be too grand a word, but it's worth a peek. It's a small museum, so don't plan to spend more than about 30 minutes here. You'll easily take it all in within that time.

PETER MAERKY/SHUTTERSTOCK ©

Zaculeu

Zaculeu Ruin

UNIQUELY RESTORED BY UNITED FRUIT

Anyone who's visited some of Guatemala's other ruins will find the restoration of Zaculeu oddly unique, and that's because it was not done with the careful oversight of archaeologists, but rather (and rather bizarrely!) by the United Fruit Company. Thus, it has a distinctly different look and feel to it: structures are off the horizontal, they're usually cemented over and the land between ruins has been cleared and flattened, with the structures sticking out of what could otherwise be a football field.

Structures that are worth finding are the ballcourt, which is enormous, and the main pyramid (Estructura I), which is interestingly topped with columns. Unfortunately, it's hard to know what was original and what was 'creatively' restored by United Fruit.

 WHERE TO STAY IN HUEHUETENANGO

Hotel Zaculeu
This centrally located icon is stately, clean and reasonably priced. There's also on-site parking. **$$**

Royal Park Hotel
Close to the main plaza, shops and restaurants. Rooms may not be 'royal' but it's nice. **$$**

Hotel El Centro
A no-frills, inexpensive option for basic rooms, with tile floors and televisions. **$**

Delightfully, on sun-filled Saturdays or Sundays, it's full of locals, who come with their families to picnic or let their kids kick a ball around. You'll see grandmothers in full *traje* (traditional outfit) slowly climbing up to get a bird's-eye view from atop a pyramid.

If you care to strike up conversations, you'll find it's a welcoming place to meet new friends. Some may even ask if you'd mind being part of a selfie. It was one of the many sites visited by explorers Stephens and Catherwood, though when they visited in the 1840s, the site had no structures in shape enough to be drawn. From Zaculeu, the two would continue northward, leaving Guatemala and entering the state of Chiapas, Mexico.

Cueva del Mamut

A MAMMOTH FIND

On the outskirts of Huehuetenango a farmer was digging a well and came up with something totally unexpected: the bones of a mammoth, buried some 20ft underground. Even more interestingly, the bones showed evidence that the creature did not die from ripe old age, but was rather killed and eaten, and the carcass discarded in this spot after the humans were through.

This find shed light on an aspect of prehistoric Maya culture, one that might have deeper archaeological significance, but it's been set aside by science for the time being. Perhaps, given funding, more might be done with it.

Today you can visit the site, **Cueva del Mamut**, and look down on the bones from a covered enclosure. There's also a small museum. If he's there, the owner will be happy to give you a tour and discuss how he found the bones and the research that became of it.

Inside the humble museum are some various artefacts, such as mammoth molars (they're big, I tell you!) and items from other creatures, such as fossilized scales of a glyptodon, a kind of prehistoric armadillo. The walls have worn, with faded artist renderings of what some of the creatures might have looked like.

MISSING MAMMOTH MYSTERY

Interestingly enough, this is not the first time a mammoth was discovered in this area. In their wanderings, explorers John L Stephens and Frederick Catherwood write of mammoth bones found in a riverbank that eroded near the site of Zaculeu, and how they went to see these bones, which had been taken out of their river location and put somewhere in town. Yet mysteriously, these bones have disappeared. When the mammoth was discovered by the rancher, it was thought to be the first one found in this area, but it wasn't. Not unless Stephens and Catherwood were telling tall – no, make that *mammoth* – tales.

GETTING AROUND

Huehuetenango is amply served by express buses, and *tuk-tuks* zip around inside the city. To get to spots further away, you may need to plot the route carefully in shared minibuses, or find private transportation.

Beyond Huehuetenango

A sweet, quaint, quiet part of the country, away from the hustle and bustle.

Huehuetenango may seem like it's all traffic and exhaust, but get outside and you'll be able to stop and smell the flowers. There are lovely fields to explore, beautiful purples and yellows and pinks dot the landscape, and you'll spot abandoned shacks among the picturesque patchwork of cornfields. A few Maya ruins are out there to explore, and the pine-topped ridges are excellent for sunsets, but for the most part this is not heavily touristed and you'll be on your own. For many, that's the whole reason to spend additional time here. Whether you stay or go, always be respectful of people who may not have met many foreigners before.

Mirador de
Juan Dieguez
● Olaverri
Chiantla ●
Viejo

● Huehuetenango

TOP TIP

Unless you've arranged a homestay, Huehue will be your place to find restaurants and hotels.

Sunrise, Huehuetenango

BRUNO ADRIAN/SHUTTERSTOCK ©

Cows grazing in the mountains of Huehuetenango

 ## Chiantla Viejo

A REMOTE RAVINESIDE RUIN

Some key parts of **Chiantla Viejo** have already dropped off and been lost in the sheer ravine that protects it on one side, but the remaining structures are worthy of visiting for anyone with an interest in ticking off yet another ruin. Part of the fun is just getting here, up a winding mountain road with some sections so steep that you'll need a 4x4 to get over them.

When you reach the ruin itself, you'll find it's small, but interestingly, researchers believe that the ruin here was based in many ways on what existed in Zaculeu, with similar structures that were modified for the much smaller scale. So you may enjoy trying to figure out which structures match those of Zaculeu if you've already been there. There's a pyramid, a ball court (this has basically been bisected by erosion, unfortunately), and several other structures. This may have been one of the locations the Mam people were relocated to after the Spanish conquest. Researchers think perhaps this modest site was built from memory as a way to continue Mam traditions. Curiously, archives from the Spanish indicate Chiantla Viejo was burned by the Mam themselves around 1530 CE, showing that Maya traditions continued beyond the conquest. Much of that remains unclear, and new research may overturn those theories.

 ### THE MAM

The Mam kingdom's center was Zaculeu, near modern-day Huehuetenango. The kingdom extended to Quetzaltenango and as far as Chiapas, Mexico. The Mam were a dominant power in the region up until the Spanish came, though like all Maya civilizations of the time, their dominance was threatened by near-constant warfare with other competing kingdoms, such as the K'iche'. When the Spanish arrived, they laid siege to Zaculeu for months, eventually defeating the Mam through drought and starvation. Inside the city, survivors had been forced to eat the dead.

Today, Mam language is still spoken in many of these regions, especially in small towns and villages. Barriers and discrimination, both lingual and geographic, exist even today.

 WHERE TO EAT IN HUEHUETENANGO

Museo Café
A coffee shop with lots of interesting coffee memorabilia, knickknacks and photographs. $

La Tinaja
Dine here in a famous author's house more for the experience and decor than the food. $$

La Fonda de Don Juan
A 24-hour diner with wooden booths, chrome and cheap-yet-tasty food. $

CAFE DEL CIELO

You'll be out of luck if you're arriving for sunrise or sunset, but if you come to Mirador de Juan Diéguez Olaverri during the day, you'll have the option of a meal or a coffee at the aptly named Cafe del Cielo (Cafe of the Sky). It's got both indoor and outdoor seating and is open 8am to 5pm daily, with surprisingly tasty food considering that all too often, a place with a great view (and the view here is great!) can skimp on quality. The coffee and hot chocolate are particularly nice after shivering in the cold while waiting for the sunrise. The only shame is when fog rolls in, which it often does...obscuring that precious view.

VLOM7/GETTY IMAGES ©

Mirador de Juan Diéguez Olaverri

View From a Mirador

SUN WORSHIPPERS BRING YOUR CAMERAS

High above Huehuetenango is a line of steep cliffs that are impossible to miss if you're driving: you'll either come down through them as you arrive or they'll be looming ahead of you if you continue. If you're in a car with a small engine, plan on creeping up and 'enjoying' some hairpin curves along the way. This lookout spot, **Mirador de Juan Diéguez Olaverri**, is stunning, well worth the visit, and it's pretty any time of day. It's most popular, however, for sunrise, where you'll get even more atmospheric photos and possibly look out on a 'cloud sea' below you, as the sun has yet to burn off the valley's nighttime humidity. Far in the distance you'll even be able to make out some of Guatemala's cinder cones, including Volcán Tajumulco, the tallest mountain not only in Guatemala, but in all of Central America. Off to the southwest, it's striking at sunset.

Depending on whether you're alone or part of a number of others, the experience can be anything from a solitary vigil in honor of a new or passing day, or a boisterous party where you'll either make new friends or wish people would quiet down. There's an atmospheric farmhouse, long disused, which stands as a kind of landmark, a parking area, and several monuments. You may even get to befriend a passing sheep or two. But the real majesty here isn't what's on the peak, but what's there beyond it: the mountains, the sky and the sun.

GETTING AROUND

Steep hills and 360-degree hairpin turns make driving anywhere around Huehue a challenge. Take it slow, avoid driving at night and beep (it's polite, really!) when you're about to go around a blind corner. If you're not driving yourself, you'll need to inquire at your hotel for the best way to get to the *mirador* at sunrise, as it's not served frequently by public transportation.

QUETZALTENANGO

Perhaps the highlands' most charming city and certainly its largest, Quetzaltenango (also known as Xela) is a bustling, vibrant gem on the western side of Guatemala, surrounded by volcanoes that are often obscured by clouds. One moment, the massive cinder cone is there; the next, it's gone as if by magic. The proximity to volcanoes has played a more active part in the city's history, with an eruption as recent as the early 1900s causing death and destruction. Tourists come to enjoy the clean mountain air, the delightful crispness in the air – winter temperatures can dip below freezing! – and a relaxed, tranquil city vibe. It has a number of language schools and many people spend weeks or months here. The varied food scene, the great coffee and the lovely architecture all make it a top spot to visit, second only to Antigua in terms of popularity.

Quetzaltenango • Guatemala City

TOP TIP

As these are key festival days in Guatemala, it's no surprise that most restaurants close on Christmas Day and New Year's Day. If you're here during that time, plan ahead so you don't go hungry. Either ask at your hotel if they serve meals, or make alternate dining plans.

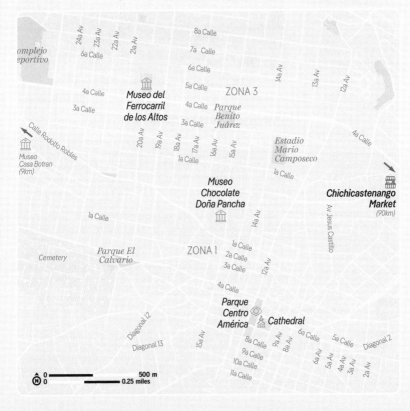

XELA, XELAJÚ OR QUETZALTENANGO?

This naming all gets pretty complex. The city of Quetzaltenango was originally known as Xelajú by the native Mam. Yet the Mam, by the time of Spanish contact, had themselves been conquered by neighboring K'iche' Maya, who annexed it into the region of Q'umarkaj. Yet when the K'iche' fell to the Spanish, the city (and all the other '...tenangos') were names used by the Nahuatl-speaking Maya who had allied themselves (if only temporarily) with Pedro de Alvarado. Today, many Guatemalans and in-the-know foreigners abbreviate Xelajú to Xela, which, if nothing else, is a little easier to spell.

Quetzaltenango

Parque Centro América

LOVELY ARCHITECTURE AND GREAT FOOD

Quetzaltenango's most iconic park, Parque Centro América was one of the spots visited by explorers Stephens and Catherwood, the latter of whom recorded the view in his artwork. Though the plaza has changed substantially since the 1840s, it is still recognizable.

The cathedral's facade is impressively ornate and echoes back through the centuries, and the inside has relics and effigies worth a peek.

But the park offers more than just architecture: it's a site for community events such as marathons or public speakers, and it's a spot where parades and dances are held. At night,

WHERE TO STAY IN QUETZALTENANGO

Lar Antiqua
Inexpensive but clean, with a beautiful terrace and courtyard. **$$**

Mucha Arte Hostal
A hostal with private rooms, free breakfast, a nice garden and lots of art on the walls. **$$**

Hotel Pensión Bonifaz Quetzaltenango
A high-end option right near the Parque, with dining, a pool and spacious rooms. **$$$**

especially with the fountain lit up, the park is even more impressive and a great place for evocative photos.

More sobering is the massive statue in honor of Justo Rufino Barrios, born in nearby San Marcos, who served as president of Guatemala in the latter half of the 1800s.

He is credited with legalizing the privatization of Maya lands and concentrating wealth in the hands of his allies, many of whom weren't Guatemalan.

It's a complex, troubled history of exploitation that still reverberates through Guatemala today. In the center of the park is an iconic rotunda dedicated to Rafael Álvarez Ovalle, who composed the Guatemalan national anthem.

Though this park is full of people during the day, it can be a bit dicey in the wee hours, so use caution if venturing out late at night.

Dance of the Venado

MERRY NEW YEAR CRAZINESS

If you're lucky enough to be in Xela around the New Year, inquire when the Dance of the Venado will be held. This grand festival is held throughout the highlands and even into Mexico, and brings out marching bands, costumed dancers and a procession of bearers with an effigy of Jesus, passing up and down streets filled with throngs of cheering onlookers.

The dancers – dressed as either deer or monkeys – shake maracas and light fireworks, sometimes choosing to dance (or bless) a crowd member by stamping feet and moving the antlers. It's a wild, frenetic, high-energy festival that definitely is something to write home about.

It's a tradition that – like so many fascinating Guatemala customs – blends both Christian and Maya beliefs. Here, the deer are offering themselves to hunters so that the latter may thrive. It's a form of gratitude to nature, as well, a kind of competition, as other animals also want to eat the deer.

Though this has become mostly ritual today, in ancient times the dance would be followed by a feast. In Xela, the dancers are followed by a marching band and reposing Christ effigy. There's cheering, laughter and a bit of drunkenness, but mostly it's just a great excuse to have a good time.

NOT TO MISS

Museo del Ferrocarril de los Altos
Though the railway only lasted for a few short years, there's a fascinating museum here that shows its tragic glory.

Museo Chocolate Doña Pancha
A small museum dedicated to that wondrous product that comes from cacao.

Museo Casa Botran
If rum is your passion, this out-of-the-way museum will be well worth stopping by. Learn the history of (and get to taste!) this popular Guatemalan rum.

Parque Centro América

GETTING AROUND

Quetzaltenango/Xela is served by a multitude of express buses, and micro-buses on various routes serve the city itself. *Tuk-tuks,* however, unlike much of the rest of the country, aren't common here, so you'll need to arrange for taxis or use buses to get around the city.

Beyond Quetzaltenango

Great day trips around the city will have you at stunning markets, quirky churches or atop sacred peaks.

San Andrés
Xecul   Chichicastenango

● Quetzaltenango
● Volcán
Cerro Quemado

Quetzaltenango (Xela) is located centrally and thus makes a great spot to use as a base camp while you explore during the day. There are plenty of hiking and nature opportunities in the volcanoes nearby, and further to the west is the Pacific. This proximity means the weather changes rapidly, so whatever your plans are, make sure you take precipitation into account. For those looking to find great souvenirs, the Chichicastenango market will enthrall, delight and surprise – it's the largest in all of Central America. The remoteness of the region has led to some very odd architecture, especially the folksy yellow church of San Andrés Xecul. There's plenty more to explore, too.

TOP TIP

If you'll be doing any hiking, make sure you have footwear that ties securely, as the volcanic rock is sharp.

Sanés Xecul church

TIAGO_FERNANDEZ/GETTY IMAGES ©

LAURA G.ROBE/SHUTTERSTOCK ©

Chichicastenango market (p208)

Volcán Cerro Quemado

RITUALS AND BEAUTIFUL VIEWS

If there's one thing you need to do in Xela, it's visit **Volcán Cerro Quemado**, an active volcano revered by the Maya as a pilgrimage spot. Its most recent eruption was in 1818, but a previous one about a century earlier destroyed a nearby town. Whole extended families ascend the steep, rocky trail, carrying garlands of flowers to place as an offering before they pray. Entire church groups sit in circles, some with loudspeakers blaring, chanting or sobbing for Christ's forgiveness. Other prayers are more personal: a grandmother and grandfather on their knees, softly chanting, oblivious to any passersby. Couples make the climb hand in hand. Some hike up in somber solitude. Not everyone makes it to the summit; some simply stop on the way, decide this is the spot for their makeshift altar, put down their flowers and pray.

The summit rewards you with a sweeping view of the city below amid a stunning backdrop of mountains. Look in the other direction and you'll see there's a black lava flow that extends for hundreds of yards, dotted everywhere with flowers, crosses, offerings and trash. If you yourself want to partake,

SAN ANDRÉS XECUL

Less than an hour's drive from Xela is the small town of **San Andrés Xecul**, famous for its church. Bright yellow and decorated elaborately with folk-art-style figurines, it's one of Guatemala's most singular Catholic churches and another area specialty that really needs to be seen to be believed. The entire front facade is filled with figures, mostly angels, but also vines and tendrils, leaves, flowers and so on. Small doll-like figures sit casually on the ledges with their legs hanging down. One is a minstrel, playing a tiny lute or guitar. It has a childish quality, but this is exactly why it's so endearing and has become the primary – or the only – reason tourists come to this small town.

 PLACES TO EAT IN QUETZALTENANGO

Baviera Café
A delightful spot near the Parque, with delicious breakfasts and lunches, and great espressos. **$$**

Restaurante Tertulianos
A fancy, romantic Italian standby considered by some to be the best in the city. **$$$**

Xelapan
A local chain of tasty breads, pastries and coffees that opens early and closes late. **$**

feel free to purchase flowers at the trailhead from the many vendors who supply them. The road up is delightfully lined with flower fields. It's awe-inspiring in some ways and troubling in others, but is a fascinating peek at modern Maya life and a ritual that's been happening for centuries.

Chichicastenango's Market

CENTRAL AMERICA'S BIGGEST MARKET

Chichicastenango's market is one of Central America's oldest, and its biggest: a sprawling, chaotic and beautiful scene held twice weekly, on Thursdays and Sundays. Preparations begin the night before. Vast sections of the city shut down, poles and tarps are erected, and merchants ready their wares. You can find nearly anything here, from dry goods to plastic pails to piñatas, but most of the tourism is centered around the fabrics, textiles and outfits that one can find here.

If you've dreamed of purchasing a *traje* (traditional outfit), this may be your best chance, and prices can be reasonable, though some key things bear keeping in mind. There are more people here who speak only K'iche' Maya than who speak only Spanish, and more than half speak both. You're more likely to hear K'iche', as less than two percent of residents are outside that ethnic group. Wandering the narrow, crowded alleys, you'll be surprised how few people call you to make a sale. It's because for the most part, these vendors are here to sell to other locals. So it's a little more relaxing than similar for-tourism spots in Guatemala's bigger cities. Plan to spend at least a few hours here if you want to see more than a small portion. Just like a big box store, there are separate areas for things like flowers, hardware, a 'food court,' and so on.

IGLESIA DE SANTO TOMÁS

Chichicastenango's oldest church, Iglesia de Santo Tomás, dates back to 1545 and its steps today are used for the market as a spot for selling flowers. In addition to its Christian role, it is still a site for modern Maya ceremonies as well. The church was a stop for explorers Stephens and Catherwood when they made their visit, and interestingly, it was the site where the Maya's sacred *Popul Vuh* text was first transcribed. The site, originally a Maya temple, was razed to build the church, but the platform was left intact. Its 18 steps symbolize the 18 months of the Haab' (Maya) calendar.

BARGAIN ETHICALLY

For more on how to bargain in a way that leaves the world a better place, see page 174.

GETTING AROUND

Tours to Chichicastenango leave from as far away as Guatemala City and Antigua, as well as Lago de Atitlán towns and Xela/ Quetzaltenango. Around the city, you can walk, ride-share, or take a taxi or *tuk-tuk*.

NEBAJ

Traditional Nebaj, officially known as Santa María Nebaj, is tucked in the middle northwest of the country, often overlooked by tourists and the Guatemalan government alike. It was the site of horrific atrocities during the Guatemalan civil war, and though decades have passed, many people here live with its memory close at hand, and many families have lost loved ones. Estimates vary, but as many as 75,000 people may have been killed. The 2018 census calculates that 78,000 people live in Nebaj municipality, which gives a chilling sense of scale to the government's lethal measures here. The distinctive red *cortes* (skirts) worn by the Nebaj women are said to symbolize the blood of those lost in the civil war. The people here are understandably suspicious of the government and of visitors, yet they are also friendly, funny and kind. The language here is Ixil, one of the least spoken of all of Guatemala's indigenous languages.

TOP TIP

There is still concern about cameras here, so do not take photos of anyone without asking permission first, and you may need to pay for doing so.

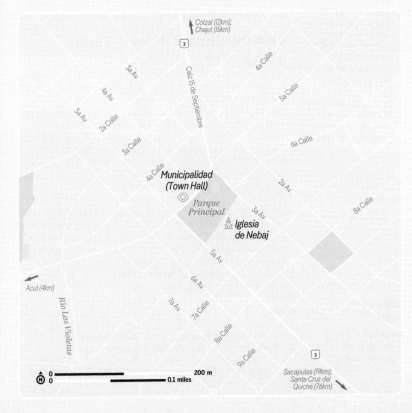

THE IXIL TRIANGLE

Three towns make up
the Ixil Triangle, which
was feared – many
believe needlessly
– during the
Guatemalan civil war
due to a belief that the
Ixil were supporting
the guerillas.
Xenophobia, politics
and racism surely
all played a part,
but even today this
region is infrequently
visited and often
misunderstood.
Santa María Nebaj,
San Juan Cotzal and
San Gaspar Chajul
make a thin isosceles
triangle that remains
one of the poorest
and least educated
areas of Guatemala.
That should not be
taken to be putting
the region down:
it's beautiful, and
there's a great pride
that runs through its
Ixil-speaking people.

Central Nebaj

THE HEART OF THE CITY

Nebaj is best explored on foot, with camera in hand, though be mindful that many – if not most – people prefer not to be photographed. The town square is a wide, airy open place where the community comes together for celebrations. A small rotunda offers a space for politicians to speak, for people to educate others or – as is often the case – life to go on unaffected and unchanged. A crumbling facade still stands on the plaza's south side, next to a stunning mural and the Catholic church, the **Iglesia de Nebaj**. Across on the other side is the **Nebaj Municipalidad** (Town Hall), a stately structure with columns that befits a town government. It's surprisingly wide and open compared to some other Guatemalan plazas, with little in the way of foliage, structures or seats. A small fountain offers some decoration, but the austerity is somehow fitting in a place where the memory of so many 'disappeared' still lives strong.

Only a short walk away is the main **Nebaj market**, which is a wonderful feast of colors, smells, clothes and activity. If you had to miss the Chichicastenango market due to timing or some other misfortune, you'll get a taste of what it's like here but on a smaller scale. At one end is the bus depot, where colorful buses wait to hurtle their way towards their destinations.

Visit the Cheese-Making Farms

CHEESE, COWS AND RURAL LIFE

In the hills and fertile farmland that surround Nebaj are a number of small hamlets, many of which produce cheese. You can visit these farms (especially in the town of Acul, over the mountains) and see how the cheese is made, and you can even stay there. Some ranches are more tourist-friendly than others, but if this is your cup of...milk...then consider looking for one and spending an extended time here. Cows aren't the only product, however. Some also breed roosters, which, though gorgeous birds, may be part of a darker cock-fighting trade. In a place where outsiders are already viewed with suspicion, you may not want to ask too directly about it, especially if you're hoping to tour the farm. There's an almost Swiss feel in places, with cows grazing peaceably on steep hillsides covered with vivid green. In fact, there's a reason you might make the connection: the founders of some of these farms were European immigrants, some from the Alps region. So they came here, found a place that felt very much like home, and started making cheese.

 WHERE TO STAY IN NEBAJ

Hotel La Fe
A charming, simple, friendly spot with parking, hot water and comfortable beds. **$**

Hacienda San Antonio
An Acul option if you're looking to get away from Nebaj and make cheese. **$$**

Hotel Villa Nebaj
Centrally located multi-story hotel with an on-site restaurant, though service is slow at times. **$$**

JEREMY WOODHOUSE/GETTY IMAGES ©

Central Nebaj

Ray Bartlett, writer

I love Nebaj (and the whole Ixil Triangle) in part because I didn't really expect to. I've always gravitated toward other parts of Guatemala, such as the jungles of Petén or the Highland cities. Nebaj took me by surprise. I loved the market, loved wandering the streets, and the vibrant red *cortes* (skirts) of the women seem so stylish somehow. The wide red and thin stripes are so distinctive – to me the clothes seem to embody the spirit of the Ixil: their fierce pride despite all that's happened to them.

The cheese itself, well, you may love it or you may find it's an acquired taste. People tend to react to it the way some do to *chèvre* goat's cheese. It's either tasty or it makes you recoil. Regardless of whether you like it or don't, this 'artisanal' cheese is popular with locals and they're rightly proud of it.

Hiking to Acul

SPECTACULAR SCENERY, SUN AND SKY

Hiking is one of the main activities for tourists here and of the many possible treks one can do, few are more rewarding than the one from Nebaj to Acul. If you have a 4x4 with good traction (and even better brakes!) you can make this same route by car, but for most, it's a delightful, fun jaunt and a great excuse to get outside for a while. The walk begins in Nebaj and may take a bit of trial and error at first, but when you're on a road that's leading west, up the precipitously steep mountain in front of you, you'll know you're on the right path.

✖️ WHERE TO EAT IN NEBAJ

Le Jardin
A quiet, slow restaurant with decent meals that's open all day. $

Hotel y Restaurante La Cabaña de Juanita y María
A delightful log cabin vibe here in this farmhouse turned hotel and cafe. $

Nebaj Market
Expand your culinary horizons in the market by finding food that suits your fancy. $

WHEN THINGS GO AWRY...

It's important to realize that in remote, off-the-grid areas like Nebaj you may not find the kind of ritzy accommodations you would find elsewhere, such as in Antigua. Part of the point of exploring these areas is to *not* be getting the same thing you've come to think of as routine. If you find yourself disappointed or the room, parking or food isn't what you'd expected, it is best to try not to change things on the spot or complain. Remember that you're the visitor here, experiencing a place and a lifestyle that's quite comfortable to the people who live here.

VOJTECHVLK/SHUTTERSTOCK ©

Nebaj cheese (p210)

From there, it's just a matter of going up and up and up, and then down and down and down. You'll pass coffee farms, cow pastures, forested patches, farmhouses and perhaps even a farmer or two. Many villagers head up here to cut wood, so you may pass a few people with impossibly large loads of firewood on their backs. Goatherds meander through here as well. It's a good spot for birding, if that's your thing, too. Eventually, after an hour or so of steep uphill, the road flattens out, and if you think you're almost there, there's some bad news: you've got to go all the way back down again on the other side. The curvy road between the summit and Acul is impressively steep, and you may need to rest a bit just to give your calves and Achilles tendons a break. But eventually you'll reach the bottom, the road flattens out and you'll be in Acul. From there, you can take a micro-bus or even hitch a ride around the north side, skirting the mountain and returning to Nebaj.

GETTING AROUND

Tuk-tuks are the go-to method for getting around Nebaj, and it's not uncommon to see one putting up some impossibly steep hill with determination that defies both logic and physics. Big express buses barrel wildly between the cities and towns.

Beyond Nebaj

Todos Santos
Cuchumatán
Chajul
Nebaj
Xexocom • • ● San Juan
Acul Cotzal

The entire Ixil Triangle and beyond is a gem waiting to be experienced, explored and understood.

This region may seem closed in some ways to the casual tourist, and at times it can be hard to find people who speak Spanish enough to communicate with you. It still has undeniable poverty, a place forgotten – even persecuted – by the Guatemalan government, and people here don't simply open up to outsiders (Guatemalans or otherwise) for the heck of it. They do open up to acts of kindness, to friendship, to generosity and to respect. If you need help or have a question, chances are that someone will go out of their way to assist you. It's delightfully pastoral here, with a tranquility and beauty that's impossible to overlook.

TOP TIP

Drivers beware of potholes, even at modest speed. Definitely don't drive at night if you can help it.

Huipil, San Juan Cotzal (215)

J MARSHALL - TRIBALEYE IMAGES/ALAMY STOCK PHOTO ©

AMAZING MURALS

Chajul is also the site of several valuable murals that were discovered quite recently when builders began renovating a family home. Between the layers of the wall were drawings that dated back to the time of Spanish conquest. Some were in excellent condition, having been preserved for centuries beneath the plaster. They were brought to the attention of archaeologists, who were thrilled: murals made at that time were usually of religious ceremonies, but in these one can see both Maya and foreign figures in a variety of settings, playing music, eating or drinking. While these murals are fascinating, they are part of someone's actual home: it's up to the owner to decide whether you can come in.

STUDIOLOCO/SHUTTERSTOCK ©

Chajul

Visit Chajul

TINY TOWN, BIG DREAMS

Visiting tiny **Chajul** (San Gaspar Chajul, officially) is partly delightful because just getting there requires a bit of slow going over pothole-dotted roads, but you hardly notice because it's so pretty.

Cornfields burst with yellow and purple flowers on the brown stalks, bright green bunches of weeds push out against the paved road, and the views of small farmhouses and cows, pigs and chickens seem almost like one's driven into a movie. When you reach the town it's quiet, but there's a bustling market scene, and people wait in line to cash their paychecks at the Banrural office at the main plaza.

 WHERE TO HIKE AROUND NEBAJ

Acul	**Xexocom**	**Todos Santos Cuchumatán**
Excellent accommodations in this cheese-making hamlet.	A friendly 25-household hamlet a day's hike from Acul.	A popular terminus for extended multi-day hikes.

That's where you'll find Felipe Rivera, the director/caretaker of the future Ixil Museo Maya, which is currently just a collection of artefacts, traditional clothing, and other items, along with sobering tributes to important men who were killed in the civil war. It's housed in and outside a building that Rivera hopes will soon have exhibits and displays.

To take a look, go to the office and introduce yourself, and when he's free (in 15 or 20 minutes), he'll come out and show you the museum, as well as murals that were found inside some house walls. You can also get in touch via email: museomayaixil@gmail.com.

Multi-Day Hikes

GORGEOUS PASTORAL SCENERY

Using Nebaj as a hub, you can do several extended, multi-day hikes through the region. Though you can do them on your own, it's not a bad idea to have a guide, and you may learn more about the area, the plants and the families if you do. But to hike over a few days like this is in some ways the closest one can get to the way it would have been experienced by explorers Stephens and Catherwood, who covered this entire country on foot, mule or horse.

These towns – quite surprisingly – have plans for when visitors from the hills arrive, and while they may not often have hikers, when they do, they're able to welcome them with somewhere to sleep and meals to eat.

You may end up in a spare hammock or perhaps you can bring your own. But the hospitality in these tiny hamlets is amazing and it's heartwarming that people are so willing to share their time and space. What you make of the hospitality is really up to you.

Some hikers just need a meal and a place to sleep. Others leave having made lifelong friendships that bridge socio-economic barriers. You can make yourself even more welcome by bringing gifts for the kids, such as pencils, paper or crayons.

Candy is another option but less ideal for teeth. And make sure your shoes are well-worn in before you start, because you won't be able to get a different pair until you're back in a big city.

SAN JUAN COTZAL

Whether you hike there or drive, tiny **San Juan Cotzal** deserves a mention for its spot as a vertex in the Ixil Triangle. It's a small yet densely packed town with – you guessed it! – a bustling market that's not at all for tourists. Buy a live chicken or a bag of dry beans or fruit; no mugs with 'I Love Guatemala' on them here. Instead, hunt for the small women's cooperative, which, just like the more famous ones in Atitlán and elsewhere, helps backstrap loom weavers earn a living through their craft. The store is piled high with fabrics, textiles, *huipiles* (tunics) and decorations. You may find something that's far more meaningful than a coffee mug.

GETTING AROUND

Roads here are undeniably terrible, so take it slow, drive during the day and don't get distracted. If you're on dirt, be aware that rain can turn hard ground into mud quickly, making for for unsafe conditions.

TOOLKIT

The chapters in this section cover the most important topics you'll need to know about in Guatemala. They're full of nuts-and-bolts information and valuable insights to help you understand and navigate Guatemala and get the most out of your trip.

Arriving
p218

Getting Around
p219

Money
p220

Accommodations
p221

Family Travel
p222

Health & Safe Travel
p223

Food, Drink & Nightlife
p224

Responsible Travel
p226

LGBTIQ+ Travelers
p228

Accessible Travel
p229

Nuts & Bolts
p231

Language
p232

Volcán Acatenango (p176)

Arriving

Most visitors arrive at La Aurora airport, about 6km from Guatemala City's Parque Central. International flights all use one terminal. Some flights to and from Flores, Petén, use a smaller terminal nearby. The usual assortment of money changers, cafes and car rental agencies are on hand.

Visas

Citizens of the EU, UK, USA, Australia and many other countries do not require a visa and will be given a 90-day permit on entry. Check with your embassy if you're unsure.

SIM Cards

Small kiosks throughout the arrivals area sell pay-as-you-go SIM cards, and the attendants are happy to help you set them up.

Border Crossings

Guatemala has land and/or sea borders with Mexico, Belize, Honduras and El Salvador. Try to cross early in the day, dress respectfully and (as always) be polite to officials.

Wi-Fi

The airport has free, unreliable wi-fi. Elsewhere, cafes, hotels, restaurants and many other businesses offer free wi-fi. Just ask for *la contraseña* (the password).

Public Transport from Airport to City Centre

	Guatemala City	Antigua	Quetzalteneango
TRAIN	N/A N/A	N/A N/A	N/A N/A
BUS	N/A N/A	90 mins **Q10**	5 hours **Q100**
TAXI	15 mins **Q80**	60 mins **Q400**	4 hours **Q1000**
SHUTTLE	N/A N/A	60 mins Q80	4 hours Q350

MOVING ABOUT

Very few people choose Guatemala City as their primary destination and many make a beeline straight for Antigua. Public transport is available, but you'll need a Q80 taxi to get to the bus stop, so you might as well opt for the direct Q80 shuttle at the airport. Long-distance bus stations (for Quetzaltenango, Petén, Río Dulce etc) are scattered around town, many in Zona 1 – you'll need a Q80 taxi to get there as well.

Getting Around

Every transport option imaginable exists, but for longish distances, most travelers opt for the bus – they go almost everywhere and are very affordable (if not always comfortable).

TRAVEL COSTS

Rental
From US$30 per day

Gasoline
Q37 per gallon

Chicken bus ride
Q15 per hour

Bike rental
From Q30 per hour

Chicken Bus

The workhorse of the Guatemalan public transport system is noisy, smelly, cramped and cheap. Travelers love them or hate them. Whichever way you lean, a chicken bus ride is a slice of life that every visitor should experience once.

Pullman Bus

Here you get a reserved seat, a possibly working toilet (number ones only, please), meal stops and some sort of entertainment on the TV. Pullmans tend to run between major cities and don't do unscheduled pickups.

FINDING YOUR BUS

Guatemalan bus terminals can be intimidating places – they're chaotic, noisy and have little to no signposting. Every bus has an *ayudante* (helper) whose job it is to yell out their bus's destination, help passengers with luggage and collect fares. These people are a font of knowledge – if you can't find your bus, they're the ones to ask. They'll quite often take you there and hook you up with their counterpart. A small tip is appreciated, but a *muchas gracias* will suffice.

TIP

On longer bus rides, snack vendors board at towns along the way. The food can be delicious. The hygiene? Well…

Shuttle Bus

Increasingly popular are these shared private minibuses that offer door-to-door service between fixed destinations (Antigua to just about anywhere, Flores to Semuc Champey, and Quetzaltenango to Guatemala City are a few popular routes) – book a ticket almost anywhere in town. You'll see the signs.

Boat

Boats take the place of buses where roads aren't an option. Some of the popular routes are between villages on Lago de Atitlán, from Río Dulce or Puerto Barrios to Livingston and some of the coastal spots like Monterrico or Tilapita.

Plane

The only really reliable domestic flights run between Guatemala City and Flores; a decent option if you want to get to Tikal in a hurry. Flights from the capital to Quetzaltenango, Retalhuleu and Puerto Barrios are sometimes offered, depending on demand.

DRIVING ESSENTIALS

Drive on the right

Don't drive at night

Drive defensively, regardless of 'the rules'

 # Money

CURRENCY: **QUETZAL (Q)**

Credit Cards

Accepted in most hotels and restaurants, gas stations and tourist-oriented businesses in larger towns. But cash is king – never assume that you'll be able to pay with card (or that the machine will be working) and have a Plan B.

Changing Money

US Dollars and Euros are accepted in many tourist-oriented businesses. Other currencies can be changed in exchange houses or banks, but it's safer to use ATMs. The quetzal is stable against the US dollar.

Tipping

Restaurants 10% in 'nicer' restaurants; a few coins elsewhere.

Taxis Negotiated in advance, the fare will almost certainly include a tip.

Elsewhere You may get asked for a little something ('*para la gaseosa*' – for a soft drink). Before you get worked up, a *gaseosa* costs Q5.

HOW MUCH FOR...

week of Spanish classes (20 hours) from Q1800

entry to Tikal Q150

shoeshine from Q10

movie ticket from Q40

HOW TO... Save Some Quetzals

The unwritten 'gringo tax' is hard to avoid – if you look foreign, chances are you'll be overcharged at some point. This is common where prices are fluid, such as on public transport and in markets. One strategy is asking a local what a reasonable price is and aiming for that. Another is to keep things in perspective – does paying an extra Q10 really make a difference?

THE LOWDOWN ON ATMS

Withdrawing from ATMs (*cajeros automáticos*) is by far the most convenient way to get cash in Guatemala. The exchange rate is decent, you can find a machine in all but the smallest of towns and they all accept international cards.

Unfortunately, card-skimming is equally prevalent. One precaution is to cover your hand when you're entering your PIN.

The other is to avoid machines on the street that are easier to tamper with – inside supermarkets, shopping malls and banks themselves is your best bet.

LOCAL TIP

Guatemalans have many nicknames for money – *billetes* and pesos are both quetzals, *plata* and *pisto* is money in general and a bit of change is unas *monedas* (some coins).

Accommodations

No Place Like Home

For that true cultural immersion, nothing beats a homestay. Set up mostly for students at Spanish schools (but welcoming anybody) this network of families offer spare rooms to travelers. You get to eat and hang out with the family and practice your Spanish to your heart's content. Serious party animals may want to check the house rules before committing.

Farmstays

Agrotourism is a burgeoning industry here, and life on the farm is an option for all budgets, ranging from super-rustic, no-electricity options all the way up to super-swank, hacienda-fantasy fulfilment. Either way, the settings are usually magnificent, the food delicious and fresh, and the insights into a little-seen aspect of Guatemalan life fascinating.

Renovating Colonial-Style Homes

All over the country, old colonial-style homes are being converted into upscale accommodation. These places are atmospheric and not that much pricier than the generic hotel down the road. Think thick walls, serious art, heavy furniture and rooms arranged around a leafy central patio with wide eaves – an ideal place to while away the midday heat or a rainy season deluge.

Budget Sleeps

Basic digs are easy to find in Guatemala – anywhere near the bus station is always a good bet. You'll probably end up with a concrete box with a bathroom, a TV and maybe a window. It's often worth shelling out another Q20 – the comfort levels rise significantly once you're off rock bottom

HOW MUCH FOR A NIGHT IN...

a homestay
Q45-85

a hostel dorm
Q60

a Finca Ixobel treehouse
From Q150

Hostel Life

Until recently, Guatemala only had a few backpacker hostels, but now they're here in force. These are your serious all-service affairs, offering restaurant, bar, tour agency, laundry – basically anything you want. Regular activities (salsa classes, pub crawls etc) are on offer, as are convenient shuttles to the next hostel down the road. Dorm rooms tend to be cramped, but you're really here for the social scene.

LOVE HOTELS

There are two types of businesses even the smallest towns are almost guaranteed to have: a church and an autohotel. Nominally a motel, the autohotel is a favorite for young lovers without a place of their own, people having affairs, and anybody else who needs a bed for a few hours. Ranging from the downright seedy to over-the-top, '70s sleaze decor, these places are all about discretion, with enclosed garages (so no-one can see your car) and attendants who take your money through a hole in the wall (so no-one can see your face).

Family Travel

Guatemalans love kids and tend to have a few of their own, so most places welcome the little ones even if they're not family-oriented in the strict meaning of the term. The vibrant colors, exotic landscapes and cultural anomalies capture even the most jaded youngster's attention, and practicalities like smaller portions, extra beds and daytime activities are easily arranged.

Sights

Child concessions to museums and archaeological sites apply up until 15 years of age. Scrambling around Maya ruins is a favorite for most age groups; exploring the crumbling colonial buildings of Antigua, not so much. Active volcanoes dotted around the country make for exciting, reasonably safe hikes, and there are plenty of places to ride horses.

Facilities

- Very few places have diaper-changing facilities.
- Cots are unknown in all but high-end hotels – if it's important to you, make sure you inquire well in advance.
- Diapers, formula and other baby necessities are available everywhere from corner stores to supermarkets.
- Dedicated rooms for breast-feeding are non-existent, but breastfeeding in public is commonplace. Bring a shawl.

Eating Out

Guatemalan fare tends to be simple and there's almost always something kid-friendly on the menu – spaghetti, fried chicken and, if you're lucky, your kid will love beans, tortillas and eggs. There's usually a high-chair somewhere around – if it's not offered, ask.

Getting Around

Children pay for their own seat on public transport – if you can have them on your lap, they ride for free. Safety seats are rare – if you're hiring a car and one's important, make sure you specify at booking time and reconfirm.

KID-FRIENDLY PICKS

Parque Acuático Xocomil (p90) World-class water park boasting the classic range of waterslides, lazy rivers, dunking games and much more.

Autosafari Chapín (p109) A drive-through zoo where you can get up close with African and native animals from the comfort of your car.

Museo de los Niños (p51) Guatemala City's kids museum leans heavily on the education theme, but is generally a winner with kids and parents alike; featuring exhibits like the earthquake simulator.

GOING BILINGUAL

If you're going to be in one place for a while, one option you might consider to keep the kids entertained is enrolling them in Spanish school.

Young kids' brains are like sponges for languages and you'll be amazed by how much they progress after even a couple of weeks of classes.

The one-on-one format of Spanish lessons here suits kids particularly well, as it feels more like they're making friends than sitting in a classroom.

And the fact that putting the kids in class gives the parents a few hours of grown-up time per day? Some would see that as a bonus.

Health & Safe Travel

INSURANCE

Travel insurance is not required for entry, but it's a good idea to get some. Something that covers flight cancellation is great and, while basic medical care is inexpensive, long hospital stays or evacuation back home can be very costly. Petty theft is a problem, but rarely worth claiming due to excess fees.

Natural Disasters

Hurricanes, earthquakes, floods and volcanic eruptions – Guatemala has them all, and on a regular basis. Keep an eye on the news and follow official advice and warnings, particularly when it comes to evacuation orders. In an earthquake, find a sturdy doorframe to stand in – don't run into the street.

Swimming

The wild rip tides of Guatemala's Pacific coast claim multiple victims every year. Few beaches are patrolled by lifesavers and many of them simply patrol from the shoreline – don't rely on someone rescuing you if you get into trouble. If you see waves coming in diagonal to the shore, it means there is a particularly strong rip, but some are invisible. Take care.

SOLO TRAVEL

Women traveling alone will get unwanted attention and offers of company. Don't do anything you wouldn't do back home.

ROAD RULES

Left side indicator
it is safe to overtake

Passenger flapping hand out of window
driver is about to cut in front of you

Branches on road
broken down vehicle blocking the road ahead

Hazard lights flashing
driver is about to do something completely random

Drugs

Being a staging point between Colombia and the US means cocaine and cannabis are prevalent. They are also illegal and multiple foreigners are doing drug-related time in Guatemalan prisons. Be wary of strangers offering you drugs on the street – this is a classic undercover sting that often ends in a shakedown for a bribe, if not prison time.

MOSQUITOS

In the lowland coastal and jungle areas, mosquitos are numerous. They carry malaria and dengue fever, and there have been outbreaks of the zika virus. There are malaria tablets, but the best defense is to avoid getting bitten – staying above 1500m altitude helps, as does wearing long sleeves and long pants, using a DEET-based repellant and avoiding being outside during sunrise and sunset.

Food, Drink & Nightlife

When to Eat

Desayuno (8–10am) Breakfast is a relatively heavy affair, usually including eggs, beans, tortillas and fried plantains.

Almuerzo (noon–2pm) Lunch is usually the main meal. Set lunches include soup, a main course (rice, meat and salad) and dessert or fruit.

Cena (6–8pm) Dinner can look a lot like breakfast, but 'international' foods like pasta and pizza are generally on offer.

Where to Eat

Comedor (diner) Literally an eatery, these simple shops are everywhere, often offering cheap breakfasts and set meals to office workers and travelers.

Restaurante (restaurant) Generally more comfortable and formal, these places will have nicer decor, higher prices and usually a wider menu than a *comedor*.

Cevicheria (ceviche restaurant) If you're game to try seafood pickled in citrus juices (way more delicious than it sounds), these places specialize in it.

Comida rápida (fast food) No surprises here.

MENU DECODER

Plato del día set meal
Refacción snack
Carne de vaca (or simply carne) beef
Pollo chicken
Cerdo pork
Vegetariano vegetarian
Caldo stew
Sopa soup
A las brasas flame-grilled
Frito fried
Huevos revueltos scrambled eggs
Mosh porridge
Queso cheese
Crema cream
Plátanos plantains
Licuado Blended fruit drink
Jugo juice
Leche milk
Agua water
Entrada entree

Plato main course
Postre dessert
Helado ice cream
Frío cold
Caliente hot
A tiempo room temperature
Taza mug/cup
Vaso drinking glass
Botella bottle
Vino wine
Vino blanco white wine
Vino tinto red wine
Cerveza beer
Gaseosa soft drink
Mesa table
Silla chair
La cuenta the bill
Propina tip
Mesero/a waiter/waitress
Para llevar take away
A domicilio home delivery

HOW TO...

Get a Decent Cup of Coffee

Despite producing some of the finest coffee beans, Guatemala has a history of disappointing caffeine enthusiasts. The classic Guatemalan drink is weak and filtered that you can drink it at any hour and fall asleep ten minutes later.

Coffee culture is spreading in Guatemala, though, and larger places more accustomed to tourists tend to have espresso machines and staff who know how to use them. A few Starbucks-style chains are popping up and McDonalds outlets that have a McCafe serve good coffee using Guatemalan beans. Guatemalan coffee shop lingo is mostly imported, using terms you'll most likely be used to – espresso, cappuccino, cafe latte. A large black coffee is an *americano*. The same with milk is *cafe con leche*.

HOW MUCH FOR...

glass of wine
Q20

imported steak at a steakhouse
Q150

cup of coffee
Q15

soft drink at a corner store
Q5

set lunch in a comedor
Q30

serving of ceviche and crackers
Q60

HOW TO... Order a Steak

Guatemalans love steak. Even the smallest towns will have a 'steakhouse' (or something resembling one) and true carnivores will be pleased to hear that the commonly available *desayuno finquero* (farmer's breakfast) features six or eight ounces of grilled beef, usually topped with a couple of fried eggs and accompanied by the usual fixtures of beans, cheese, plantains, etc.

Until recently, pretty much everywhere served up steak grilled until it was bone dry and gray, but with the rise of more refined steakhouses featuring imported cuts, waiters have started asking how you want your meat done (el término de la carne). Generally, Guatemalans stick to these terms:

Jugoso rare
Medio jugoso medium-rare
Medio medium
Tres cuartos medium-well
Bien cocido well done

Specific cuts can be harder to pin down as the restaurant may be using Guatemalan terms or the names used by their importer. Generally speaking, these are some things you're likely to find on a steakhouse menu:

Longaniza sausage
Chorizo spicy sausage
Tripa intestines
Panza tripe/stomach
Chuletas chops
Lomito tenderloin
Puyazo sirloin
Churrasco minute steak

Filling the Petén

The Petén region was largely unpopulated until the government started offering subsidies to farmers to move there to start up cattle ranches. The region is now one of the country's main beef-producing zones.

GOING OUT

Going out in Guatemala is basically the same as back home, with a few key differences. The first one you'll notice is that you'll get patted down for weapons by the bouncer at the door. Don't be put off by this – it's actually kind of reassuring to know that nobody else in the club is carrying, either. If you do happen to have your pistol on you, you'll be asked to leave it in the lockers in the lobby while you're inside.

The next thing you'll notice is that everybody dances and they're all really good. Salsa, merengue and reggaeton are the big dance floor fillers, and it's worth taking a few classes, either back home or once you get here, so that you can at least fake it until you start making it.

Another one to watch out for is closing time. For some years now, Guatemala has had the Ley Seca (Dry Law), which prohibits the sale of alcohol after a certain time. This time moves around a bit, but is generally 1am. After parties definitely exist, but anybody found in an establishment selling alcohol after the stipulated hour can be fined Q5,000. Make your plans accordingly.

A final word on venues: *cantinas* tend to be fairly rough places, not at all the sort of place a woman would want to go for a drink on her own. Nightclubs (more generally spelt 'nigthclub') are strip bars. If you're looking for a place to go dancing, ask for *la discoteca*.

Responsible Travel

Climate Change & Travel

It's impossible to ignore the impact we have when travelling, and the importance of making changes where we can. Lonely Planet urges all travellers to engage with their travel carbon footprint. There are many carbon calculators online that allow travellers to estimate the carbon emissions generated by their journey; try resurgence.org/resources/carbon-calculator.html. Many airlines and booking sites offer travellers the option of offsetting the impact of greenhouse gas emissions by contributing to climate-friendly initiatives around the world. We continue to offset the carbon footprint of all Lonely Planet staff travel, while recognising this is a mitigation more than a solution.

Volunteer

Guatemala is packed with NGOs, many of which accept volunteers for varying lengths of time. Short-termers should try to avoid placing a burden on organizations by expecting extensive training. See entremundos.org for more details.

Shop Small

Fancy stores and fixed prices have their appeal, but if you want to support local craftspeople, there's nothing like buying direct from the source in the market.

Chow Down

Sample the delights of traditional Garifuna cuisine like *tapado* at Buga Mama (p61), a restaurant set up to train local young people for careers in hospitality.

Get into the Community

Community tourism is really in its infancy in Guatemala and won't survive without support from tourists. This is a fascinating way to get off the beaten track and enjoy a more authentic experience.

Don't Get Greenwashed

Like everywhere else in the world, 'green' can be a cynical marketing ploy in Guatemala – try to do a little investigation before accepting a company's ecological claims as a reason for them to get your custom.

Literally drop into the caves of B'ombi'l Pek (p78), where the easiest access is a long abseil down into the darkness. The income from this tourism project supports the local community.

Set the turtles free, warm your heart (and maybe win a prize!) at the Saturday night liberation party held by turtle-conservation project ARCAS (p142) outside of Monterrico.

THINK BEFORE YOU CLIMB

It's tempting to climb on top of pyramids and other Maya ruins (pictured), but your footsteps (added to everybody else's) pose a real risk of wearing away and damaging the stones. If there's a separate lookout, consider using it.

TRY THE NATURAL HIGHS

Illegal drugs are widely available in some parts of the country. Buying them not only opens you up to a terrible run-in with the law, it also incentivizes young Guatemalans to become drug dealers.

Giving It Away

Be prepared for beggars, some of whom are shockingly young. If you're uncomfortable giving money directly, consider dropping off a big bag of colored pencils and other school supplies at a local school.

Get Cooperative

When looking for a guide, consider hiring one from a cooperative – they're generally present around the larger tourist attractions and it's a fairly safe bet that they will be both professional and fairly paid.

Learn how coffee is cultivated in an agricultural cooperative at the Cooperativa Chicoj (p73).

Support the community by shopping for handmade textile gifts at the Atitlán Women Weavers collective (p191).

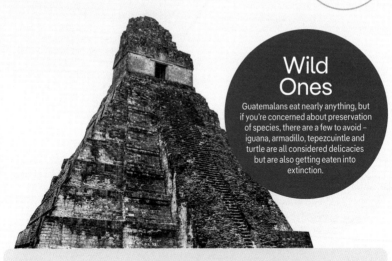

Wild Ones

Guatemalans eat nearly anything, but if you're concerned about preservation of species, there are a few to avoid – iguana, armadillo, tepezcuintle and turtle are all considered delicacies but are also getting eaten into extinction.

RESOURCES

idealist.org
Searchable database of volunteering opportunities.

arcasguatemala.org
Guatemalan NGO, dedicated to animal protection.

safepassage.org
Guatemalan NGO, heavily involved in development work.

LGBTIQ+ Travelers

Homosexuality was decriminalized in Guatemala in 1871, but there's no point pretending – of all the things Guatemala is, LGBTIQ-friendly is just not one of them. Coming in at 132 on the Spartacus Gay Travel Index, the country obviously has a long way to go when it comes to tolerance, equality and other such issues.

Accommodations

LGBTIQ+ couples who are travelling together won't have any trouble getting a room, but outside of specifically targeted accommodations in the more cosmopolitan areas such as Antigua or Guatemala City, you will most likely raise some eyebrows if you ask for one double bed – it's back to the old days of pushing the beds together or making do with what you've got. As with any situation here, discretion is the best strategy.

'HONEY TRAPS'

As is the case in many conservative, highly religious countries, many married Guatemalan men lead a 'second life'. Be very wary when making casual acquaintances – 'honey traps' are not unheard of and violence against LGBTIQ+ people is common and not taken all that seriously by authorities.

HOMOSEXUALITY & THE MAYA

One little-known fact is that homosexuality was largely tolerated amongst the Maya. Homosexual acts featured in various religious rituals, shamans were known to use them as healing practices and the cave art of Naj Tunich near Poptún shows representations of homosexual acts and relationships.

Out & About

Guatemala has a few nightclubs worth checking out, which are lesbian-friendly but really oriented towards men. Antigua is probably the most relaxed place in the country and Frida's bar, at 5a Avenida Norte 29, has a regular queer night and special events throughout the year. The scene in Quetzaltenango is small and ebbs and flows.

TAKING IT TO THE STREET

Pride festivals and parades are nowhere near as large-scale as in many parts of the world, and tend to be cancelled or resurrected according to the political and social climate of the day. When they do run, chances are they will be in one of the country's two largest cities, Guatemala City or Quetzaltenango.

The Politics

Progress is slow, but it is happening. Sandra Morán, Guatemala's first openly LGBTIQ+ legislator, was elected to congress in 2016 and began to introduce reform bills. Since then LGBTIQ+ candidates have become more common. Support for same-sex marriage is growing, but with opposition from religious groups.

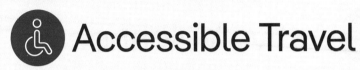 Accessible Travel

Guatemala lacks basic infrastructure in many senses. There are efforts to make life here more accessible, but progress is slow. There are many competing priorities for very few resources, and accessibility advocates find themselves getting told to take a number quite frequently.

Challenges

Outside of the capital, accessible public transport is all but non-existent. Sidewalks are uneven, if they exist at all, and cobblestone streets can pose a challenge for mobility-impaired travelers.

Airport

Guatemala City's Aurora Airport was refurbished in the mid-2000s and meets basic international standards for accessibility. Elevators are available both in and outside the terminal and most walkways are ramped, not stepped.

Accommodations

Budget accommodation will present a challenge, with at least one step somewhere. Older, colonial-style hotels are probably the best bet, with larger rooms on the ground floor, set around a patio with wide walkways.

GETTING HELP

Guatemalans are extremely helpful and hotel staff in particular will go out of their way to assist somebody in need. Don't be afraid to ask – if help isn't offered, it's probably just a case of shyness.

Navigating Antigua

Antigua's sidewalks are inlaid with cute tiles featuring wheelchair icons – getting into the street is easy enough, but how you manoeuvre a wheelchair over those cobblestones is anyone's guess.

Three Wheelers to the Rescue

Even for short hops, many travelers opt for a *tuk-tuk*. These three-wheeler taxis zip around everywhere for pennies and their low, open design makes them relatively easy to enter and exit.

ARCHAEOLOGICAL SITES

Perhaps surprisingly, Guatemala's more heavily visited archaeological sites are some of its most accessible places. Walkways are generally wide, flat and wheelchair-friendly, and guides can help navigate. Unfortunately, access to lookout points is often via flights and flights of stairs.

RESOURCES

A range of useful general information for travelers who have access issues or a disability can be found in Lonely Planet's free guide to **Accessible Travel Online Resources**.

Antigua-based **Transitions** is an NGO that is dedicated to accessibility advocacy and promoting programs that are aimed at employing people with diverse capabilities.

TRANSPORT

First-class buses are better and less crowded than a chicken bus, but the stairs are still tricky. Consider hiring a car or driver if you're planning on moving around the country a lot.

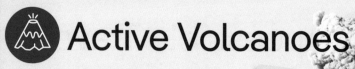

Active Volcanoes

Defining the landscapes of much of western Guatemala and sacred to the Maya, volcanoes are one of the first exotic sights you are likely to encounter. Beautiful to look at and fun to climb, you must remember that these aren't just lovely shaped mountains – they can (and do) erupt.

GUATEMALA'S ACTIVE VOLCANOES

Of Guatemala's 33 volcanic peaks, three are classified as active.

- **Fuego** *near Antigua* 2022 (last eruption)
- **Pacaya** *near Antigua* 2013
- **Santa María** *near Quetzaltenango* 2013

Of these, Fuego is by far the deadliest – it is constantly active at a low level and the 2018 eruption caused the loss of at least 159 lives, thousands of evacuations and the closure of the international airport. It's also the volcano whose eruption in 1717 contributed to the moving of the capital from Antigua to its present-day site at Guatemala City.

Types of Eruption

Eruptions come in a few flavors: magma eruptions are the deadliest and the type that occupies the common imagination. Steam blasts aren't to be underestimated, though – the famous eruption of Mount St. Helens belonged to this category.

Nor does it give you any real timeline, although magma eruptions tend to build up for longer periods – weeks or even months – whereas steam blasts can happen suddenly.

Evacuation Orders

Wherever you are and whatever you're doing, if there's an official evacuation order to leave the area, take it very seriously. These situations can escalate rapidly and you don't want to be acting at the last minute.

Updates

If you'd like to keep an eye on volcanic activity in Guatemala, the US Geology Service (usgs.gov) publishes regular updates.

WARNING SIGNS

Volcanic eruptions aren't as random as they may seem. There are various indicators that volcanologists have identified as warning signs that an eruption is imminent.

An increase in frequency and severity of earthquakes
Located on three tectonic plates, Guatemala is prone to the shakes – this is probably the easiest symptom for the layperson to spot.

An increase in steam emissions or general heating of ground areas
You're probably not going to notice this one unless you're climbing volcanoes regularly.

Swelling of the ground surface
Unless you've got some serious measuring equipment at hand, the changes here are probably going to be too subtle to notice.

Changes in lava flow
Both Pacaya and Fuego dribble lava at regular intervals – this is part of the attraction of climbing them.

# Nuts & Bolts

OPENING HOURS

Banks 9am–5pm Monday to Friday, 9am–1pm Saturday

Bars 11am–11pm

Cafes and restaurants 7am–9pm

Government offices 8am–4pm Monday to Friday

Shops 8am–noon and 2–6pm Monday to Saturday

Tap Water

Some locals drink the tap water. Visitors should not. The most practical, sustainable way to stay hydrated is to bring a water bottle and fill it up from the *garrafón* (water cooler) in the lobby of your hotel/hostel, Spanish school, etc. Failing that, supermarkets and corner stores sell purified water by the gallon.

GOOD TO KNOW

Time Zone
GMT/UTC -6

Country Code
502

Emergency Number
110 (tourist police: 1500)

Population
17 million

PUBLIC HOLIDAYS

New Year's Day (Año Nuevo)
1 January

Easter (Semana Santa) March/April

Labor Day (Día del Trabajo) 1 May

Army Day (Día del Ejército) 30 June

Assumption Day (Día de la Asunción)
15 August

Independence Day (Día de la Independencia)
15 September

Revolution Day (Día de la Revolución)
20 October

All Saints' Day (Día de Todos los Santos)
1 November

Christmas Eve (Víspera Navidad)
24 December

Christmas Day (Navidad)
25 December

New Year's Eve (Víspera de Año Nuevo)
31 December

Weights & Measures

The metric system is the default; fresh produce is sold by the pound.

Smoking

By national law, smoking is prohibited in any enclosed public space.

Electricity 120V/60Hz

Type A
120V/60Hz

Type B
120V/60Hz

Language

Spanish is the national language of Guatemala, and knowing some very basic phrases is not only courteous but also essential, particularly when navigating through rural areas. That said, a long history of North American tourists has made English the country's unofficial second language.

Basics

Hello. Hola. *o·la*
Goodbye. Adiós. *a·dyos*
Yes. Sí. *see*
No. No. *No*
Please. Por favor. *por fa·vor*
Thank you. Gracias. *gra·syas*
Excuse me. Con permiso. *kon per·mee·so*
Sorry. Perdón. *por·don*
What's your name? ¿Cómo se llama usted? *ko·mo se ya·ma oo·ste*
My name is ... Me llamo ... *me ya·mo ...*
Do you speak English? ¿Habla inglés? *a·bla een·gles*
I don't understand. Yo no entiendo. *yo no en·tyen·do*

Directions

Where's ...?
¿Adónde está ...? *a·don·de es·ta ...*
What's the address?
¿Cuál es la dirección? *kwal es la dee·rek·syon*
Could you please write it down?
¿Podría escribirlo? *po·dree·a es·kree·beer·lo*
Can you show me (on the map)?
¿Me puede enseñar (en el mapa)? *me pwe·de en·se·nyar (en el ma·pa)*

Signs

Abierto Open
Cerrado Closed
Entrada Entrance
Salida Exit
232 **Servicios/Baños** Toilets

Time

What time is it? ¿Qué hora es? *ke o·ra es*
It's (10) o'clock. Son (las diez). *son (las dyes)*
It's half past (one). Es (la una) y media. *es (la oo·na) ee me·dya*
morning mañana. *ma·nya·na*
afternoon tarde. *tar·de*
evening noche. *no·che*
yesterday ayer. *a·yer*
today hoy. *oy*
tomorrow mañana. *ma·nya·na*

Emergencies

Help! ¡Socorro! *so·ko·ro*
Go away! ¡Váyase! *va·ya·se*
I'm ill. Estoy enfermo/a. *es·toy en.fer.mo/a*
I'm lost. Estoy perdido/a. *per·dee·do/a* (m/f)
Call ...! ¡Llame a ...! *ya·me a ...*
a doctor un doctor. *oon dok·tor*
the police la policía. *la po·lee·see·a*

Eating & Drinking

Can I see the menu, please?
¿Puedo ver el menú, por favor? *pwe·do ver el me·noo, por fa·vor*
What would you recommend?
¿Qué me recomienda? *ke me re·ko·myen·da*
Cheers! ¡Salud! *sa·lood*
That was delicious.
¡Estuvo delicioso! *es·too·vo de·lee·syo·so*
The bill, please. La cuenta, por favor. *la kwen·ta por fa·vor*

NUMBERS

1
uno *oo·no*

2
dos *dos*

3
tres *tres*

4
cuatro *kwa·tro*

5
cinco *seen·ko*

6
seis *seys*

7
siete *sye·te*

8
ocho *o·cho*

9
nueve *nwe·ve*

10
diez *dyes*

DISTINCTIVE SOUNDS

Note that *kh* is a throaty sound (like the 'ch' in the Scottish loch), *v* and *b* are like a soft English 'v' (between a 'v' and a 'b'), and *r* is strongly rolled.

DONATIONS TO ENGLISH

Numerous – you may recognise armada, aficionado, embargo, fiesta, machismo, patio, plaza ...

To Lisp or Not to Lisp

If you're familiar with the sound of European Spanish, you'll notice that Latin Americans don't 'lisp' – ie the European Spanish *th* is pronounced as *s* in Guatemala and elsewhere in Latin America.

Modern Mayan

Since the pre-Columbian period, the two ancient Maya languages, Yucatec and Cholan, have subdivided into more than 20 separate Maya languages. Indigenous languages are seldom written, but when they are, the Roman alphabet is used.

Where the @!*# is it?

Spanish-language and English-language keyboard layouts differ because the two alphabets aren't quite the same. This shouldn't generally be a problem, but for one pesky – all too useful in the age of email – key. The @ ('at') symbol – in Spanish this symbol is called *la arroba* (la a·ro·ba) – isn't necessarily labeled on keyboards or may not be accessed by simply pressing the keys you're used to. Try the F2 key, use an ALT code – or ask for help:

Where's the @ key? *¿Dónde está la arroba?* (don·de es·ta la a·ro·ba)

The Host with the Most

If you're invited to share a meal in a Guatemalan home, your solicitous hosts will ply you with food and drink. Remember that politeness is highly valued in their culture, so be sure to extoll the virtues of your hosts' cooking. This phrase should do the trick:

The food is very good! *La comida está muy rica!* (la ko·mee·da es·ta mooy ree·ka)

SPANISH AROUND THE WORLD

Though it's a distinct variety of Spanish, Guatemalan does share many similarities with its Latin American siblings, which set it apart from the mother language, Castilian Spanish. Guatemalan Spanish was influenced by the southern Spanish dialect of Andalucia, from where the first Spanish conquistadors sailed to the New World.

300 million people speak Spanish as their first language

Spain
Mexico ● Guatemala
El Salvador ● Honduras
Nicaragua ● Cuba
Guatemala ● Puerto Rico
Panama ● Dominican Republic
Colombia ● Venezuela
Ecuador ● Equatorial Guinea
Bolivia
Chile ● Paraguay
● Argentina

100 million people speak Spanish as their second language

233

STORYBOOK

Our writers delve deep into different aspects of Guatemala life

Sololá Market (p181)

SL PHOTOGRAPHY/SHUTTERSTOCK ©

A HISTORY OF GUATEMALA IN
15 PLACES

Guatemala's history is a series of dramatic events to say the least – cataclysmic natural disasters, political intrigue and coups, a rigid class system left over from colonization and a decades-long civil war are amongst the defining points that still echo through the country today, writes LUCAS VIDGEN.

THERE'S A FEELING of timeless continuity to everyday Guatemalan life – it seems as if this is the way it has always been and the way it will always be. The reality is, though, that Guatemala has gone through a very distinct set of phases to get where it is today.

Broadly speaking, these phases would be the reign of the Maya, Spanish conquest and colonization, independence, the civil war and modernization. Guatemala holds a special place in the region – it's the largest and most populous country in Central America, with the most vibrant economy, and yet for all the historical ties it shares with Mexico to the north, they are very different places.

Development in Guatemala is hard – corruption is endemic and foreign investors are wary. Some facets of society see the need for real change, a move away from the fragile subsistence farming that much of the population relies on to survive. Against the forces of change are a powerful elite whose lineage can be traced back to colonial days – with control of the land, the military, congress and industry, they don't seem to be in a hurry to shake things up too much.

1. Lago de Atitlán
WHERE IT ALL BEGAN?

Between 11 million years and 2 million years ago, the area where Lago de Atitlán now sits saw a period of sustained volcanic activity, culminating in the collapse of the earth's surface and the formation of the caldera that the lake now partially fills. Volcanic growth continued in the area, forming the three volcanoes that ring the lake today – San Pedro, Tolíman and Atitlán. Some Maya believe that these three volcanoes are the three stones that were placed by the gods at the beginning of time, which has been linked to the custom of using three hearthstones to support cooking vessels over an open fire.

For more on Lago de Atitlán, see page p183

2. Tikal
HIGH POINT OF THE MAYA

There is some dispute over where exactly the Maya culture started, but it's undeniable that it saw its greatest achievements realised in city states like Tikal in the Petén region. Tikal's heyday lasted around 1000 years, and in 900 CE it was all but abandoned. However, in many ways, it remains one of the most impressive sites in the country – it is relatively easy to get to, extensively excavated and reconstructed, with towering temples and sprawling residential complexes shrouded by jungle, and it's connected by easy walking paths through a lovely, park-like setting.

For more on Tikal, see page p116

3. Takalik Abaj
A MIX OF CULTURES

The Maya were the most prevalent pre-Columbian civilization in Guatemala, but hardly the only one living here. Archaeologists working on sites on the Pacific Slope have found evidence that the Olmec of southern Mexico migrated here, most likely fleeing persecution from the ruling Aztec nation. The massive carved stone heads – emblematic of the Olmec civilization – which were found at Takalik Abaj are the most compelling argument for this theory. There's also evidence that the Pipil migrated through (themselves fleeing the Olmecs) and settled for some time along the coast before moving southwards and eventually settling in what would become El Salvador.

For more on Takalik Abaj, see page 90

4. Rabinal
THE MAYA FIGHT BACK

The popular misconception is that the Maya civilization was so weakened by the time that the Spanish arrived that the conquerors basically just walked in and took over. This is far from the truth. Legendary warriors like Tecún Umán, the last king of the K'iche', put up spirited resistance to the invaders and delayed the final conquest for many years.

El Castillo de San Felipe

One of the last regions to be conquered was around Rabinal in Baja Verapaz. Unable to conquer the region militarily, the Spanish tried another tack – the Dominican monk Fray Bartolomé brought locals under some form of control by converting them to Christianity.

For more on Rabinal, see page 78

5. Antigua
THE FIRST REAL CAPITAL

Guatemala's former capital wasn't the colonizers' first choice – the previous two had been abandoned due to indigenous uprisings and a volcanic eruption. But in 1543, Santiago de los Caballeros was founded on the site of present-day Antigua. It remained the capital for over 200 years - the seat of power for a kingdom that took in much of modern-day Central America plus what became the state of Chiapas in Mexico. The city thrived until a devastating series of earthquakes inspired the decision to move the capital to its present-day site. The previous capital began to become known as Antigua Guatemala (Old Guatemala), commonly shortened to Antigua.

For more on Antigua, see page 166

6. El Castillo de San Felipe
KEEPING THE PIRATES AT BAY

As present-day Guatemala was finding its feet and the indigenous populations were largely subdued, another threat to prosperity emerged, this time from the seas. Pirates, mostly of English and Irish descent, but also hailing from as far away as South America, became active in the Caribbean and regularly plundered cargo ships travelling from the Spanish colonies on their way back to Spain. Warehouses set up on the shores of Lago de Izabal to store goods waiting for transport became regular targets of pirate ships. The fort at San Felipe was constructed in 1651 to repel these ships until the early 1800s.

For more on El Castillo de San Felipe, see page 69

7. Guatemala City
THE CAPITAL FINALLY FINDS A HOME

The present-day capital was founded in 1776 after Antigua Guatemala was abandoned due to a series of earthquakes. The site occupies what was the Maya city of Kaminaljuyu. The city grew quickly and maintained the importance that the Spanish had placed in the old site. In 1821, Central America's independence from Spain was declared from here and the city was the first capital of the brief-lived United Provinces of Central America (later, the Federal Republic of Central America). Much of Guatemala City was razed in a couple of devastating earthquakes in the early 1900s, with some buildings around the central plaza having been saved and restored.

For more on Guatemala City, see page 48

8. Quetzaltenango
THE SECOND CITY BREAKS FREE

Shortly after independence from Spain was declared, a new state declared secession from Guatemala. The Estado de los Altos was declared in 1838 and had its capital in Quetzaltenango. It comprised the departments of Quetzaltenango, Totonicapán, Sololá, Suchitepéquez and the Mexican region of Soconusco, Chiapas. The division was driven by Western Highlands liberals who were unhappy with the power being accumulated by Guatemala City conservatives. The secession was briefly accepted, but Guatemala City was never really happy about it, and the region was forcefully reincorporated in 1849. The highlands still feel somewhat separate from the rest of the country and Quetzaltenango retains the name Ciudad de los Altos.

For more on Quetzaltenango, see page 203

9. Retalhuleu
THE RISE OF BIG AGRICULTURE

The Declaration of Independence did little to improve the lot of the indigenous population. Land that had previously belonged to the Church and Spanish administrators was largely granted along racial lines. Criollos – those born in Central America of mostly/purely Spanish heritage - received huge tracts. Ladinos (mixed Spanish/indigenous heritage) received smaller or no parcels. The indigenous were left out. The huge farms and ranches you see around Retalhuleu today are a remnant of that time. Land rights issues have been problematic ever since, with widespread reform (unsuccessfully) attempted in 1957 and again in the Peace Accords of 1996.

For more on Retalhuleu, see page 86

10. Champerico
THE HIGHLANDS' LINK TO THE OUTSIDE WORLD

Resulting from the growing friction with the capital, farmers and industrialists from the highlands started highlighting the need for a second Pacific port, as Puerto San José was seen as largely servicing the capital and too distant to be of use to the highlands. In 1881, the port of Champerico was inaugurated, taking its name from Champer & Co, a German company that had previously operated in the area. Highlands coffee and lowlands cotton was exported from the port, aided by a railway that ran from Retalhuleu to Champerico. The port was nationalized in 1955 and continues to export coffee, sugar and timber.

For more on Champerico, see page 91

11. Uspantán
A FIGHTER IS BORN

Unremarkable in almost every other way, the small town of Uspantán gave birth to arguably Guatemala's most famous daughter – Rigoberta Menchú Tum in 1959. She was politicised as her mother and other members of her family were tortured and assassinated during the civil war, and she joined the Indigenous Rights movement in the '70s. Like many opposed to the military regimes,

Posters of missing people, Guatemala City

Menchú went into exile in Mexico, where she published her autobiography, later winning the Nobel Peace Prize. The resulting fame allowed her to return to Guatemala and eventually act as mediator in the peace talks between guerrilla factions and the military.

For more on Rigoberta Menchú Tum, see page 244

12. Puerto Barrios
BITTER FRUIT

This port town was the flash point for what was to become the longest civil war in Central American history. US-backed forces supported by the CIA started off protecting the interests of US-based concerns like the United Fruit Company. Before long, the situation had spiralled out of control, with covert US actions deposing dictators and supplying arms and support to anti-communist military dictatorships, and peasants, students and unions forming guerrilla resistance. The war lasted 36 years, leaving scars that are only starting to heal today (pictured). Combined sources estimate around 200,000 people were killed.

For more on Puerto Barrios, see page 63

13. Nebaj
THE DARKEST DAYS OF THE CIVIL WAR

The highlands area saw some of the worst excesses of the civil war, and particularly hard hit was the area around Nebaj, where dictator Rios Montt practiced his 'scorched earth' policy of simply eliminating villages instead of going to the bother of trying to investigate which of the inhabitants were sympathetic to the resistance. Estimates are that between 70% and 90% of villages in the Ixil Triangle, where Nebaj is located, were eliminated during this time. Mass graves are still being uncovered today and the painstaking work of identifying corpses could go on for decades.

For more on Nebaj, see page 209

14. Esquipulas
TALKS OF PEACE

In 1986, in the sleepy pilgrimage town of Esquipulas, the presidents of five Central American nations began talks that would culminate in the end of the civil wars that had plagued the region for decades. Amongst the final terms of the agreement were a cessation of hostilities, the holding of free elections, the end of government funding of paramilitary groups, arms control and refugee aid. It would take some years for fighting to officially end, but late in 1996, the parties signed the Agreement on a Firm and Lasting Peace, and life in Guatemala began the slow process of getting back to normal.

For more on Esquipulas, see page 56

15. Volcán Fuego
HISTORY REPEATS

Early on a Sunday morning in June 2018, residents living in the foothills of the Volcán Fuego (pictured) on the outskirts of Antigua awoke to an alarming sight: a 15km-high column of smoke was forming above the volcano.

Within hours, there were reports of flying rocks the size of baseballs, and car tyres melting as lava flows threatened local villages. Emergency services called for residents to evacuate and began trying to rescue those who were trapped.

Rescue efforts continued, hampered by heavy rain that caused volcanic mudslides. The exact death toll is unknown – estimates range between 159 to 2,900 people.

For more on Volcán Fuego, see page 176

MEET THE GUATEMALANS

A reflection of a complex history and diverse cultures and landscapes, the Guatemalan population almost defies definition. DIANA PASTOR introduces her people.

IT'S NOT DIFFICULT to strike up a conversation with a Guatemalan. You can talk to your seatmate on the bus or to the bread seller. However, Guatemalans struggle to be direct, reflected by the use of 'fíjese que' (which means nothing, but is necessary to start stories, explanations or excuses). Generally, Guatemalans are friendly and willing to help if someone requires it. 'No tenga pena' (don't worry) is a phrase you'll often hear.

Guatemalans aren't always on time, but neither are they champions of unpunctuality. Since most Guatemalans cannot travel, many will be happy to learn about you and your country.

The United States continues to be the largest immigration destination for Guatemalans. Most immigrants are indigenous, young and immigrate illegally to earn money to send back to provide for their family or build a home. Families aren't as large as before. The birth rate has dropped and women now have about 2.48 children.

Children often have two first and last names. Nicknames are also common. The most common names in Guatemala are José and María – a reflection of the strong influence of religion in the country. Other common names are Ana, Juan or Pablo; but English names or celebrities' names like Bryan, Michael or Jennifer are more common in younger generations.

Not all Guatemalans are religious, but the majority are Christians. Atheism is frowned upon, as are abortion and gender and sexual diversity. Guatemala is a conservative country, and religion and family relationships are important, but so are parties. It's common to hear loud music in houses or on the street, together with fireworks to celebrate the Day of the Catholic Virgin, a birthday, wedding, or anything anytime.

Besides religion and family, Guatemalans are passionate about soccer. An important match means a barbecue at home with the family or eating (and drinking) with friends at a restaurant. People love barbecues, but they also love fried chicken. It's true that tortillas, eggs and beans are important in the Guatemalan diet. Life tends to be faster where the economy is stronger; in Guatemala city, the action starts at 5am, but in small towns everything goes slower, though this also depends on the weather. In the coastal or tropical areas of the north, there's not much to do in the midday heat. In these areas, people tend to speak with a more 'Caribbean' accent. Coastal accents tend to be less clear than in urban areas, and this is true in towns where indigenous languages are prevalent, too.

Who & How Many

Guatemala's population is 17.4 million people; 45% are indigenous. Many Maya people migrate to urban areas, and stop using their language and wearing traditional clothing – they aren't included in this figure. The reasons for this lie in structural and systemic racism.

I'M GUATEMALAN, BUT IT'S COMPLICATED

Like many other families, I come from a (Maya K'iche') family that migrated in the '70s from rural to urban areas for economic reasons, and fortunately was not affected by the genocide of indigenous peoples. I was born in Quetzaltenango (Xela), and I have lived there for most of my life. I grew up in a large working-class family and was raised with a lot of freedom and tolerance for change.

I studied social work because it was an affordable degree and because I care about human rights and justice. My relationship with Guatemala is a never-ending difficult love story: on the one hand, I get mad seeing working children and seniors, stray animals and trash everywhere; on the other hand, I am in love with the beauty of nature, the simplicity of every day and the kindness of some Guatemalans, despite their hard lives.

MAYA:
THEN & NOW

A brief introduction to the timeless culture of the Maya.
By LUCAS VIDGEN

THE REGION COVERED by modern-day Guatemala, Belize, Honduras and Southern Mexico was, is and always will be the heartland of the Maya: a culture that has endured flood, famine, drought, colonization, persecution, civil war and government neglect. Still it persists and is kept alive through rituals, dress, language and culture.

Beginnings

According to the Maya creation story, it all began on August 13, 3114 BCE. This is the first day of the Long Count calendar. The Popol Vuh ('council book') tells of seven deities who wanted to create creatures who could 'keep the days'. They succeeded in creating a human from white and yellow maize. Corn still plays a central part in Maya diet and ritual, and many modern-day Maya still refer to themselves as *hombres de maíz* (men of corn).

Developments in toolmaking and agriculture led to stable communities forming in the Preclassic period (2000 BCE to 250 CE). As standards of living improved, populations grew and larger villages formed in the Copán valley in modern-day Honduras and the jungles of the Petén and Mexico's Yucatán Peninsula. The Classic Period (250 to 900 CE) is seen by many as the high point of Maya culture. Elaborate monuments and temples were raised. The most powerful and impressive sites endure today – Tikal, Calakmul, Palenque and Copán among others. Populations swelled and trading activity by overland, sea and river routes boomed, with salt, cacao and gems such as jade and obsidian being amongst the most commonly traded items.

Then around the mid-900s, something strange happened. These civilizations began to collapse. One by one, they stopped building monuments, food ran out and populations dwindled. Archaeologists still can't agree on one cause for this, but it's likely that it was a combination of factors. Overpopulation, war, famine, disease, drought and the ruling classes' reluctance to abandon tradition have all been cited as possibilities. What we do know is that within the space of 100 years, the great capitals were all but abandoned, left to be enveloped by jungle or occupied by squatters.

New trade networks formed as smaller cities developed, many in the highlands in Guatemala's west. These new settlements were often located in more strategic lo-

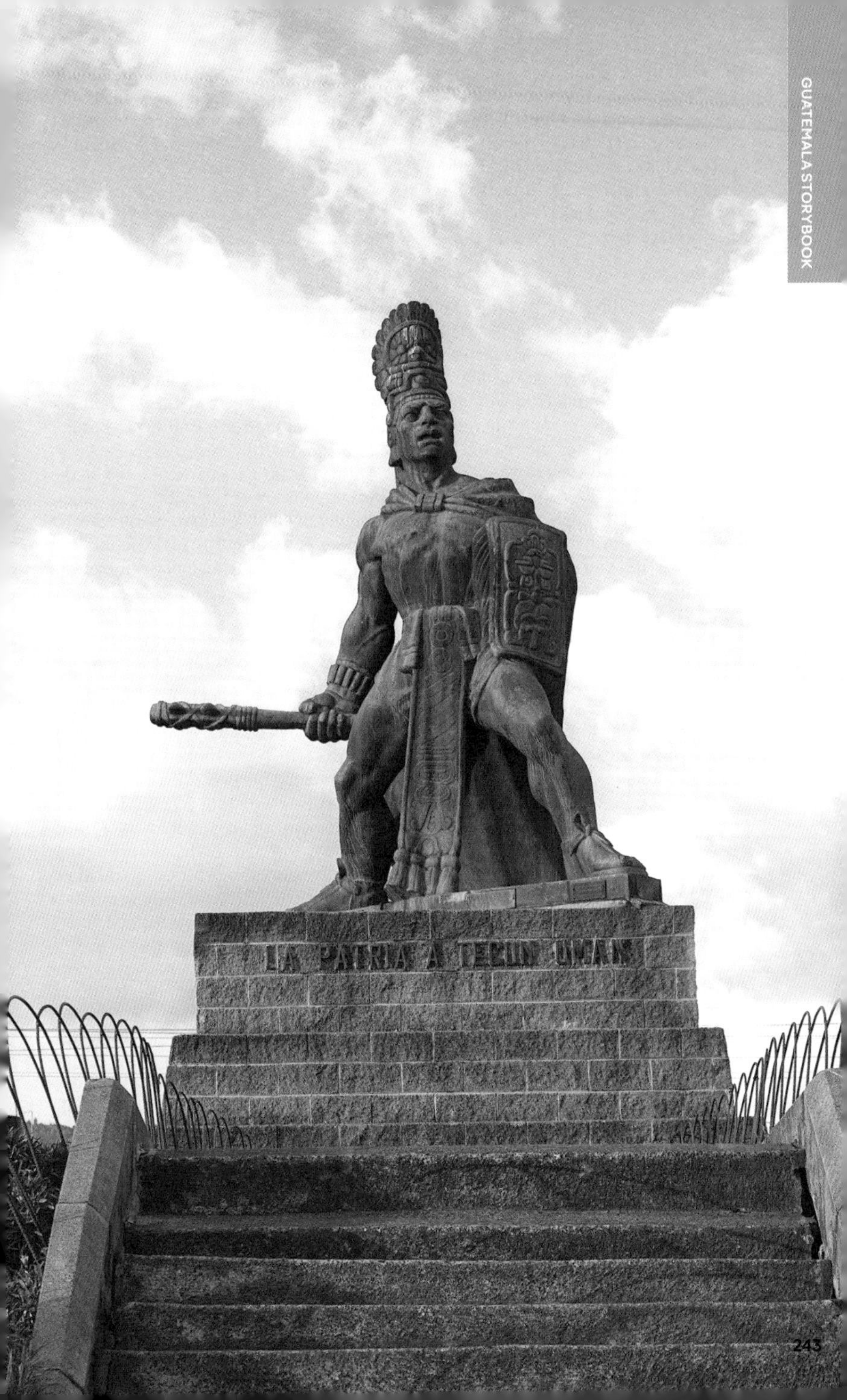
LA PATRIA A TECUN UMAN

cations with natural defences, such as on hilltops or surrounded by ravines. Conflict between cities continued, but there were no dominant players in the region. Some form of peace was maintained by a regional council, with members hailing from regions as disperse as Mexico's Yucatán and southern Guatemala.

The Spanish Arrive

This was the fractured state of the Maya peoples when the Spanish turned their attention to the region in the early 16th century. The popular myth is that the Spanish had an easy time conquering Guatemala, but in reality they met with fierce resistance in many parts of the region. The Petén region held on for 170 years after Cortés first arrived there and there were lengthy battles all through the highlands, one of which culminated in the death of famed warrior and national hero Tecun Uman, whose name you will see all through the highlands and whose statue stands at the entrance to modern-day Quetzaltenango.

Eventually, though, Maya resistance crumbled. The Maya lacked technology such as gunpowder and steel weaponry and were highly susceptible to diseases brought by the conquering forces. Superior Spanish military tactics and their ability to enlist conquered Maya into their forces is also thought by many to have been a decisive factor in their eventual victory.

Many Maya were forced into *reducciones*, somewhere between a farm and a slave camp, to provide agricultural labor for their new rulers. Life on the *reducciones* was brutal. The class system was strictly defined along race/color lines. At the bottom of the heap were the darker, full-blooded indigenous. The lighter-skinned ladinos, with mixed Spanish and indigenous blood, made up something approximating the middle class. At the top of the heap, occupying the positions of power in the government, military and church, were the creoles – Spaniards and their descendants. With very few notable exceptions, this hierarchy exists today.

The *reducciones* were run like independent kingdoms and many owners took it upon themselves to eradicate whatever vestiges of Maya culture that they could. Spanish was encouraged, if not enforced, and much energy was spent trying to convert the Maya to Catholicism and get them to abandon their traditional beliefs.

Present & Future

It would be nice to say that independence from the Spanish brought improvements for the Maya, but that wasn't really the case. The land that had been taken by the Spanish was parceled out to the creole ruling class and the class system stayed firmly in place. Many Maya continued on in agricultural labor or survived through subsistence farming, and so it continued through the 19th and 20th centuries.

The civil war took a particular toll on the Maya population as the military conducted 'scorched earth' campaigns, murdering or kidnapping the entire male population of villages. Those who spoke out against these atrocities were similarly targeted. The population further dwindled as many escaped persecution, fleeing to southern Mexico where large refugee communities exist to this day.

While there were concerted pushes to eradicate Maya languages, dozens survive – many of which are spoken as a first language in some parts of the country, with Spanish being a distant second. The elaborate weaving and colorful dress of traditional Maya women is the culture's most outwardly noticeable expression, and Maya religious beliefs live on, too, though at times the rituals were performed in secret, for fear of reprisals.

The Maya Pride movement started gaining momentum in the 1970s, along with civil rights movements elsewhere in the world. Author and activist Rigoberta Menchú Tum won the Nobel Peace Prize in 1992 for her work promoting indigenous rights. At the end of the civil war, international and local NGOs began springing up all over the country, many dedicated to improving the lives of the indigenous population. They've got a long way to go – on nearly any indicator (health, education, income, life expectancy, standard of living etc), the indigenous population score markedly worse than Guatemalans in general, despite making up nearly 60% of the population.

THE
GARIFUNA

An amazing survival story of a journey through time and space. By
LUCAS VIDGEN

WITH ITS BEGINNINGS on a small Caribbean island, the Garifuna diaspora now spans the globe. The global population is around 400,000 people, with the majority living in the United States and Honduras. Guatemala's Garifuna population numbers around 5,000.

Some History

Most Garifuna trace their origins back to the island of Saint Vincent. How they got there is a matter of dispute – some say the Garifuna were survivors of a wrecked slave ship and therefore never technically enslaved, others say they arrived here having been traded from other Caribbean islands. What is known is that many who escaped slavery on other Caribbean islands came to Saint Vincent where they could live freely. Regardless, DNA testing says that modern Garifuna originally descended from West Africa, later mixing with European, Latino and indigenous people from Central America and the Caribbean, most notably the Arawak from whom their language heavily derives.

The Garifuna took a circuitous route to get to Guatemala. Having been caught up in the wars between the British and the French over possession of Saint Vincent, they were eventually expelled from the island by the British and relocated to the island of Roatán in Honduras. From there they moved to the mainland, eventually arriving in Livingston in the mid-19th century. Having lived as a minority wherever they have been, the Garifuna have regardless maintained strong ties to their traditional culture. The language, dance and music of the Garifuna were included on UNESCO's Intangible Heritage List in 2008.

The Garifuna Language

Despite popular misconception, the Garifuna language has very few ties to African languages – one academic study found a total of five African loan words in the entire lexicon. The same study found that the language is about 70% Arawak, with other words coming from French, Caribbean Creole, English and Spanish.

The four main variations of the Garifuna language coincide roughly with their **245**

Garifuna parade, Guatemala City

geographic bases, and the Garifuna can easily distinguish if a speaker is from Belize, Honduras, Nicaragua or Guatemala. Some linguists have flagged that a fifth variation, American Garifuna, is emerging from the large populations of Garifuna who live in New York, Miami and Los Angeles.

The Garifuna language is complex and despite having loan words from various languages, it is considered a fully fledged language in its own right, not a pidgin or creole dialect.

Garifuna Food

Throughout their journeys, the Garifuna have almost always lived by the coast, so seafood plays a predictably strong role in Garifuna cuisine. A couple of other ingredients that feature heavily in Garifuna dishes are coconut, green plantains and cassava – in fact, one theory says that the name Garifuna is derived from the Arawak meaning 'cassava eaters'. You can try all these ingredients together in the wonderful traditional seafood stew called *tapado.* You sometimes see it on menus around the country, but the best place to try it is, of course, Livingston. Street vendors in Livingston also sell *pan de coco* (coconut bread), which is an absolute treat when freshly baked.

The traditional alcoholic drink of the Garifuna is *gifiti,* a bitter drink that uses rum as its base and is infused with herbs and spices for extra flavour. *Gifiti* is taken traditionally as medicine, but is also a social drink, most often taken in shots. There are very few commercial producers of *gifiti,* but you can see it for sale in the street markets in Livingston.

Garifuna Music

The source of fame for the Garifuna culture outside of Central America is their music. The main genre of Garifuna music is fast-paced *punta* – the accompanying dance features lots of hip swinging and gyration that would surely have scandalized the Europeans back in the day.

In the 1970s, Punta Rock emerged from Belize, mixing Punta with soca, calypso, reggae, merengue and salsa. Punta Rock is really responsible for popularising Garifuna music and culture and was definitely part of the Garifuna Pride movement that began around the same time. More recently, Garifuna bands have begun to incorporate hip-hop lyrical styles into Punta Rock pieces.

The other main style is *parranda,* which is slower than *punta* and often features a guitar (which *punta* does not). *Parranda* lyrics tend to be more sorrowful, too, often telling of struggles and hardships – you could think of it as Garifuna folk music.

The Garifuna Today

Conditions for Guatemala's Garifuna community could be much better. Livingston appears in nearly all tourism promotions about the country, making heavy use of the town's colorful appearance and vibrant culture, but it suffers from serious governmental neglect – basic infrastructure like roads, schools, hospitals and water systems are in serious need of attention.

If they decide to leave Livingston, the Garifuna have a hard time integrating into mainstream Guatemalan culture. The class system is stratified and works very much along racial lines – the lighter your skin, the more likely you are to be accepted into the upper echelons. For the most part, the dark-skinned Garifuna struggle to find employment other than as manual laborers and tend to be treated with suspicion in much of the country.

Just like many Central Americans, large sections of Garifuna youth confront this lack of opportunity by migrating north to the United States. Some stay for a few years, saving money and sending it home, then return. Many decide to stay and, as a result, the Garifuna population is both decreasing and ageing.

The Garifuna language hovers on and off UNESCO's list of endangered languages. While Garifuna has recently been recognized as one of Guatemala's official minor languages, for many years it was forbidden to teach it in schools. Some classes in Livingston are now held in Garifuna, but many young people see English as the language of opportunity and would rather learn that as a second language.

Despite all of that, it's unlikely that you'll meet a more proud and (outwardly at least) happy people than the folks in Livingston – they will generally welcome you with open arms should you decide to make the trip. **247**

Natural textile dyeing
PHIL CLARKE HILL/IN PICTURES VIA GETTY IMAGES IMAGES ©

INCREDIBLE GUATEMALAN TEXTILES

Guatemalan identity expressed in warp and weft. By RAY BARTLETT

OF ALL THE arts, crafts, and traditions that define Guatemala, perhaps none represent the country's individuality as perfectly as its textiles. They are one of the most striking aspects to foreigners, visible even as you pass through the airport doors.

Art One Can Wear

People wear Guatemalan traje as a normal way of life, not – as in other parts of the world, such as Japan – only for special occasions. Not only are the clothes a visual feast, the vibrant colors and detailed embroidery place a wearer in a certain region – or even a specific town. Sometimes it's a message 'spelled out' boldly in the fabric's pattern or color (who can miss the proud, defiant blood-red crimsons of the Nebaj region, for instance?). Other times it's something as simple and subtle as the use of sparkles or the scallop indentation in a neckline.

When I enter a shop packed floor to ceiling with these stunning works of art, I'm reminded of Daisy in F Scott Fitzgerald's The Great Gatsby, breaking down after being overwhelmed by the beauty of the hundreds of shirts in Gatsby's closet.

I confess I've never felt that way about a wall of button-downs. But I feel it quite intensely every time I visit Guatemala. The Maya may have abandoned their grand cities, but they didn't forget to take their incredible clothes with them. Their fabric traditions are still just as alive and vibrant today as when their gleaming cities ruled the Maya world. In fact, many depictions of life in the murals and friezes show that the clothes worn then are very similar to what's still worn today.

To understand these beautiful fabrics is to delve into the core of Maya identity, to realize that these patterns and colors and products are not simple souvenirs. They are a culture. An identity. And purchasing any part of the *traje* (outfit ensemble) is more than just a transaction. Older items, often found in markets like that of Chichicastenango, were likely never crafted for general sale, and thus, are being sold because of a family's financial situation. To haggle the vendor down may be taking advantage of your power as a purchaser. So if you're buying these items, do so with reverence,

caution, respect and care.

What Is the Traditional Guatemalan Traje?

Women's *traje* is usually comprised of three, possibly four parts:

A headpiece, the *cinta*, can be as simple as a thin strip of cloth or quite substantial, as in the Ixil Triangle and Nebaj.

A shirt, the *huipile*, usually with sleeves, is often elaborately embroidered or decorated in a style distinct to the town or region.

A skirt, the *corte*, is commonly made by hand on a backstrap loom. The length is adjusted by folding the top edge, then it's wrapped around the waist and secured with the *faja* – a decorative, colorful belt that ties the ensemble together.

Though most of the modern focus is on women's *traje*, some parts of Guatemala still see men in traditional garb as well. Men wear a hat, a backstrap-loom-woven shirt, pants that are often unique to the town or region, and a bag slung across a shoulder.

The Incredible Backstrap Loom

If you're lucky enough and have time, visit a women's weaving collective and learn how to use a backstrap loom.

First, the threads – warp are the long threads; weft is the sinuous, back-and-forth one – are chosen, and in some collectives, even the threads are made by handpicking cotton from cotton trees, dying it with natural dyes, and spinning it to the right thickness into skeins.

Next, the warp is stretched out into the loom, and the magic here is that the wearer becomes part of the loom itself. By wrapping the bottom of the loom around one's back and tying the top to a cord attached to the ceiling, the wearer adds the necessary tension to the loom, whereas normally this is done with a complex framework that's part of a machine. This simple method allows one to craft incredibly rich fabrics with only a few sticks, some careful counting and the thread itself. It's astonishing how simple a backstrap loom

is, yet its mastery is truly an art.

Sit down, let the teacher wrap the loom around your waist and tie it firmly, and instantly the threads take form. Presto! It looks like a fabric suddenly. You can lean forward or backwards to add or release tension, and the next challenge is that there's a different process one must do depending on whether you're passing the bobbin from the right to the left, or the left to right. For the former, you scrape the threads with a particular motion to lift one side; for the latter, you have to pull and release them. The tiniest mistake, or even a single thread missed, and the pattern won't look right.

Doing a short scarf takes hours, even days. The teachers are patient and will carefully fix your mistakes but by the time you finish you'll understand how mastering this requires years or decades.

Learning More about Guatemalan Textiles

There are three ways to delve deeper into the incredible world of the Guatemalan traje. You can take classes at a women's weaving collective, as mentioned above. You can peruse the markets in Chichicastenango (p208) or Antigua (p166), or more traditional weaving markets such as San Antonio Aguas Calientas (p174). Or you can visit the Museo Ixchel (p50) in Guatemala City.

The Museo Ixchel is not for everyone and might be boring for kids, but for anyone keen to learn more about Guatemalan fabrics, it's a must-see. There are several permanent collection rooms and a visit – especially shortly after you arrive – will give you a great overview of what to expect as you venture out to other parts of Guatemala.

Of particular interest is the museum's collection of paintings by Carmen L Pettersen, whose beautiful watercolors capture various traditional Guatemalan styles in a snapshot of the 1970s. Over 50 paintings of her work are in the collection, and by viewing them you'll get a sense of the variety and beauty of traditional Guatemalan wear.

INDEX

251

Map Pages **000**

'Guatemala deserves to
be explored in depth and
in detail. Each time I visit
I find something new
that amazes me.'
RAY BARTLETT

'Love it or hate it, there's
an undeniable buzz to
Guatemala City that you
won't find in the rest of
the country.'
LUCAS VIDGEN

31901069896886

THIS BOOK

Design Development
Marc Backwell

Content Development
Mark Jones, Sandie Kestell, Anne Mason, Joana Taborda

Cartography Development
Katerina Pavkova

Production Development
Sandie Kestell, Fergal Condon

Series Development Leadership
Darren O'Connell, Piers Pickard, Chris Zeiher

Destination Editor
Alicia Johnson

Production Editor
Graham O'Neill

Book Designer
Eoin Loughney

Cartographer
Rachel Imeson

Assisting Editors
Mani Ramaswamy, Maja Vatric

Cover Researcher
Mazzy Prinsep

Thanks Ronan Abayawickrema, James Appleton, Andrea Dobbin, Karen Henderson, Ania Lenihan

MIX
Paper from
responsible sources
FSC™ C021741
www.fsc.org

Paper in this book is certified against the Forest Stewardship Council™ standards. FSC™ promotes environmentally responsible, socially beneficial and economically viable management of the world's forests.

Published by Lonely Planet Global Limited
CRN 554153
8th edition – September 2023
978 1 78868 431 6
© Lonely Planet 2023 Photographs © as indicated 2023
10 9 8 7 6 5 4 3 2 1
Printed in China